Anna

with best wishes

CHURCHILL'S ABANDONED PRISONERS

The British Soldiers Deceived in the Russian Civil War

Rupert Wieloch

RUPERT WIELOCH

CASEMATE

Oxford & Philadelphia

Published in Great Britain and the United States of America in 2019 by
CASEMATE PUBLISHERS
The Old Music Hall, 106–108 Cowley Road, Oxford OX4 1JE, UK
and
1950 Lawrence Road, Havertown, PA 19083, USA

Hardcover Edition: ISBN 978-1-61200-753-3
Digital Edition: ISBN 978-1-61200-754-0

A CIP record for this book is available from the British Library

Printed and bound in the UK by TJ International

Typeset in India by Versatile PreMedia Services. www.versatilepremedia.com

For a complete list of Casemate titles, please contact:

CASEMATE PUBLISHERS (UK)
Telephone (01865) 241249
Email: casemate-uk@casematepublishers.co.uk
www.casematepublishers.co.uk

CASEMATE PUBLISHERS (US)
Telephone (610) 853-9131
Fax (610) 853-9146
Email: casemate@casematepublishers.com
www.casematepublishers.com

Front cover: Teddy the Siberian Pup with his Saviours in Moscow, with permission from the artist, Araminta Blue

Contents

ARCTIC

NORWAY

SWEDEN

FINLAND

Helsinki

Terrijoki

POLAND

•Warsaw

BYELORUSSIA

St Petersburg
(Petrograd)

Archangel

Dvina

• Moscow

Kiev

UKRAINE

Dnieper

Kazan

Kama

Perm

Volga

Sevastopol

Ufa

Ekaterinburg

Tobol

Tobolsk

U R A L   M O U N T A I N S

Tor

Omsk

Novosibirs
(Novo-Nikhol

Black
Sea

*Caspian
Sea*

KAZAKHSTAN

GEORGIA

AZERBAIJAN

Baku

UZBEKISTAN

TURKMENISTAN

Dedicated to the memory of Angus MacMillan,
"Never fear, scholar dear,
In the morning of the year
Was not all the sunny beauty made for you?"

Foreword

I have a personal reason for finding Rupert Wieloch's gripping account of hitherto unrevealed dramatic adventures in the time of the Russian Civil War a work of remarkable interest. In it he describes the often-terrifying experiences of a handful of British soldiers who found themselves serving with the White Russian Army of Admiral Kolchak in Siberia fighting the Bolsheviks in 1918. Following the eventual Bolshevik victory, these British soldiers found themselves adrift amid the chaos and cruelty ensuing on that victory. After many perilous adventures, against all odds they eventually found their way home.

The first article of the 1920 Treaty of Copenhagen provided for mutual repatriation of British and Russian prisoners. Some returned home courtesy of the Royal Navy, others subsequently on board SS *Dongola*. Also on board the latter vessel was my nine-year-old father Dmitri, who had been smuggled out of Soviet captivity by his English nanny Lucy Stark, under pretence of his being her illegitimate son. But for Lucy's astonishing courage and devotion, I would not be here to read about the exploits of my father's fellow-passengers.

Wieloch's story is very much a personal one, following as it does in vivid detail the travails of Britons who, in differing circumstances, volunteered to assist in Winston Churchill's heartfelt support for the White campaign to (in Churchill's words) "destroy Bolshevik buffoonery in its lair." Their backgrounds were remarkably varied, ranging from the American Emerson MacMillan, who volunteered to join the British Army, to the future Lieutenant General Sir Brian Horrocks, who commanded 30 Corps at the ill-fated battle of Arnhem.

The vast region of Siberia controlled by Kolchak during the period of his leadership comprised in reality little territory beyond a few miles north and south of the vast length of the Trans-Siberian Railway. The problems he faced were immense, and in the end tragically proved insurmountable. Siberia's brief liberation originated in the uprising of the emigrant Czech Legion, recruited among prisoners of war in order to further Russia's war effort. Ultimately, however, their loyalty naturally lay in the cause of their own country, which made them uncertain allies. Much blame, too, has been unfairly accorded Kolchak in consequence of appalling crimes of the murder and banditry perpetrated by the independent Ataman Semeonov. In fact, far from being a supporter of Kolchak, Semeonov pursued an independent policy of rapine under the cynical aegis of the Japanese occupiers of eastern Siberia.

The heroes (and that they were) of Wieloch's tale were at the time naturally little aware of such major considerations, being preoccupied with acting their varied parts in ensuring the success of the anti-Bolshevik forces. Ultimately, they sought desperately simply to survive amid the chaos of the dissolution of the White Army, and their subsequent brutal treatment at the hands of the victorious Reds.

Arguably, however, the most inexcusable betrayal was inflicted on them by their own government. Lloyd George, anxious to appease the Bolshevik regime and enter into profitable economic arrangements with Russia's despoilers, was it appears happy to abandon British subjects whose presence in Soviet hands had become an embarrassment. Again, when they were eventually released, not the least unpleasantness inflicted on the gallant protagonists of this history was the fact that, while they were officially forbidden to talk about their tribulations at the hands of their Bolshevik captors, early British appeasers of the regime remained at liberty to extol Soviet humanity to the skies.

These, however, are more serious considerations. The great merit of *Churchill's Abandoned Prisoners* is the attention it pays to the remarkable individual vagaries experienced by the British prisoners. This largely chaotic episode in world history repays being studied at the microscopic level of individual humanity, where the chaos is most evident and disturbing. I am confident that it will afford readers the same intense interest as it did me.

Nikolai Tolstoy

Acknowledgements

My gratitude to the many people who have in some way helped me to write this book starts with those who taught me Russian and Soviet history at school and university. It extends to family friends scarred by the 1917 revolutions and to distinguished historians and memorable authors, who wrote about the extraordinary events that took place in Russia one hundred years ago.

I am particularly indebted to Angus MacMillan for providing the spine of this story, which is based on the letters, diaries, photographs and unpublished documents belonging to his parents, Emerson and Dallas. These are supported by the diary of the inspiring commander, Leonard Vining and memoirs of the renowned war journalist Francis McCullagh and the illustrious World War II general, Brian Horrocks. They all shared their time as prisoners of war in Siberia with Emerson and their vivid recollections led me to the main source of research, the National Archives. I pass special thanks to the friendly staff at Kew, who helped me access Cabinet Papers, Foreign Office Reports, War Office Diaries, Admiralty Weekly Intelligence Summaries, Government Maps, London Gazettes and the military records of many of the soldiers who served in Siberia from 1918 to 1920.

There are no surviving British captives, who were incarcerated in Moscow in 1920, but there are three volumes of interviews with prisoners that were recorded at 22 Carlisle Place by Lord Emmott's Committee to Collect Information on Russia. I heartily thank the Warden and Fellows of Nuffield College, University of Oxford and to Mr Martin Simon, Lord Emmott's great grandson for the opportunity to cross check the soldiers' recollections with the evidence in these volumes.

I am especially grateful to the Pro-Chancellor and Senate of the University of Leeds for access to their Special Collection, which holds the papers of several important characters in the book, including one of the prisoners, Eric Hayes, who saved Horrocks's life and later became a distinguished commander in World War II. The full list of sources from Leeds is in the bibliography, but I extend thanks to Matt Dunne and the staff, who supplied me with copious box files full of intriguing documents from the Liddle and Russian Collections.

For political sources, I am grateful to the compilers of Hansard Online and to Annie Pinder at the Parliamentary Archives for finding space for me to trawl through the Lloyd George Papers during the refurbishment of the House of Lords. Whilst in London, I appreciated the help of Jacqui Grainger at the Royal United Services Institute, Edward Bishop at the Wellcome Library, Hannah Cleal at the Bank of England Archive and the guardians of documents at the Imperial War Museum for sight of the Jack Papers.

For access to most of the histories, memoirs and newspapers listed in the bibliography, I thank the staff at the much-visited British Library. Two of these books written by Professor Jon Smele, *The Russian Revolution and Civil War 1917–1921: An Annotated Bibliography* and *Civil War in Siberia: The Anti-Bolshevik Government of Admiral Kolchak 1918–1920*, are contextual touchstones and I am particularly grateful to him for his generous help and guidance. I also owe special thanks to Colonel Colin Bulleid and the Royal Hampshire Regiment Trust for allowing me to delve into 9th Battalion's files and albums in Winchester and for permission to reproduce photographs. Colin spent several years in the British Embassy in Moscow, so he was a terrific help with Russian terminology and checking Hampshire military details. I am also grateful to Robert Glynn, who provided the evidence that Dukhovskaya was the only battle honour awarded to a British regiment in Siberia.

No one knows Russia completely, but everyone has a view about the largest nation in the world, that spans 11 time zones. When I visited Russia to broaden my knowledge and see the Moscow prisons for myself, I was guided by Violeta, a scholar of Moscow State University and helped by Elena and the delightful staff of the Prince Galitzine Memorial Library in St Petersburg. I am extremely grateful to them and to my son Hastings who, with his friend Patrick Gilday, drove from St Petersburg to Irkutsk and provided photographs of the route taken by the British prisoners. I also thank Princess Katya Galitzine and Count Nikolai Tolstoy for their kindness, encouragement and guidance on Imperial protocol.

On the other side of the Atlantic, where a significant part of the story resides, Dr Jennifer Polk helped enormously with the challenges of checking American and Canadian archives for Red Cross and YMCA references. I am also appreciative of the websites of many government and academic institutions, including the Johns Hopkins Nursing Historical Collection at the Alan Mason Chesney Medical Archives, the Hoover Institution and the Universities of Columbia, Stanford and Toronto.

More than 150 characters touch this tale. I have not been able to do all of them justice, but I owe thanks to several descendants and dedicated volunteers who keep alive the memory of many ordinary heroes whose lives were changed forever by World War I. Through the excellent Great War Forum website, I connected to George Lillington, the grandson of Bob and Ludmilla Lillington, who married in Omsk in 1919. Through the admirable Bedfordshire Regiment website, Steve Fuller put me in touch with Rex Carthew's great niece, Stephanie Rose. The Royal Marines Historical Society put me in touch with Lieutenant Colonel Alastair Grant of the Royal Marines, the grandson of Major General Tom Jameson, who provided me with a photograph of the gallant leader of the Kama river expedition. Andrew Pentland and the Air History website helped me discover more about Dwyer Neville. Mike Sampson and the dedicated Tiverton Civic Society brought the story of the Yates family to life. Joe Devereux, one of the Volunteers of the Soldiers of Gloucester Museum, provided me with the letter written by Private Lionel Grant that is quoted in Chapter 16. Sadly, I haven't traced what happened to all of Emerson's fellow prisoners, but I would be delighted to hear from any descendent who is related to the characters in this book, or who holds relevant stories that connect to the British campaign in Siberia.

For the background to the two officers who ran British intelligence operations in Omsk, I looked initially to their regiment and school. I owe particular thanks to Lieutenant Colonel (Retired) Peter Garbutt, the Regimental Secretary of The King's Royal Hussars for his help with John Neilson and to Dr Jonathan Smith, the archivist at Rugby School for help with Leo Steveni. My thanks go also to Katrina DiMuro and the staff at the Liddell Hart Centre for Military Archives at King's College London for access to Steveni's unpublished memoir. I am grateful to *The Times* for allowing me to use contemporary reports from their correspondents in Siberia. I also appreciated the outstanding World War I memorial website created by Harrow School, for background to several characters, including the last chief of the British Military Mission in Siberia, Charles Wickham.

Finally, I thank Clare Litt, Ruth Sheppard, Isobel Nettleton, Declan Ingram and Connor Reason at Casemate for their encouragement and hard work; my daughter, Araminta Blue, for her art work; and my sister Drusilla and my wife, Perry, for their much-needed proofreading talents that were used extensively.

The UK material which is not under private copyright is unpublished Crown-copyright material and is published by kind permission of the Controller of HM Stationery Office. The author and publisher have undertaken every effort to trace copyright holders. If any copyright holder believes that they have not been consulted, they are urged to contact the publisher directly.

Prologue

On Wednesday 17th November 1920, Prime Minister David Lloyd George chaired a tense Cabinet meeting about Britain's relationship with Soviet Russia. The Foreign Secretary, Lord Curzon and the War Secretary, Winston Churchill, both confirmed that matters were in hand to send 300 British troops to Lithuania under control of the League of Nations for peacekeeping duties. The discussion then turned to the prisoners of war still held by the Bolsheviks, with Curzon and Churchill arguing to delay the resumption of trade until they were all repatriated to England.

The prime minister was exasperated. He cut short the foreign secretary and brushed aside Churchill's protests about Russian propaganda. He knew that even the most anti-Bolshevik Members of Parliament had "shewn the white feather" in the House of Commons at the prospect of further military adventures in Russia. But there still remained the question about the Moscow inmates, which the government had kept secret from the public.

It was not just the prime minister who had been inconvenienced. The beleaguered British economy desperately needed a Russian stimulus to help it out of the doldrums. However, the thorny problem of prisoners had prevented the Board of Trade from fulfilling the commitment made at San Remo in April, to reopen commercial links.

Lloyd George had spent a disproportionate amount of time on this issue in 1920. Following the return of the British battalions from Russia, he had sent the Labour MP, Jim O'Grady, to sign a much-acclaimed deal with Lenin's envoy, Maxim Litvinov, in Copenhagen. The two governments had agreed to the conditions and a mass prisoner exchange followed in April. However, when trade negotiations stalled, the 15 soldiers of the British Military Mission to Siberia were deceived in Irkutsk and sent 3000 miles to the headquarters of the secret police in Moscow, in Lubjanka Square.

The situation was compounded when the train carrying a Royal Navy maintenance team on its way from Constantinople to Enzeli was detained at Baku. Throughout June, Lloyd George was pressed in the House of Commons by honourable and gallant members who appeared to be better informed about these men than the prime minister. The government had been skating on thin ice for some time. Calls for Churchill to be impeached over British operations in Siberia were followed by the prime minister misleading Parliament when answering awkward questions about the fate of the British prisoners.

Meanwhile, the 15 soldiers were starting the final leg of their 10,000-mile journey across Russia. A year before, they had been ordered to "remain until the last" in Omsk to organise the evacuation of Admiral Kolchak's capital. They helped thousands of terrified citizens to escape and just managed to leave on the last train out of the city before Trotsky's Red Army overwhelmed it.

Embarking on a frantic dash to freedom by train and sleigh, they witnessed the tragedy that ensued with tens of thousands of desperate refugees dying in the harsh Siberian winter. In one incident at Achinsk, a waggon load of dynamite in a freight train exploded in the centre of a dozen refugee trains standing on parallel tracks. One of the British soldiers observed that: "the dead were piled up like cord-wood. There were hundreds of them, but they were luckier than the injured who still lived and who could not possibly receive medical attention." In ordinary times this would rank as one of the world's worst disasters, with several thousand burned badly, but here people just shrugged their shoulders and said, *Nichevo*!

This incredible story traces the Allied intervention in Siberia from its flawed inception to the disastrous finale. It follows the exploits of Emerson MacMillan, who joined the British Army in Philadelphia at the same time that the first British battalion arrived in Vladivostok. Parting from his betrothed, Dallas Katherine Ireland, he avoided the fearsome German submarine attacks on his way to England, where he trained with the Inns of Court Officers Training Corps. After a 16,000-mile journey, he arrived in Omsk where he began work for the commander of the British Railway Mission. When Admiral Kolchak's White Army retreated and the Provisional All-Russian Government collapsed, he boarded the last train out of the city and wondered whether he would ever see Dallas again...

PART I

Pennsylvania to Siberia

CHAPTER I

Philadelphia Parting

When in Europe, I always experience a peculiar feeling of walking through the beautiful alleys of a great cemetery where every stone reminds me of a civilisation which committed suicide on August 1st 1914.

GRAND DUKE ALEXANDER OF RUSSIA

Philadelphia in May 1918 was full of the New Hope characterised by the flourishing Pennsylvania art movement. Dallas Katherine Ireland[1] looked at the poster for the latest exhibition in the Art Club on South Broad Street, but the inspirational impressionism of Robert Spencer's *Waterloo Place*, could not reignite her faded hopes.

Her journey by rail from Baltimore that day had started so well. After spending a hectic week at Johns Hopkins Hospital Training School, she was looking forward to seeing her betrothed, Emerson Augustus MacMillan. However, when he announced his intention to enter the "war to end all wars" by joining the British Army, a deep sense of foreboding overwhelmed her.

She understood the pressure on him to do his duty. The media was full of jingoistic patriotism and threats of white feathers if young men didn't sign up. However, the news from Europe was not good. After the Bolshevik Government signed the Brest-Litovsk peace treaty on 3rd March, 50 German divisions were released from the Eastern Front and General Ludendorff dispatched these formidable troops to reinforce his fearsome attack on the Western Front.

The German commander timed his Spring Offensive whilst there were only four battle-ready American divisions on the front line, hoping to win the war before the full deployment of the United States Army later in the year. As the Teutonic hordes advanced in a series of attacks, President Wilson called again for able-bodied men to join up and Emerson, a 26-year-old electrical engineer, felt compelled to do his bit.

Emerson preferred to join the ranks of "Tommy Atkins" rather than "Johnny Doughboy" because he was very proud of his Scottish heritage and felt allegiance to King and Country. With her Irish roots, Dallas did not share this unequivocal loyalty, but it was not in her nature to wait meekly in the "wings". Whilst Emerson's papers were being checked at the British Embassy, she investigated what she could do to assist the war effort. However, there seemed to be very few ways for a North American woman to serve on the front line in France. The US Army did recruit 233 female bilingual telephone operators to work at switchboards near the front, but the main employment for women was nursing. She decided to apply for front-line service, but first she would have to complete her training course which was due to end before Christmas.

Six weeks later, in the hottest recorded summer in Philadelphia, when the mercury reached 106 degrees Fahrenheit, Emerson was called forward to swear an oath of allegiance before catching a train to Nova Scotia. As he bade a fond farewell to Dallas, she wished that he was a bit more tactile, but she knew his abrupt character well and forgave this awkward parting. The send-off from his work colleagues at the Stroudsberg Traction Company was much more uplifting and, with a resolute spirit, he headed for the station to catch his train to Canada.

Arriving at Windsor, he reported to the guard room at the Imperial Recruits Depot, close to the birthplace of ice hockey. The officer in charge told him that he was being posted to a "mixed foreign platoon", but before he was commissioned, he must complete his training with the Inns of Court[2] Officers Training Corps at Berkhamsted. In the meantime, whilst waiting for a ship to transport him across the Atlantic, he was given the temporary rank of corporal and set to work at Fort Edward as a drill instructor attached to the Jewish Legion that was bound for Palestine.

Emerson's passage to England was delayed several times due to the threat of German submarine attacks. He did not enjoy waiting for the ship to sail because the port of Halifax resembled the aftermath of a battlefield following the worst maritime disaster in the world. Two thousand people were killed when a French ammunition ship exploded in the narrows after colliding with a Norwegian vessel. The devastation was compounded by a tsunami that wiped out the Mi'kmaq community in Tufts Cove and obliterated the shore line around the harbour.[3]

Emerson was thankful that the Atlantic crossing was calm and the captain of his ship successfully dodged the minefields and torpedoes. He felt much relief when he eventually arrived in London, but was shocked at the damage caused by the German air bombing raids to the historic buildings of Lincoln's Inn. After completing more paperwork, the quartermaster handed him a pile of army clothing. Emerson was tall and skinny and he wondered whether the tailor had worked in the zoo before the war, but at least his boots fitted "like a pair of gloves." He was given a rail warrant and instructed to go straight to Euston station, where he boarded a train bearing the London and North West Railway livery, bound for Berkhamsted.[4]

The Inns of Court Officers Training Corps' camp was located at the foot of the Chiltern Hills.[5] At the beginning of the war, Lord Brownlow gave permission for the commanding officer to use a field near to Ashridge Park for a nominal six weeks, but four years later, they were still camped on what was known as Kitchener's Field. The instructors prided themselves on taking a more considered approach to training than the "Sandhurst method" of instilling mindless obedience. However, by the time Emerson arrived, the syllabus had adapted to the type of warfare waged in Flanders, which required neither thought, nor initiative. Theirs was not to reason why, but to advance from trenches through mud and barbed wire against dominant machine gun emplacements.

Emerson's commanding officer was a 45-year-old South African, Lieutenant Colonel Herbert Stevens of the Welch Regiment, who had been awarded the Distinguished Service Order after temporarily commanding a battalion in the trenches. His appearance at Berkhamsted was marked by a low flying air salute, which frightened a young cow so much that it fell into the labyrinth pit whilst attempting to escape the noise. Watching the cadets' forlorn attempts to extricate the heifer made Stevens realise how much there was to do to make them ready for the front line.

Emerson was a hard worker and good at drill, which made it easy for him to settle in. Many of the senior sergeants were veterans of the South African War. They were quick to detect any signs of shirking, or ruses to avoid unpleasant duties. However, in October 1918, they had to face a new disciplinary challenge.

Following a change in policy, the first detachment of female soldiers had arrived to take up some of the administrative posts in the headquarters. The women wore the cap badge of Queen Mary's Army Auxiliary Corps[6] and were employed under the steely eye of a keen female officer. They were accommodated in a pair of large houses converted into hostels and their presence rapidly changed the dynamics of the camp, as Cupid emptied his quiver of golden arrows on a daily basis.

That month, Emerson "passed out of the recruit class into the company proper" and wrote that "work is more interesting as we are getting into the specialities." These included poison gas training and trench work, but there was only a limited amount of riveting because the sergeants told him that "a week in France would teach him more than several months of playing at it in England." He especially enjoyed field firing with the Lewis gun at the Ivinghoe range and musketry in the grounds of the Black Prince's castle. His platoon was issued with a new pamphlet about the bayonet, but this did not meet with favour at the War Office, so they were told to hand it back and warm their hands when all the copies were burned in a pyre.

As an engineer, Emerson had an innate ability to solve problems, but he was not a natural infantryman. He discovered that he belonged to that large group of men whose leadership skills needed to be nurtured like "a slow growing plant." However, he did enjoy the night exercises, "blowing up" railway bridges and setting ambushes on the Watford to Tring road.

Recruits were paid one shilling and sixpence per day, equivalent to 35 US cents. He described his pay in a letter to his elder brother, Albert, as "feeding strawberries to an elephant, so inadequate is it to our legitimate expenditure." He said that the food was "substantial", but there was a shortage of items "that might be called luxuries", complaining "We carry little tablets of saccharine for our tea … it is a coal tar product and intensely sweet, but lacks the food value of sugar."

Soon after Emerson arrived, there was an outbreak of the Spanish flu, which he recalled "hit us hard." The disease began with a cough and pain behind the eyes and ears. The victim's heart rate, body temperature and respiration rose rapidly, leaving them vulnerable to pneumonia. Emerson avoided contact with the victims, who were quarantined in the Voluntary Aid Detachment hospital run by the formidable matron Mrs Haygarth Brown. Many recovered under her care, but sadly 14 died during the pandemic, including one of the recently-arrived female soldiers.

On 31st October, the recruits moved from the tented camp to billets in town. The citizens of "Berko" obliged the Corps by taking in the unkempt soldiers with good grace and humour. It became normal for long-suffering home owners to find their favourite garden seat occupied, their bathroom door locked and their pantry ransacked. Despite these minor irritations, many of them felt glad to be associated, however remotely, with the soldiers who they knew might only have weeks to live.

Emerson was billeted with three other cadets in a comfortable house with an open fire and a gas light, for which they each paid half a crown extra per week. His landlady offered to do their laundry and gave them hot water for shaving and tea, but he had to "go up town" for a bath. One of his billet mates came from South Africa and was grateful for the supplies of candy that Albert sent over, but he had "never before heard of maple sugar."

Emerson and his fellow cadets had every intention of doing their duty on the Western Front, but the Armistice put paid to these thoughts. The joyous announcement on 11th November was greeted with an especially loud cheer because everyone was given a holiday. He joined a large group who accompanied the band on its way to the High Street where it played an impromptu concert. After a gallant resistance, Queen Mary's detachment joined them round a great bonfire that was built on Kitchener's Field, where the celebration continued long into the night.

There was much uncertainty about what would happen now the war had ended. Emerson had signed up "for the duration and six months after if required," so he was presented with three options. He could wait for demobilisation in England, serve in the fledgling British Army of the Rhine, or join the campaign in Russia, which became the main focus for anyone intent on earning the War medal. Emerson felt he had come so far that he didn't wish to go home without seeing some action and so he put his name down for *post bellum* work in the Far East.

In December, he travelled to London and joined a huge crowd celebrating the visit of the French Marshal, Ferdinand Foch. He was also selected as one of the Corps' guards of honour for the visit of Sir William Robertson, noting that it was "probably more for my height than my facility in presenting arms." He was driven in a lorry to Lord Rothschild's estate at Tring, where the former Chief of the Imperial General Staff, whom Emerson described as a "big block of granite", unveiled a monument to the fallen.

At Christmas, he was grateful for the knitted socks that Dallas sent him and her letter which informed him that after graduating as a Red Cross nurse on 24th December, she would sail to Ireland to visit her relatives. Emerson volunteered for duties over the festive period to allow his friends to spend time with their families. Meanwhile, he made plans for a journey to the Emerald Isle in the New Year.

Emerson took his leave just as Winston Churchill became the Secretary of State for War and Air and the *Daily Express* ran a feature with the headline: "Are we to be committed to a War with Russia?"[7] The anti-war mood made him think that he would not be sent to the Far East and he travelled across the Irish Sea eager to see Dallas. Their reunion after months apart was better than anticipated. Revelling in each other's company, they laughed and gasped at their remarkable stories as they recounted their adventures of the past six months.

Dublin provided a magnificent backdrop to their romance and Emerson was delighted that the food was "more plentiful and varied than in England." On 20th January, they enjoyed a fine evening in a republican pub where everyone talked enthusiastically about Sinn Féin's surprise victory in the General Election, winning 73 of Ireland's 105 seats. They heard that there would be a gathering at Mansion House the next day and were swept up with the tumultuous crowds as the new Members of Parliament proclaimed themselves as the Dáil Éireann and declared independence for the Irish Nation.

Three days later, Emerson was back at Berkhamsted on his first day in Number 11 Officer Cadet Battalion, where he put a white band around his peaked cap. At that moment, he believed he would return to

Philadelphia in the spring, where he would marry Dallas and return to work as an electrical engineer. However, the following week, he heard from the War Office that they were transferring him to the Railway Operating Division of the Royal Engineers and that he would deploy to Russia to help "repair and operate the Trans-Siberian Railway."

The news was a shock. It meant that he would travel as a sergeant major, which was disappointing since he had completed so much of the officers' commissioning course. On the positive side, his pay was increased to ten shillings per day. He was also given the right to immediate discharge and to repatriation if it did not work out and the prospect of a field commission was dangled in front of him. This persuaded him to accept the challenge and he wrote: "I may regret my decision, one often does, but I shall at least have satisfied my curiosity and something good may come out of it."

At the beginning of March, he was given a clothing supplement that included a fur coat and leather jack boots and he received orders to report to the SS *Stentor* on the River Clyde, for his journey across the world. His emotions fluctuated between trepidation and excitement as he boarded the train for Glasgow, humming "It's A Long, Long Way To Tipperary" and contemplating the prospect of a 14,000-mile voyage to the unknown.

Major Leonard Vining of the Royal Engineers; the officer commanding the British soldiers ordered to "remain until the last" in Omsk and organise the evacuation of refugees in November 1919. (Courtesy of Leonard Vining, St Catherine Press)

Warrant Officer Emerson MacMillan of the Royal Engineers; appointed the quartermaster of the prisoners of war captured in Krasnoyarsk on 6th January 1920. (Courtesy of Angus MacMillan)

Dallas Katherine Ireland, betrothed to Emerson; graduated from Johns Hopkins Hospital Training School in Baltimore as American Red Cross Nurse number 34286. (Courtesy of Angus MacMillan)

Major General Alfred Knox, appointed by Winston Churchill to command the British Military Mission to Siberia. He departed from Omsk on 8th November 1919, leaving behind Vining, MacMillan and the other soldiers who became the last prisoners of war in World War I. (Courtesy of The National Archives)

The Prime Minister David Lloyd George, with the Secretary of State for War and Air, Winston Churchill, at the Paris Peace Conference.

Winston Churchill, briefing HRH The Prince of Wales while the British campaign in Russia was at its most active in 1919.

Kitchener's Field near Berkhamsted where Emerson lived when he started training with the Inns of Court in 1918. (Courtesy of Angus MacMillan)

CHAPTER 2

It's a Long Way to Vladivostok

If you truly wish to find someone who you know and who travels, there are but two places where you but need to sit and wait, and sooner or later your man will come there: the docks of London and Port Said.

RUDYARD KIPLING

The SS *Stentor* was due to sail from Glasgow on 8th March, but was delayed six days and this allowed Emerson to visit his clan in Greenock. Returning to the dockyard on the eve of departure, he witnessed the "infinite" industry of post-war ship-building on the Clyde before reporting to the officer commanding the troops, Major Leonard Vining.[1] There seemed to be hundreds of hulls in various stages of construction, including the "last word" in battleships, HMS *Hood*. That night he was restless with anticipation and whilst others slept, he wrote to Dallas and his brother, posting their letters before the ship slipped its mooring in the morning:

> In a few hours we expect to sail for Hong Kong via the Suez and the rest of it. We will go by rail from Hong Kong to Vladivostok. The first port of call will be at Havre and after that at every corner. We may arrive at Vladivostok in two months. There are just six of us for Siberia – three officers and three non-coms – all specialists. Two are interpreters. One officer is a locomotive designer, one a general superintendent and the other a traffic superintendent.

He explained that as one of the non-commissioned ranks,[2] he could either be assigned to the operating division or to maintenance support, depending on the wishes of the head of the British Railway Mission, Colonel Archibald Jack. Believing this uncertainty might worry Dallas, he continued reassuringly: "If I don't like it I will return *toute de suite* via Vancouver as I have the privilege of discharge and separation at any time."

At 9a.m. on 14th March, their ship steamed towards the Ailsa Craig on its way to its first halt in Normandy. Whilst the passengers stood on the deck gesturing at the bystanders on the wharf, their eyes were drawn skywards as a huge airship flew towards them. They gasped in astonishment at the size of the blimp and pointed to the crew who waved back to them. Emerson had heard how the Royal Air Force was making an attempt at the non-stop trans-Atlantic crossing and was thrilled to see the R-34 on its maiden flight, taking this to be a good omen.[3]

Emerson also struck lucky with his cabin mate, "Mac" MacPherson. "I am travelling with an old white-haired bombardier who is completely internationalised. He speaks about seven languages and is a bit of a connoisseur of liqueurs. He has been all over the world in every direction by numbers." Mac had been the chief engineer to a big transportation company in Russia before his property was seized by the Bolsheviks in Petrograd. He had joined the Army to see whether he could recover his losses and been given the honorary rank of sergeant major. He took Emerson under his wing when the Royal Navy Petty Officers welcomed them into their saloon for a raucous first night at sea.

At Le Havre, they were joined by 450 men of the Chinese Labour Corps released from their war duties. They had crossed Canada on their way to the Western Front in 1917 and fulfilled a vital role when manpower was haemorrhaging in the middle of the war. Wearing their characteristic pigtails and wooden shoes, they noisily boarded the ship and attracted much mirth from the other passengers because several of them had stuffed orange peel up their noses to avoid catching Spanish flu.

Unfortunately, there was a mixture of Northern Chinese and Cantonese men in this company. It was well known that they despised each other and on the first night a knife fight broke out below decks. Major Vining handed out rifles to Emerson and the other soldiers in order to protect the crew and other passengers whilst the fight raged. Eventually, the English missionary officers, who spoke Mandarin, managed to calm down the protagonists, but the incident made everyone wary for the remainder of the journey.

In the Bay of Biscay, the ship caught the raw edge of a storm and most of the passengers retired to their cabins for three days. The weather moderated as they passed Lisbon and by the time they reached the Rock of Gibraltar and the majestic coast of Morocco, the days began to dazzle. As the temperature warmed, they spent their evenings on deck sipping their tot of issued "grog" and singing sea shanties accompanied by an ill-tuned banjo, or flute.

The Mediterranean was glorious as they passed Libya and approached Port Said at the head of the Suez Canal. In the saloon, Emerson heard amazing tales from the old hands who served in the "Dardanelles Campaign" or the "Jutland Fight". He didn't know whether his leg was being pulled when they told him about a cargo ship full of caterpillar tractors that was torpedoed, with the ensuing explosion hurling one so far that it landed on top of the submarine and sank it.

As the climate changed, the petty officers and Royal Marines all brought out their white uniform. Unfortunately, Emerson's kit was loaded down with fur coats and wool clothes, so they laughed at his discomfort in the heat. Looking out to sea, the colour changed from blue to green and the rigging and funnels of an occasional sunken ship appeared from the deep.

The statue of De Lesseps stood solemnly to starboard as the Pilot came on board. Glancing towards the harbour, Emerson caught sight of hundreds of masts and was reminded of Kipling's stories of swarms of dhows and small craft darting between the steam ships. Since the piers were all full, they dropped anchor and this allowed the barges ferrying baskets of coal and food to come alongside to replenish the ship. When he went ashore, Emerson was delighted to accompany the experienced sailors, who knew how to bargain with the ferrymen.

They soon discovered why there were so many battleships in the harbour; they had arrived in the middle of the Egyptian Revolution. The security situation was very fraught with serious uprisings occurring at Asyut and Zagazig and the New Zealand troops retaliating after one of their officers was killed. They found the Arab part of town had been placed out of bounds, but they still managed to visit the souks and bazaars where discontented *dragomen* lurked in shadowy doorways.[4]

Just before Emerson set foot in Egypt, the new Special High Commissioner, General Allenby, arrived on board HMS *Carlisle*[5] and placed the country under military law. The next day, he met with a renowned group of nationalists, who persuaded him to release the revolutionary Wafd leaders and to permit their journey to Paris. As a result, the people stopped their demonstrations and the tension eased throughout the country.

Emerson avoided any fracas during his short stay and on Monday 31st March, SS *Stentor* started its passage through the Suez Canal. Steaming through the swampy section, he marvelled at the "neat and efficient structure" of the El Ferdan railway bridge and the slow Palestine Military Railway trains carrying freight to Jerusalem.

At Kantara, he was delighted to see a Ford car and a caravan of camels close to a camp of Armenian refugee children. Nearby, 3rd Battalion Gurkha soldiers were squatting in a circle, performing a religious ceremony. Further south lay miles of British tents storing tonnes of ammunition and matériel. Here, the bored guards called forlornly to each ship, asking passengers where they were headed. "There and back again," called Major Vining. "Poomba, Poomba," came the reply.

As the heat increased, tarpaulins were erected and the decks were put under canvas to protect the passengers from the merciless sun. Emerson and the other soldiers wore their pith helmets, short trousers and puttees and quickly turned an "angry prawn" colour from their solar exposure.

In the Red Sea, they were inspired by the vision of Mount Sinai and the sunset view of the "beautiful Arabic city of Mocha."[6] Each day heralded impressive new sights from the "impregnable nest of rocks where the British base of Aden sits at ease like some somnolent Buddha" on 4th April, to the isolated island of Socotra,[7] which was the last land they sighted before Ceylon.

At night, it became too hot in their cabins, so everyone slept on deck, but this meant waking early because the decks were hosed down at sunrise. At latitude 16, Emerson gazed alternately at the Southern Cross and the Pole Star and thought of home. On moonlit nights, he meandered aimlessly along the decks. His pining face reflected his sentimental thoughts about Dallas and he developed an unfortunate reputation for being lovesick. However, his demeanour improved each morning as the rising sun encouraged the flying fish to skim the surface alongside the ship, avoiding the purposeful porpoises at the bow and the surly sharks at the stern.

In the Indian Ocean, Emerson paid a visit to the boiler room to check on the back-breaking labour of the Chinese stokers. As he descended the steps the scene resembled Dante's Inferno and the heat hit him like a brick wall. The firemen had furled wet towels round their heads as they raked and tended the furnace. It was relentless, dangerous and dirty work and the crew fully warranted their nickname of the "black gang". Back on deck, he couldn't believe how cool it appeared and he never again complained about the equatorial heat.

Approaching the southern tip of Ceylon, the ship was met by hundreds of picturesque catamarans with Cingalese crews selling fish from their skiffs. Fish had been on the menu three times a day since Glasgow, but it was always cooked well and inspired Emerson to write: "I have never lived better since I arrived in England."

The highlight of the voyage was the enchanting trip through the Malacca Strait and the "indescribable fragrance from the abundant tropical vegetation that covers the illimitable small islands off the Malay Peninsula." They sighted Penang as the sun descended and enjoyed the riot of colour before the moon rose over the water. Soon after sunset, they beheld the profile of the Chinese junks sailing to their fishing sites, lit by luminescent waters that glittered like molten silver.

Emerson enjoyed the break on the island and marvelled at the rubber, coconut and betel-nut plantations. Re-embarking on 18th April, he brought his bedding on deck again, but was caught out when torrential rain woke everyone in the middle of the night. The thunder and lightning that accompanied the storm compelled the captain to go "dead slow."

Three days later, they arrived in Singapore and went ashore. Raffles was fully booked, so Emerson stayed in a nursing home that was spotlessly clean and tidy. He was struck by the cosmopolitan population, with large Malay, Indian, Chinese and Japanese communities living next to each other in peaceful harmony. He found a topsy-turvy world of jinrikishas, money changers, sweetmeat vendors and naked children. He discovered hundreds of shoe factories, but everyone went barefooted, including the police. He also found very good tailors who provided him with some tropical uniform to replace the heavyweight wool he had endured since leaving Scotland.

Setting off again on 26th April, the *Stentor* nervously passed through a live minefield laid by the infamous German raider SMS *Wolf*.[8] This had reportedly sunk four Japanese steamers, so Emerson and the other passengers had their life vests close at hand whilst their ship inched its way forward, guided by alert observers at the bow and sides.

The next morning, there was uproar on deck. At Singapore, one of the merchant seamen had heard that a Spaniard was embarking on the ship for the passage to Hong Kong and volunteered to share a cabin because he had lived in Argentina and knew some words of Spanish. Unfortunately, it turned out that the man, named Spargoni, was in fact Portuguese and did not understand the clumsy attempts at communication. In disgust, the matelot took his bed out on deck for the night, but in the morning returned to find that Spargoni had been seasick. In fact, he had been so ill that not only had he decorated the walls of the cabin, but every piece of clothing and pair of shoes belonging to the British passenger.

The seaman's companions silently and sympathetically withdrew from the cabin whilst he vented his spleen. Back in the saloon, they had to hold each other up whilst tears of laughter ran down their cheeks as they heard the uproar continue for half an hour. During the remainder of the passage, the new cabin mates were not on speaking terms for two reasons: "one being they knew no mutual language; and the second, it would make no difference if they did."

Arriving in Hong Kong on Wednesday 30th April, they picked up their pilot shortly after passing Clearwater Bay. Emerson was thrilled to collect a large package of letters from Dallas and his family and dutifully sent his replies the next day, apologising for the poor-quality paper he had bought. He was keen to choose some presents for Dallas from the cheery Chinese shops, but was very conscious that he was going on active service and his baggage was restricted.

Roaming round Chinatown, Emerson was impressed with the long display boards painted in every imaginable colour, with gold, silver or black lettering in Chinese characters. He was taken to an opium house, but declined the offer as he was told that the effect was the same as if he smoked three full strength Capstan cigarettes.

The intention for the Siberia party was to continue on the Canadian Pacific Railway's *Empress of Russia*[9] to Shanghai and Yokohama before taking the best route to Vladivostok, where they were due to arrive on 1st June. However, the growing ill-feeling between Britain and Japan was assuming alarming proportions and rivalled the "most regrettable friction between the British and the United States." Plans were changed and they found themselves back on board the *Stentor* a few days later.

Continuing along the Chinese coast, they dodged the pirate junks that preyed on unsuspecting craft through the Formosa Strait. Three days later they arrived at Tsingtao in thick fog and anchored opposite the light house. The next morning, they tied up at the wharf and welcomed on board a Japanese officer wearing "shining" armour and a "clanking" sword. The port had been a bright jewel in the German Empire, but had been seized by the Allies[10] and was now administered by Japan. This officer and his medical team checked each of the Chinese, who were still on board from Le Havre and supervised their pay and demobilisation as they disembarked.

The cold thick fog marked a change in lifestyle and prevented any further sleeping on deck, or wearing of tropical uniform. Throughout the next 48 hours, the *Stentor's* hooter sounded for seven seconds every minute and this played on the passengers' nerves as they wended their way slowly south. Eventually, they entered the Yangtze River on 10th May and ironically anchored alongside the *Empress of Russia* at the entrance to the harbour.

The British soldiers were disappointed not to transfer aboard the Canadian steam ship, but the predicted weather made for another change in their plans. In the morning, a Navy launch picked them up and took them into town where the British consul advised against further sea travel and handed them passports to travel overland to Russia on the railway.

Emerson was accommodated in the comfortable Hanbury Institute, where the consul handed over international travel tickets, by Thomas Cook and Sons, for the train journey to Vladivostok. He took the opportunity to write another letter to Dallas: "I am trying to listen to some music as I write and revise the errors. It is not Chinese – music – you see I put a hyphen there to ease my conscience because although it is obviously Chinese, but it most emphatically is not music... Shanghai is a fine town despite that."

After drawing mosquito nets and a new issue of uniform from the British forces' stores, they set off on 13th May at 7.50a.m. They were excited about the journey ahead and peered avidly out of the carriage windows as they passed through the flat countryside that appeared to be cultivated every foot of the way with fields of rice. Emerson observed that "pagodas are plentiful," but "there is a noticeable absence of timber and the dwellings are chiefly mud huts."

Six hours later, they arrived at Pouchow where they crossed a canal by ferry. Boarding another train bound for Tientsin,[11] they stopped for dinner before their Pullman style sleeper train departed at midnight. Emerson "blushed" to note how the Chinese Government Railways gave them better accommodation than the same institution at home might. The other passengers were fascinated that the British soldiers disrobed and wore pyjamas in bed. Annoyingly, there was always a cosmopolitan crowd peeking at Emerson and the others when they undressed at night. However, this was not their worst complaint; that was saved for the dining car, where other male passengers cleared their throats into the spittoon whilst they were eating.

They awoke the next morning to a change of scene as they passed through a rugged district that was "intensely cultivated by the terrace system." For many miles, they followed the Great Wall of China and at all the stations there were Chinese soldiers on guard. Some were very smart, but the varying standards depended on the whims of the non-commissioned officer in charge of each station.

Entering Inner Manchuria,[12] they completed the 275-mile stage to Mukden[13] at 7.30p.m. and stayed at the Yamoto Hotel for 36 hours before returning to their train. The next major halt at Changchun marked an important watershed in their journey. Here, the Japanese authorities took a lively interest in their movements and suspiciously checked their paperwork several times as they walked around the town. It started to pour with rain and this turned the street into a quagmire, so they retired to the hotel by the station in a droshky drawn by a pair of worn-down ponies.

That afternoon, they caught the dirtiest train that Vining had ever seen. The lavatories "were so filthy and the effluvia so strong, that a pigsty full of pigs which had never left the premises for six months would compare very favourably." There was no dining car, so the soldiers had to join the lengthy queues for a glass of tea and a loaf of bread during the protracted stops. Up to this stage, Emerson could have been on an extended holiday, but as he entered the war zone the reality struck home in a peculiar way:

> We got aboard the train for Harbin and my travelling companion – MacPherson, is in his element. He talks Russian to the guards and passengers. We are fixed up quite comfortably in a very substantial coupé. They run corridor trains with compartments for sharing. The track gauge is about four inches wider than our standard and the rolling stock is very heavy. It is seen however that everything is booked through to chaos as the windows are either dirty or broken. The coaches are unbelievably dirty and the mechanical equipment gets its fine work in with the aid of binding-twine and hay-wire.

On 17th May, they arrived at Harbin after dark. This cosmopolitan city was rumoured to include every nation in the world, but the main population comprised 30,000 Russians and a similar number of Chinese. It was the junction point between the Chinese Eastern and the South Manchurian railways, so there were many businesses and dens of iniquity, which gave it a reputation as a "wicked" town. No one met them, but the station master told them about a military base within walking distance. They groped their way along the railway line for a mile and a half in the dark and found a well-lit building full of American officers, enjoying a dance organised by the YMCA.

The Americans welcomed their British cousins with open arms and plied them with Bourbon. Vining was pressed to dance with a local Russian girl and since he seemed a good sort, their hosts invited his party to stay the night. However, two of the British group had remained at the station to guard their luggage, so they all returned and spent a cold night without bedding in an empty train.

The next morning Vining took everyone to the American base and after washing and shaving, they enjoyed a hearty breakfast. After more delays, a train bound for Vladivostok arrived in the afternoon, but there was space for only two of their party, so Emerson and five others stayed behind. Their frustrations were mitigated by an evening spent at the Cafe Charmant. They particularly enjoyed a performance of Russian dancing and the sight of a Cossack officer with a shaven head, swaggering about in his splendid blue uniform with a silver dagger, pistol and sword hung from his belt.

On 19th May they left Harbin in a crowded train, guarded by Chinese and Russian soldiers. There were no tunnels or bridges across the valleys, so the train took a leisurely 36 hours to complete the final stretch, following the contours of the hills. The next night they arrived in Vladivostok, which Emerson described as an armed camp with "a high-tension, hair-trigger atmosphere that means business."

To their relief, they were met at the station by the two officers who went ahead from Harbin. They had been held up at gunpoint by eight bandits, who were surprised to meet any resistance, but when their Czech guards returned fire, the attackers fled into the night. They brought Emerson to the billets opposite the station, but the first priority was to wash the grime from their bodies, so they all adjourned to the Russian baths and enjoyed a long soak in the salt water.

CHAPTER 3

Diehards and Tigers

There was no British policy, unless seven different policies at once can be called a policy.

ROBERT BRUCE LOCKHART[1]

Although he was aware of the war raging in Russia from the newspapers, it was not until Emerson arrived in Vladivostok that he was informed fully about the British involvement there. He learned that a party of the Royal Marine Light Infantry landed on 9th April 1918 as part of an Anglo-Japanese force.[2] The Marines' task was to prevent Allied war matériel from falling into enemy hands.

Two factors transformed the British position from protecting supplies to active engagement in the civil war. The first was the perceived imperilment of the Czech Legion[3] as it attempted to extract 70,000 soldiers along the Trans-Siberian Railway. The second was the Bolshevik government's unwillingness to re-open the Eastern Front in the wake of their treaty with Germany, Austria-Hungary, Bulgaria and the Ottoman Empire, known as the Central Powers.

The War Cabinet was divided over the question of military intervention. The Prime Minister, David Lloyd George, was not in favour of a large-scale deployment of British troops whilst the War Secretary, Winston Churchill, argued for a massive commitment. Lord Curzon, in the Foreign Office, represented the middle ground, keen to ensure that Russia would pose no future threat to India and other British dependencies. Despite his reservations, the prime minister agreed to push significant resource into North Russia, the Baltic and Caucasia. However, the most important battleground was in Siberia and the key to this strategic region was the Trans-Siberian Railway, running from the Pacific Coast to the Ural Mountains.

Churchill appointed an experienced Russophile, Major General Alfred Knox, as the Senior British Military commander in Siberia. Before the revolution, Knox had been the Military Attaché in St Petersburg working for the ambassador, Sir George Buchanan and after he returned to London, he advised the war secretary about Bolshevik movements. His original directive, received on 28th August 1918, was confined to liaison, but this was amended by a telegram shortly afterwards to "assist reorganisation of the Russian Army."

Emerson discovered that the first meaningful action in the Eastern theatre of operations occurred whilst he was with the Inns of Court at Berkhamsted. The leading role was occupied by the 25th Battalion of the Middlesex Regiment, which arrived at Vladivostok in the SS *Ping Suie* from Hong Kong. The 25th was founded by its commanding officer, John Ward, a Member of Parliament and former trade union leader. At 52, his age, background and prior service in Khartoum earned him the unquestioned loyalty of his soldiers, but his military ideas were thought to be outdated by the headquarters staff, who had served on the Western Front. However, he was not sent to Russia to fight, merely to provide garrison protection and to "fly the flag."

Ward was acutely aware of the expectations of the Russians and had a strong sense of the responsibility of being in the vanguard for the British Army. He also knew his military history. The Middlesex were branded Steelbacks as a result of their renowned resilience to flogging. However, he much preferred the nickname of Diehards from the regiment's celebrated performance in the Peninsula War at the battle of Albuera.

After a few weeks swatting mosquitos in Vladivostok, Ward moved forward tentatively to the Ussuri River with half the battalion. He arrived just in time to play a pivotal role in the key battle that removed Bolshevik resistance east of Lake Baikal.

At 1.45a.m. on 24th August, he received written orders from the Japanese[4] commander to attack the enemy with a start time of 3a.m. from a departure point north-west of Dukhovskaya, four miles away. Contrary to everyone's expectations, the battalion was complete and ready to move within half an hour. After a difficult advance astride the railway line in the dark, Ward came under fire, but his quick thinking and clever use of ground enabled his force to repel the first attack.

As they reached the outskirts of the town, the Bolsheviks, reinforced by Austrian prisoners of war, waited patiently for the British column to pass before opening a hail of gunfire at the Japanese following behind. The Diehards immediately responded and again, distinguished themselves in the ensuing battle. Their rapid shooting suppressed the enemy and forced them to withdraw into dead ground. It was a resounding success, which earned the gratitude of the Japanese commander and staved off further criticisms about the commitment and quality of British troops in Siberia.

Dukhovskaya is the only Siberian campaign entry included in the official list of the British battles of the Great War.[5] *The Times* reported that Ward had been presented with the *Croix de Guerre* after this battle. However, when Winston Churchill was asked by the Director of Military Intelligence in the War Office about publicity, he wrote: "Colonel Ward is doing admirably; but I do not think the publication necessary at this moment. Our policy in Siberia is too nebulous and our prospects too gloomy for special attention to be invited."[6]

Ward quickly realised that he needed artillery support if he was to go further and sought help from the captain of HMS *Suffolk*. In response, Captain Payne fitted 12-pounder guns to an armoured train and sent this, with a detachment of Royal Marines, forward to the Middlesex's area. However, this train did not leave Vladivostok for the front line until 30th October.[7]

Ward consolidated his position and at the end of August, moved forward again. At the same time, a detachment of three officers and 150 men from the Manchester Regiment backfilled his troops at Spasskoye. As the Diehards travelled into the unknown with a 4,000-mile line of unguarded communications, Japan opened negotiations for the absolute possession of the railway to the Urals and asked for compensation from the Russian authorities for the use of its Army.

Japan was also concerned about their commercial rivalry with the United States after President Wilson agreed to send an expeditionary force to Vladivostok. The first American contingent[8] began arriving on 16th August and they were soon followed by the force commander Major General William Graves who arrived from San Francisco. He had been handed direct orders from the president to remain impartial and not to interfere in Russian internal affairs. His arrival with 8,763 troops changed the whole dynamic within the Allied command and had a significant effect on the final outcome of the war.

★★★

Meanwhile, a coalition government[9] was formed at Omsk on 5th September. The Diehards enhanced their growing reputation and earned a further invitation to move forward from the combined Czech and Russian command. En route, Ward met the charismatic polar explorer, 44-year-old Admiral Alexander Vasilyevich Kolchak, who had been appointed as the Minister of War and Marine by the new government.

In October, the Red Army established a firm hold of the eastern bank of the River Volga with the future Marshal Tukhachevsky in command of the 1st Red Army at the age of 25. The further forward the Diehards foraged, the more they understood the divisions within the anti-Bolshevik movement. Ward describes the White Army as full of "ill-fed, half-clad soldiers struggling to save the state under intolerable conditions." Their hopes of reinforcement by vast numbers of battle-hardened Allied troops were forlorn. When he took the regimental band and a guard of 100 picked men to meet the British consul at Ekaterinburg, the Russians complained about the "long weary wait between British promises and the appearance of the first khaki clad soldier."

Once it became clear that the German Army was beaten in Flanders, the Soviet Government offered to negotiate peace with the Allies on 8th November, but this proposal was turned down. How different history would have been if London and Paris had not mis-appreciated the strength of support for the Bolsheviks, or the logistic challenges of sustaining operations in far-away places such as Omsk. They also underestimated the effect of the void in communications between their capitals and crisis centres in the Far East, in terms of accurate information and timely decisions.

Ward proved his detractors wrong. He turned out to be a bold commander who overturned the odds and did more than most to live up to the expectations of the White Russians. In Zema, he put down an armed uprising without the loss of lives by rapidly deploying his battalion to key points and reinforcing this with diplomacy, listening to the grievances and addressing the leaders' concerns. By intervening, he technically disobeyed orders, but as an MP, he had a different perspective from the average infantry commanding officer at the time.

Exactly one week after the guns fell silent on the Western Front, the coalition government in Omsk was overthrown in a *coup d'etat* by the Monarchists. Tensions had been increasing for some time. At an official dinner given in honour of the Allies, guests walked out when a Cossack officer forced the band at gunpoint to play the former national anthem "God Save the Czar". On 18th November, the Socialist-Revolutionary directory leader was arrested by a troop of Cossacks and the remaining cabinet members voted to make Admiral Kolchak the *Verkhovnyi Pravitel*, or Supreme Ruler. His first proclamation attempted to reconcile the anti-Bolshevik factions:

> The Provisional All-Russian Government has come to an end. The Council of Ministers, having all the power in its hands, has invested me, Admiral Alexander Kolchak, with this power. I have accepted this responsibility in the exceptionally difficult circumstances of civil war and complete disorganisation of the country, and I now make it known that I shall follow neither the reactionary path, nor the deadly path of party strife. My chief aims are the organisation of a fighting force, the overthrow of Bolshevism, and the establishment of law and order, so that the Russian people may be able to choose a form of government in accordance with its desire and to realise the high ideas of liberty and freedom. I call upon you, citizens, to unite and to sacrifice your all, if necessary, in the struggle with Bolshevism.

Back in Vladivostok the Allies believed the coup was inspired by the British Mission.[10] The cause of this rumour was a 34-year-old Scottish cavalry officer, Lieutenant Colonel John Fraser Neilson of the 10th Hussars. He was a refined officer, married to the daughter of a wealthy English trader in Moscow, who worked alongside Robert Bruce Lockhart before he began his famous mission as the unofficial agent to the Bolsheviks in January 1918.

General Knox, who had spent two weeks in Omsk between 21st October and 5th November, handed command of the British Mission in Omsk to Neilson when he departed for Vladivostok. Neilson lived in a carriage opposite the Russian military headquarters, known as the Stavka. When he was not working, he spent his time painting with water colours. He tried to avoid political conspiracies in Omsk and when asked by Russians, he repeated the London mantra: "we are not concerned with individuals, or the composition of governments, but we desire to see and support a government capable of restoring order and carrying on the war." However, he was the first-person Kolchak informed after assuming control and was asked to accompany the new leader when he visited the French High Commissioner's train. By appearing with Kolchak, Neilson was forever associated by the Allies as being involved, if not the brains behind, the coup.[11]

Kolchak received a mixed reception from the anti-Bolsheviks. Although the monarchists supported his appointment, angry socialist leaders denounced him and called their supporters to take action. Their agitation resulted in an uprising at Kolumzino on 22nd December that was suppressed brutally by Cossacks, who executed almost 500 protesters and subjected others to mass floggings. This drove the Socialist-Revolutionary party to open negotiations with the Bolsheviks and in January 1919 to join forces with the Red Army.

Kolchak's appointment also antagonised some of the Allies, including the Polish Rifle Division[12] and the Czech Legion. They both supported the Socialist-Revolutionary leaders and regarded Kolchak as an autocratic puppet of the British. In *The Times* of 31st December, a cable recorded that the Czech forces viewed the overthrow of the Directory "as a setback to Socialism and the triumph of reaction." The American commander also remained wary and his views were shared by President Wilson, a strong advocate of non-interference and self-determination.

Japan was also cautious, but for a different reason. The Japanese feared Kolchak would interfere with their occupation of the districts, or *Oblasts*, in the East. This was confirmed by his first decree which informed Japan that their concessions were being reduced. In response, the Japanese deployed their puppet, Ataman Grigori Semeonov, to protect their interests with hired mercenaries. This had a disastrous effect on the situation in Siberia. By placing their territorial ambitions above the Allied cause and maintaining murderous criminals in their employment, Japan created an extended area of anarchy, which ultimately made Kolchak's position untenable.

His first military test arrived within days. After the Czech Legion withdrew from the front, the Bolshevik line swept forward. Responding immediately, Kolchak counter-attacked with a celebrated winter campaign, known as the Perm Offensive. He divided his forces into three armies: General Gajda's Siberian Army in the north; General Hanjin's

Western Army in the centre; and Ataman Dutov's Cossacks with the Army of the South West.

The key battleground was between Perm, controlled by three divisions of the 3rd Red Army[13] and the capital of the Urals, Ekaterinburg, where Yukov Yurovsky and the local *Soviet* assassinated the Czar and his family. Here, General Golitzine commanding the 3rd Ural Corps restored the front line and captured a huge area which included the valuable iron industry, known as the Watkin Works. Although, he did not defeat the Red Army decisively, he was amazed to discover the factory preserved and secured by the 6,000 workers, who had rejected the Bolshevik Terror.

Kolchak's officers were not amused when they read in the English papers how the Czech, Italian and French forces inflicted defeat on the Bolsheviks when in fact they did not fire a shot. The only foreign contingent which contributed was the Royal Marines with HMS *Suffolk's* guns mounted on armoured trains. However, the Royal Navy was denied credit[14] for this and for their subsequent heroic work on the river boats, which went deeper into Russia than any of the British Army's infantry battalions.

Although Ward admired much about the Russian army and fine leaders, such as General Golitzine, he was a realist. He knew from speaking to local workers that although the excesses of the Bolsheviks made the people hanker for the comparative security of a Czar, he heard too many ordinary Russians say that "Russia will never submit to live under the old regime again."

Ward reflected the views of many observers when he wrote about a "ruthless disregard of human life by both sides in this brutal internecine strife." Omsk in the winter of 1918 was a lawless city, with neither an effective police force, nor an impartial court. Every night, as soon as darkness fell, shots were heard in the streets. The morning sanitary carts picked up between five and 20 dead with no investigations undertaken. In one incident, three conspirators disguised as soldiers entered a Siberian regiment's quarters and killed five officers. One of the murderers was captured and flogged with a knout.[15] At the 100th stroke, he revealed the conspiracy, which resulted in 50 further arrests and more executions.

Ward's biggest contribution to the campaign was his humanitarian intervention, which saved the lives of many Russians. When the Directorate of Five was arrested, he prevented their execution by suggesting to Admiral Kolchak that if the people of England thought he was murdering his rivals, he would rapidly lose the sympathy of Democratic nations. He also ensured that the journey into exile of Nikolai Avksentiev and the other Directors[16] was not disrupted.

Ward assigned a competent officer with a strong detachment to guard their train from Omsk to the Chinese border at Changchun. This platoon had to repel several lynching attempts, but eventually reached the safety of the frontier on 28th November. Ward's action was not out of any sympathy to the Socialist cause, but an example of humanitarian conscience, combined with a sense of political expediency.

★★★

A second Territorial Force[17] battalion joined the Diehards at Omsk, but not until the New Year. The 1st/9th Cyclist[18] battalion was one of 34 raised in Hampshire for World War One[19] and had served in the Punjab since 1916. It was a great surprise to the commander, Lieutenant Colonel Robert Johnson, when he received orders to sail with his whole battalion to Siberia. Thirty-three officers and 990 men assembled at Bombay and after a difficult journey on the SS *Dunera*, with many soldiers dying from influenza, they arrived at Vladivostok on 25th November.

Initially, the battalion was placed within the Anglo-Canadian Brigade of 6,000 troops under the command of Major General James Elmsley.[20] He placed the Tigers, as they were known,[21] in the barracks on the west side of Vladivostok. It frustrated Sergeant Walter Tulley that the battalion was no longer equipped with bicycles when he was forced to march ten miles to the baths, only to find the water was lukewarm. His mood improved when he was issued with the Canadian Arctic clothing and listened to "excellent" lessons by the North West Mounted Police about the best way to combat the cold weather.[22]

The battalion deployed to Omsk over a four-day period, starting on 15th December. D Company was the first to undertake the uncomfortable four-hour march to the station, wearing their wool lined coats and long boots that were far from ideal for the cobbled roads in the city.

During the 4,000-mile freezing train journey, the Tigers' reputation as hardy soldiers was put to the test. They lived in 20-man cattle trucks lit by candles and had to huddle round a barely adequate stove, eating their black bread and bully beef for 23 days. Colour Sergeant Adolphus Jupe observed that the first halt of the day was the most critical, "as men sprang from their trucks to perform the necessary functions of the body.

It was an impressive sight to witness a long line of bared posteriors their owners anxiously gazing towards the engine, ready to make a run for it at the first sign of the train moving off."[23]

There were other morale boosting moments, such as the rum and pheasant Christmas dinner bought for the troops in Harbin. However, the soldiers were not impressed when the temperature plummeted to 42 degrees below freezing in the Trans-Baikal. At least they had a Canadian YMCA truck with its tea and cake and a cinema for occasional entertainment.

The arrival of the Tigers appeased growing Russian demands for Allied support. Their appearance as the vanguard of the Anglo-Canadian Brigade, combined with the Perm success resulted in Kolchak's government refusing to attend the Prinkipo Peace Conference in February 1919. However, this was a false dawn because rather than hatching plans to flood reinforcements into Siberia, the Allies were procrastinating in their capital cities.

The Hampshire's task was to assist the White Army, but by the time they arrived in Omsk, the political situation in London had changed dramatically. Despite Churchill's enthusiasm to wage war and much support within the Army to extend their role, the Cabinet decided after the Armistice to withdraw British troops from Russia. The war secretary's letter to the prime minister on 8th March confirmed: "You have also decided that Colonel John Ward and the two British battalions at Omsk are to be withdrawn (less any who volunteer to stay) as soon as they can be replaced by a military mission, similar to that to Denikin, composed of men who volunteer specifically for service in Russia."

The same message arrived from Canada. Public opinion mirrored that in war-weary Britain and the Ottawa government forbade Elmsley from taking the brigade into battle. At the same time, the Canadian Prime Minister, Sir Robert Borden, informed Lloyd George that Canada intended to withdraw its troops from Siberia in April 1919.

It wasn't just the British and Canadians who were gun-shy. French General Maurice Janin was nominally the commander-in-chief, but his command comprised only a composite French battalion in Chelyabinsk, an Italian battalion in Krasnoyarsk, plus the Hampshire battalion and the Czech Legion. These units did no more than provide garrison security and guard the supply trains during the winter offensive.

General Knox became increasingly frustrated with the "vain pretensions of the French." His responsibilities for distributing clothing and equipment meant that he had to spend most of his time in Vladivostok, 4,000 miles from the Omsk Government. For operational information, he had to rely on a junior officer, Major Leo Steveni,[24] because Neilson moved out of Omsk following a telegram from the Chief of the Imperial General Staff in London, written in the style of Winston Churchill, which stated "You should inform Colonel Nielson that his recent activities in political matters are regarded by the Foreign Office as highly indiscreet and as tending to compromise His Majesty's Government by making it appear that they were intervening on behalf of one particular party in Siberia. While therefore Nielson's zeal and energy are appreciated he must be cautioned against further action of this nature."[25]

Steveni was popular with the Russians. However, the officers in Kolchak's military headquarters jealously guarded their information and Knox's intelligence network was not as proficient as some of the other contingents such as the excellent American team led by Robert Eichelberger. To address this imbalance, Knox posted a stream of proficient volunteers, who had seen service on the Western Front, to his operations and intelligence directorate in Omsk. These included men like Captain Rex Carthew of the Bedfordshire Regiment, who had commanded the 1st Battalion, the Hertfordshire Regiment from May until September 1918 as a 26-year-old, after his colonel had been gassed at the Somme.[26]

★★★

When the Allies failed to enter the fray, the clamour increased because the Stavka needed reinforcements to bolster their advancing army groups in the north, centre and south. On 14th March, Kolchak occupied Ufa and continued to press forward towards Samara on the River Volga. He desperately required help, but the Allies were still prevaricating, much to his dismay.

Meanwhile, the stagnation in the British battalions had a draining effect on discipline. The Hampshire officers did well to maintain morale in their companies. However, it was inevitable that there would be occasional unrest. According to Cyclist Stanley Green of 12 Platoon C Company, there was a "mini-revolt" on 26th March, when some of the soldiers demanded that the Commanding Officer "put 10 prisoners in better quarters and apologise for calling them swine." However, this was a rare exception to an otherwise highly disciplined performance.

As a former president of the Oxford Union, Robert Johnson took a cerebral approach to this challenge and introduced a programme of alternative pursuits, such as skating and ballroom dancing to the battalion's schedule. However, what he really needed was a proper military task and this arrived with the authorization from London to create an Anglo-Russian Brigade, trained and equipped by the British in the capital of the Urals, 800 miles west of Omsk.

On 26th April, the first echelon of Hampshire soldiers set off for Ekaterinburg.[27] Colonel Johnson offered his whole-hearted support to the project, saying optimistically, "we hope to march into Moscow... Hants and Russian Hants together." The force was to be commanded by the Head of the British Training Mission, Brigadier James Blair of the Gordon Highlanders, who arrived a month after a cohort of volunteer officers had established a firm presence in the elegant city.

This initiative benefited from the other training partnerships that General Knox established in Siberia. The first school was set up on Russian Island[28] and was heralded as a resounding triumph. Then in February 1919, six British officers and four NCOs under the command of Lieutenant Colonel Lyddon Morley arrived in Irkutsk. They were dismayed to find that the students spent so much time in the classroom, with only four hours practice on the machine gun and 80 hours of theory. Morley was obstructed from making any changes to the syllabus until he "donated" 15,000 sets of uniform to the 8th and 14th Siberian Rifle Divisions, after which any opposition promptly evaporated.

The third enterprise was at the Russian Cadet School in Tomsk. Here, Major Tom Kirkwood of the 17th Cavalry, Indian Army and a team of ten officers and six NCO instructors lived in the same mess as the Russian officers. With six hours each day allotted to outdoor work, the team achieved excellent results and also provided a useful base for General Knox during his regular travels from Vladivostok to Omsk.

★★★

As the spring thaw approached, the war took another turn. In April, the accumulation of filth was loaded into carts and dumped on the still frozen river to be carried away when the ice broke up. However, as the British troops celebrated Easter on 20th April, the Red Army counter-attacked Kolchak's thinly spread forces in the south.

Four days later, at about 5a.m., the ice on the River Kama started to move. The locals had done nothing about storing their felled trees because they did not expect the thaw until the first week of May. There was estimated to be over six million trees in the region, so the timber companies felt they could lose a few down river and anyway, an early melt meant good crops, which would compensate for the lost wood. A fortnight later, the snow and ice gave way to a dust storm, which according to Ward, was worse than the sands of Sudan.

Since the Anglo-Russian Brigade had not yet been formed, there was only one British unit that went into action against the Red Army on the Eastern Front in the summer of 1919.[29] This was the Royal Navy detachment that distinguished itself on the River Kama, providing fire support for Kolchak's forces. The flotilla, led by Captain Thomas Henry Jameson of the Royal Marines, comprised an oil-driven tug named *Kent* and a barge named *Suffolk*. *Kent* was armed with four 12-pounders and manned by a volunteer crew of 24, whilst *Suffolk* boasted a 6-inch gun and needed a crew of ten.

From mid-May, Jameson was in regular action, engaging enemy gunboats and firing at military targets on shore. His crews sank the Bolshevik flagship and earned high praise from Admiral Mikhail Smirnov, who was proud to fly his flag from *Kent's* top mast. Cedric Clarke, a commissioned gunner who joined the Royal Navy as a 26-year-old Boy 2nd Class in 1906, commanded the *Suffolk*. She expended all of her 256 rounds of ammunition, routing large numbers of the Bolshevik forces, before the gun was dismantled and loaded on a train commandeered at Perm[30] soon after Emerson arrived in Siberia.

When the Royal Navy detachment returned to Omsk, they dined with Admiral Smirnov at the Aquarium restaurant on 29th July. They were awarded a number of decorations by Admiral Kolchak, but the British Consul, Sir Charles Eliot, directed that they should hand them back. According to Captain Jameson: "This was a disappointment as they would have been a treasured souvenir to the recipients of this expedition and especially so when we learnt that [hundreds of] Russian awards to British servicemen on the north [and] southern fronts had been accepted."[31]

Vladivostok Harbour where Emerson inspected a freighter full of railway equipment in May 1919. (Courtesy of the Royal Hampshire Regiment Trust)

Captain Rex Carthew, sitting centre, with Captain Phelps Hodges, standing right, on their way to Omsk in April 1919. (Courtesy of Royal Hampshire Regiment Trust)

From Vladivostok to Omsk, the Trans-Siberian Railway was controlled by the Allies, but the 38 tunnels around the southern tip of the "Holy Sea" were subject to frequent attacks by Bolshevik insurgents. (Courtesy of Angus MacMillan)

The Czech Legion
liberated Irkutsk in
1918. (Courtesy of
the Royal Hampshire
Regiment Trust)

The Hampshire Regi-
ment's accommodation
in Omsk. (Courtesy of
the Royal Hampshire
Regiment Trust)

A group of Siberian
recruits in the Anglo-
Russian Brigade
being processed by
the 1st/9th Battalion
Hampshire Regiment.
(Courtesy of the Royal
Hampshire Regiment
Trust)

CHAPTER 4

American Integrity

I suppose it is the old story, Baker; men often get the reputation of being stubborn merely because they are everlastingly right.

PRESIDENT WOODROW WILSON TO THE 47TH US SECRETARY OF WAR

Emerson didn't realise how dirty the Manchurian trains were until he saw the layers of grime washing away in the Russian baths. Once he was thoroughly decontaminated, he returned to his hotel and slept deeply. In the morning, he felt revitalised and wrote: "This is Russia! The land of Cossacks and Caviar, that degenerated from Romanovs and Roubles to Revolution and Ruin…."

His excitement was tempered when he surveyed his accommodation. He was on the upper floor of a long brick building partitioned with pine boards into cubicles that held two officers. In each cell, there was a table and two iron cots with planks of wood for a mattress. In the dim corridor, a couple of rusty iron stoves were supposed to heat the place, but they were seldom lit for want of fuel. Most of the windows were broken and were stuffed with rags or paper, but from a few, he could see a view of a bleak hillside covered with refuse and latrines.

When he reported to the British headquarters, he was given no acclimatisation, but instructed to inspect a ship loaded with railway equipment that had just arrived from Japan. It was ordered from Baldwins[1] before the revolution in 1916 and had finally arrived three years later. He walked down to the *Zoltoi Rog*, or Golden Horn bay along one of two cobbled thoroughfares, lined with stone buildings that ran at right angles to each other along the western and northern sides of the harbour.

Beyond these avenues, the streets were "innocent of metal" and filled with deep ruts where droshkies picked their way past yawning holes to deposit their passengers on the rotting wooden sidewalks.

When he boarded the freighter, the second officer came up to Emerson and introduced himself as John MacMillan from Campbeltown on the Mull of Kintyre. He claimed to be a cousin and offered to celebrate their meeting with a "wee dram" for the clan. This made the dull task of checking the lengthy manifest much easier in the afternoon.

After work, he walked back to his billet along Svetlanskaya Ulitsa, where fabulous uniforms peacocked up and down the main thoroughfare. He was especially impressed by the outfits: "Every Russian regiment has a different uniform... The Cossacks are an awe-inspiring crowd and wear the cap on the right side of the head, while the left exhibits a shock of long shaggy hair."

Transit soldiers were not allowed to eat in the British Mission Mess, but were directed to a nearby restaurant where the meal took two hours to arrive. That night Emerson was invited to join a party heading for the Be Ba Bo Cafe Chantant vaudeville, where supper and a bottle of vodka cost 220 roubles, the equivalent of £1.50. However, he preferred to see some "way-fair opera", where he communicated with the manager by speaking French to an Italian, who translated it to Russian.

Emerson's arrival in Vladivostok coincided with a chaotic period of upheaval. The Diehards were returning from Omsk following a farewell parade arranged by the 2nd Siberian Regiment. After loudly applauding their dazzling display of horsemanship, the British Tommies enjoyed a lavish lunch in a Khirghiz tent followed by toasts and songs. They responded to the stern, melancholy epics about Cossack heroes, with their own renditions of popular music hall tunes. They departed to cheers from their new comrades in arms, who were confident of defeating the Red Army that summer.

The redeployment was caused by the imminent departure of 4,000 Canadian troops, who were due to return home in April. However just before their planned parting, General Elmsley found himself responding to a call from the Japanese commander-in-chief to rescue a group at Shkotova, a small village north of the city. Elmsley sent a company from the disgraced 259th Battalion[2] as part of the Allied force, which included an Anglo-Russian contingent of 149 officers and men, under the command of Lieutenant Colonel Saprikin. When they returned to Vladivostok after their successful expedition, the grateful Japanese donated a large amount of alcohol to the rescue party as an appreciation of their efforts.[3]

The Diehards took over the Canadian barracks in the west of the city, whilst the remainder of the Allies were accommodated in the lines overlooking the harbour. This area was the scene of intense activity that started at dawn. Most of the berths were filled by ships unloading war matériel destined for the White Army, but the port was also swarming with displaced society.

Anxious refugees, who had fled from European Russia in fear of the Red Terror, complained about the freighters that occupied the moorings. They desperately sought tickets on the sparse number of passenger ships available to take their families to the new lives they craved in America. Many of these unfortunates had lost money and possessions crossing thousands of miles of territory at the mercy of the marauding bandits. Now, they found themselves worse off than the ship yard workers, or those attached to institutions such as school teachers, who lived in relative comfort.

The sanitation had not kept pace with the flood of refugees and the streets beyond the two main avenues were full of filth. The city depended almost exclusively upon surface wells for its water supply, but this water was delivered in cans carried by people who had no concept of hygiene. Apart from the risk of disease, the desperate situation provided opportunities for criminal gangs who were merciless to anyone who lost their way. One seedy quarter was named "The Bucket of Blood" because it averaged a murder per night.

This anthropological dreamland was full of international intrigue. Emerson saw Hindus, Persians and Sikhs and many of the peoples who lived east of the Urals and Caspian Sea, including Bashkirs from Ufa, Tartars from Kazan, Mongolians, Kazakhs, Kirghiz, Turkmen, Tadzhiks, as well as different types of Europeans. There were Koreans in flowing white with strange stove-pipe hats; bearded Russian priests trailed by numerous offspring; fierce-looking Cossacks in mighty fur hats; Jews in gabardines; and tight-lipped American nurses in hard blue hats and billowing cloaks, who reminded him of Dallas. There were also military and diplomatic contingents from more than a dozen countries[4] including many American soldiers and sailors.

The irony that President Wilson sent nearly nine thousand soldiers to Siberia at the same time that Emerson joined the British Army in Pennsylvania was not lost on him. He felt some sympathy for the American soldiers who were scorned in the streets by some White Russian supporters. The brittle state of affairs centred on the policy of the Senior American Military Commander, 53-year-old Major General William Sidney Graves.

Graves was the son of a southern Baptist minister and had experienced a strict upbringing that served him well as a West Point graduate. Before his assignment to Russia, he had worked for five years as the Secretary of the General Staff, where he developed an intuitive eye for detail and a deep understanding of the ways of work in Washington. As a reward, he was hand-picked for the Siberian command, despite having little knowledge of Russian affairs. Before he sailed from San Francisco, he was handed an *Aide Memoire* personally written by President Wilson that forbade him from taking sides in the war.

Pitched into the melee at Vladivostok, Graves held no prejudice and was committed to a policy of impartiality. However, this not only antagonised the White Russians, but it also caused problems with some of the Allies. The coalition was divided between nations which supported Kolchak and countries that believed it was wrong to intervene in the internal affairs of another state.

By sticking to his hallowed principle, Graves earned the respect of the majority of the contingents. The Canadians and the Chinese supported him because they resented the White Russian practice of killing and torturing ordinary people. The Italians held instructions from Rome to vote with the USA on every proposal and the Czechs and Poles, struggling for their own freedom and independence, also supported American ideology.

This placed the senior military representatives of England, France, and Japan in an awkward position. General Knox and his counterpart believed the Dominion and European representatives should follow their lead and General Otani of Japan considered that he was in overall command. But Graves did not see eye to eye with them, or the British Consul, Sir Charles Eliot, because they appeared to condone the brutal measures employed in eastern Siberia.

The inconvenient truth was that the French and British were in the minority and this led to angry communiqués relayed behind Graves's back to Washington. However, the American was a wily staff officer and was able to counter their deceit because he had support from the highest level in the War Department, as well as the White House.

The American commander's competence did not stop some of the US State Department officials from undermining his authority.[5] One of the tricks they played was to ask the Head of the War Department's military intelligence branch for an officer to draft reports for the American consul. When this colonel arrived in Vladivostok with directions to bypass General Graves, it was discovered that he had in his possession a "monograph", which stated: "The American troops are in Siberia primarily to support Kolchak against Bolsheviks by keeping his line of communications open along the Trans-Siberian Railroad." Graves realised this official document discredited his statements about being impartial. He immediately sent a telegram to the chief of the Army Staff, General Peyton March, who gave him authority to burn the offending section.

Fortunately, Graves had set up his own military intelligence department, led by a talented officer who subsequently became a famous American general. Robert Eichelberger's[6] tireless energy and keen insight into local Russian conditions enabled him to stay ahead of other nations' intelligence sections. For example, he was the first to report that: "reliable information from many sources indicates that there is practically no front maintained by the Siberian Army."[7] He also ensured that his team of 15 men, recruited from educational Institutions in America, understood that they were not to "interfere" in the internal affairs of Russia.

The problem this policy caused for the American commander was how to employ his soldiers in a meaningful way. For about ten months, the US Army was engaged only on garrison duties. During this time, his soldiers were threatened and disparaged when they walked around the city and this affected the moral of his troops.

In the meantime, the state of the Trans-Siberian Railway deteriorated dramatically. The conditions were recorded by British troops, with an early illustration provided by Captain Henry Kartchkal Peacock of the Royal Garrison Artillery.[8] Peacock was half Russian and had lived in Siberia for eight years, so was well-versed in the ways and means of the country. He was put in charge of a train loaded with several million rounds of ammunition destined for the front line. Leaving Vladivostok on 28th November, his train was beset with mechanical failures, administrative delays, banditry and smuggling by corrupt officials along the route. It took three weeks to reach Omsk; twice the time of a normal journey.[9]

A less successful officer lost a third of his wagons on the 3,000-mile rail journey. Local station masters found an excuse at most stops to detach one or two wagons, which had developed mechanical problems. These were normally blamed on an overheating axle box, or a sheared bolt.

The doleful station master would explain that there was no one to carry out the repair work immediately. It was a game of bluff and counter bluff. Escort officers learned that the only response was to wait for the mechanic, or lose the wagon. If the train blocked one of his sidings, the station master usually solved the problem without much delay. Sometimes, however, it involved an overnight stop, when large notices had to be placed on all the carriages and sentries with loaded weapons had to be alert to stop the pilferers attempting to break into wagons and steal anything they could.

Between Lake Baikal and Omsk the line was subjected to frequent attacks from partisan bandits. Security threats to the railway and rolling stock increased the further one travelled from Vladivostok. Two trains loaded with 308 horses and 30 mules destined for the Jaeger artillery batteries and other regiments at Ekaterinburg were sabotaged near Tayga. This resulted in the death of 16 horses and two mules, but it would have been much worse if the guard force of Canadian Mounted Police had not reacted so well.

The Times reported again on 15th February from Omsk: "The Vice-Minister of Communications describes the condition of the railway now as being catastrophic, an enormous proportion of the engines being out of commission, partly owing to the exceptionally cold weather, which has frozen the pipes. Near Chelyabinsk, in the Ural region, there are

250 derelict engines, mostly put out of action by frost. There is a fuel and lubricating oil famine...."

However in March, after protracted negotiations between Russia and the Allies, an agreement was signed that set out how the railway would be improved.[10] The British, French and Russians had insufficient troops to protect the line, so the Americans, Japanese and Czechs agreed to do what they could in Russia, whilst the Chinese agreed to guard the short-cut through Manchuria.

When the American troops deployed forward, they were soon drawn into a fight to protect the passengers, staff and matériel from Bolshevik insurgents and White Russian bandits. The socialists complained that Graves was helping Kolchak by guarding his line of communications and those in authority, typified by the 28-year-old Ataman Semeonov, complained about the foreign interference in their territory. For the first time in history, the US Army found itself sitting between two warring factions, acting as a global policeman.

The man in the middle, charged with guarding the railway in Trans-Baikal with the 27th US Infantry, was Colonel Charles Morrow. In theory, he held Kolchak's authority to protect passengers and prevent interference with the operation of the line in his sector, but soon after his arrival, Semeonov tested him by attempting to arrest some railway employees in his sector, on the grounds that they were Bolsheviks.

The courageous Morrow informed Semeonov that he would not permit him to arrest these men unless he showed evidence that they had committed some offence. Semeonov was horrified that a foreigner could tell him what he could, or could not do in the Trans-Baikal. Morrow replied that if Semeonov's train passed a certain place, he would blow it "to perdition" and sited his 37mm guns on either side of the railway line with a sandbag emplacement around them.

Morrow's bluff worked and Semeonov backed down. This heightened the morale of the American troops and set the standard for the remainder of their operation. These small detachments that were established in isolated locations relished their work guarding the railway and managed to supplement their rations with game hunted in the woods and salmon caught in the river.

Emerson's first month in Russia coincided with a period of intense attacks on the American sector of responsibility. The most serious fighting occurred near the Suchan coal mines, which the US Army was tasked to keep open. During a battle on 12th June, a chef, Edward Evans, dropped his kitchen utensils and picked up a rifle after his section was attacked by a superior force of the enemy. He took up a position alone on the thatched roof of a shed on the flank of his platoon, from where he successfully repelled an attack by seven insurgents, thus preventing any serious casualties in his detachment. For his outstanding bravery, he was awarded one of the first Distinguished Service Crosses awarded by President Wilson to American soldiers in Siberia.[11]

A hospital train was dedicated to providing assistance to the casualties as the fighting intensified. Captain Oscar Frundt earned the only Distinguished Service Cross to be awarded to a medical officer for his skilful command of this train and care of the injured whilst under fire in June, but sadly, he was unable to save one of his fellow recipients, Private Alpha Schurter. This young hero was in a patrol group of four soldiers from 31st Infantry, led by Sergeant James Canney, when they were attacked by an enemy group of about 50 Russians in the Lower Suchan Valley. Although mortally wounded during the battle, Schurter continued to advance with the patrol and put the enemy to flight.

Battles involving American troops continued for six months. The final clash occurred at Verkhne Udinsk in January 1920. By this time, Admiral Kolchak had transferred power in the East to Semeonov, who was continuing to rob and kill in the Trans-Baikal. He sent an armoured car, under the command of General Bogomoletz, to arrest the station-master. Colonel Morrow asked the Russian General whether he was aware that the Americans had charge of that sector and he would not permit him to arrest railroad employees. Bogomoletz said: "I am not supposed to give any account to you of our actions. I will not converse with you any more in regard to such."

The American colonel replied: "Let me tell you this, I do not want to cause any trouble for you, however, I have 2,500 men here to carry out my orders. I must know why this man was arrested; he is under my protection."

The Russian responded: "I was told he was a Bolshevik and I wanted to kill him tonight, but if you insist, I shall release him. It is immaterial; if the station-master is guilty we will get him sooner or later."

The station-master was released and the armoured car continued west. About midnight on 9th January, it arrived at Posolskaya, where a detachment of 38 American soldiers under the command of 21-year-old Lieutenant Paul Kendall were on duty. An hour later, when the company was asleep, the Russian armoured car fired into their accommodation.

Kendall, who had only graduated from West Point a year before, bravely led a counter attack. One of his soldiers, Sergeant Carl Robbins, climbed onto the engine of the armoured train and in the face of pistol and machine-gun fire, hurled a grenade into the cab, which rendered the engine incapable of further operation. Unfortunately, he lost his life in this gallant action and Private Homer Tommie, who joined him in the attempt to board the train, lost his leg when he fell under the wheels of the train.

After a fierce fight, Kendall captured General Bogomoletz and 54 Russians with him.[12] There were no police or courts capable of dealing with this crime. Semeonov demanded the return of his armoured car and the prisoners, but Colonel Morrow kept them until 23rd January when the Americans finally withdrew from the region. During their detention, the Americans recorded evidence from all the individuals separately and their statements were notably consistent. It was established, beyond any doubt, that the men in this one armoured car had, between 1st and 10th January, "robbed and brutally murdered over forty men and raped and killed three women."

★★★

American military efforts were matched by the work of the Red Cross doctors and nurses involved in the humanitarian operation that Dallas joined soon after Emerson arrived in Vladivostok. It was no coincidence that this indomitable woman was in Siberia at the same time as her betrothed. When she heard that he was being sent to the Far East, Dallas immediately applied for a posting to Vladivostok and, as a talented linguist, started to learn Russian.

Volunteering to join the group of nurses due to serve with the American Expeditionary Force, she took a train to California and reported for duty. The War Department cabled General Graves and explained that a hundred female nurses were in San Francisco, and would leave for Vladivostok on the next army transport. However, Graves "did not want these nurses because of the conditions relative to accommodations, and the absence of any recreation for them."[13]

After some persuasion, he agreed to receive 25 female nurses and because Dallas spoke some Russian, she was included in a group that sailed in the SS *Nippon Maru*,[14] bound for Yokohama. When she boarded the 20-year-old ship, she noticed that the fixtures and fittings were past their best, but the commander, Captain Ocasaki, was very smart and polite.

The voyage became an apprehensive blend of emotions. It was a pleasure for Dallas to share her first crossing of the Pacific with like-minded volunteers and she befriended many of the doctors and nurses on the passage, including physician Frederick Lee Barnum and nurse Bessie Eddy Lyon. However, the stories she heard from the "old hands" returning from leave made her anxious about the future.

She was told that the prevalent diseases included the plague, typhus, typhoid and scarlet fever. Most people in Vladivostok suffered from a sore throat of some form and the illnesses affected everyone, including the troops. Sixteen Canadian soldiers had died of diseases ranging from influenza to smallpox and spinal meningitis in the first few months of 1919.

Dallas took comfort from the fact that she would be working with such professional people. She was also reassured that the Red Cross had learned many lessons since the original deployment as part of a worldwide response to the humanitarian crisis that arose in Russia during the Great War. Initially, this was led by individuals such as the Swedish nurse, Elsa Brändström, who was known as the "Angel of Siberia" for introducing basic medical treatment to the prisoner of war centres.

Britain had its own champion in this field, Lady Muriel Paget. Together with Lady Sybil Grey, she opened an Anglo-Russian Hospital at the Dmitri Palace in St Petersburg in January 1916. Its primary focus was the treatment of severely wounded soldiers and it was followed by field hospitals and food kitchens established in Ukraine, where British nurses witnessed at first hand the misery of the Eastern Front.

As the situation worsened, Lady Muriel organised a popular exhibition at the Grafton Galleries in London, which ran through May 1917 and raised thousands of pounds to support her hospital. This included a series of concerts, lectures and dramatic performances of works by Anton Chekhov. However, security worsened after the Bolshevik revolution and with no guarantees for safety, the medics at the Anglo-Russian Hospital were forced to return to England, leaving their supplies to the Red Cross. Lady Muriel remained in Ukraine, but together with the diplomat John Bagge and several medics, she was evacuated on the Trans-Siberian Railway when the civil war took hold in 1918.[15]

One of the British nurses, who completed the journey through Siberia to HMS *Suffolk*, was Florence Farmborough. Serving on the front line, she wrote about her heartache for a "beautiful land which has been laid waste" and the ghastly moments on the desolate battlefields with soldiers "lying amidst the twisted wires and shell cavities." She was one of the first women to write about her post-traumatic stress after finishing her work with the Red Cross: "I cannot express the dreadful emptiness which has come into my life. Anna Ivana found me weeping one day I could not tell her why because I myself did not know. She said it was 'reaction'. I did not contradict her, but I knew it was something much deeper than that."[16]

★★★

The American Red Cross became involved in the civil war with two commissions in North Russia and Siberia. Of these, the Commission to Siberia had by far the most profound effect. It was led by the founder of the first nursing college in Japan, Dr Rudolph Teusler. He saw it as his remit to establish hospitals and medical teams throughout Siberia and to assist the Czech Legion and the White Russian forces.

Teusler travelled from Vladivostok on 24th October 1918 at the head of a sanitary train destined for Omsk. He brought with him carriages of medical supplies, hospital equipment, and drugs. After picking up doctors and nurses at Harbin, he arrived just before the coup that brought Admiral Kolchak to power.

In the November chaos, the White authorities treated American requests with disdain. Teusler found a suitable building for a hospital, but his efforts at securing its lease were thwarted by Russian bureaucracy. The Stavka was highly suspicious about any foreign meddling and in this sense, the American Red Cross experienced exactly the same frustrations as the military missions.

The person who achieved the earliest success was the American matron, Florence Farmer. She could speak some Russian and "was a born organiser." She overcame the bureaucratic obstacles when she converted a large school building in Tumen into a model infirmary. Partitions were built; electric light and an X-ray cabinet were installed; and water was made available in all the wards.

Teusler built on this breakthrough by dealing with the greatest challenge to public health, the epidemic of typhus fever. With medical representatives from Britain, Canada, France, Japan and Czechoslovakia, he established the Inter Allied Typhus Commission. This influential body converted a train into a delousing facility that could travel to villages and towns throughout Siberia. Several cars were filled with medicines and fresh clothing. Others provided a delousing clinic, a bath car with a hot water tank and a hair cutting wagon.

Of the 31 medical professionals who embarked on the inaugural expedition that set off from Vladivostok on 2nd February, only two were Americans. The officer in charge was Captain Dallyn of the Canadian Expeditionary Force. Many of the orderlies were also Canadians, but they also employed local Russian *feldshers* and *sanitars*.[17]

They stopped at all the major towns and reached Chelyabinsk at the foot of the Urals. Their disinfection procedures were highly efficient and on a good day they were able to treat 900 people and escort those identified with the disease to hospital for convalescence. Unfortunately, Captain Dallyn and 13 others all contracted typhus by the summer of 1919, although most of them made a full recovery. When Dallyn departed, control was passed to a medic from Hawaii, Rudolf Bukeley, who continued to operate the train until the end of May 1920, when the order came from Washington to close it down.

Despite the documented humanitarian success,[18] Dr Teusler came into conflict with General Graves over the issue of impartiality. Teusler appeared to be sympathetic to the views of the State Department's representative, Ernest Harris, who supported the fight against Bolshevism. However,

Graves believed that handing over clothing and medical supplies to the White Army contravened President Wilson's policy of non-interference.

Teusler used the privileged position of the Red Cross as an independent agency to ignore Graves's instructions. In a report to Washington, he states: "The present work of the Red Cross is divided into two main lines of activity – military and refugee relief. The military relief, that is, the establishing, equipping, and operating of hospitals; the supplying of the All-Siberian Army with clothing, underwear, and other necessities, and the providing of drugs, medicine, and hospital supplies for Russian hospitals."

General Graves catalogued many occasions when the American Red Cross "crossed the line of impartiality."[19] One young officer stated in his report after returning as commander of a Red Cross train guard: "I did not get to stop at Omsk, as Kolchak troops expected a fight next day and I was rushed to the front to issue the supplies for the expected fight."

Graves condemned Teusler for acting as Kolchak's supply agent. He was particularly concerned about American troops becoming unwitting associates, so he threatened to withdraw guards from Red Cross trains. However, the doctors and nurses who arrived in 1919 were more sceptical about the mission and became more circumspect than the early evangelists. For example, one of Dallas's companions, Dr Barnum, confided to his diary: "the Russians did not want the Red Cross here … Although they did want help in the way of clothing food and supplies, the Russians had sufficient qualified and capable medical staff."[20]

Although many Russians appreciated the help when it was given with sensitivity, others were intolerant of what they considered American cultural superiority. Mrs Bessie Lyon summarised this when she wrote to her brother, Jim, on 21st August 1919: "The Russians don't like us. We are superior and we show it… If we saw a pigsty we would say, 'Poor pigs, I'll come and show you how to live, I'll stay a while and clean you up' …they resent our interference with a deep, dark, wholehearted resentment."[21]

★★★

The British also delivered medical supplies to Russian towns and cities along the railway line. For example, Captain John Alexander O'Driscoll

of the Royal Army Medical Corps distributed Red Cross stores including an X Ray unit to six military and civilian hospitals in Irkutsk. He
described the situation in his final report to General Knox,[22] explaining
that "nurses were being sent to the front in the middle of October with
no warm clothing." He praised the Russian women working under
appalling conditions, with many killed on the front line. "One of the
nurses we fitted up was going back to the front after being wounded for
the fourteenth time. She had over 24 injuries and when I saw her had
eight extracted bullets and splinters in her."

On his way back to Vladivostok, O'Driscoll visited Krasnoyarsk on
27th November and handed over to the Head of the District Medical
Services two wagon loads of medical stores and hospital clothing originally
intended for Omsk. A British lady living there, Mrs Campbell-Clark
distributed the Red Cross comforts and women's clothes to the civilian
hospital, children's refuge and families in need. Little did they know that
a future British Corps' commander would need urgent medical assistance
in that town during the following months.

CHAPTER 5

Railroad to Omsk

Those controlling the Siberian Railway control Siberia itself, for beyond the railway is only wilderness.

THE TIMES, 11TH JANUARY 1919

Emerson expected Dallas to be in Vladivostok, serving as a nurse with the American Army. When he learned that her passage from San Francisco had been delayed, he continued working in the headquarters while Leonard Vining and the others in his party headed west to Omsk. He was keen to accompany them to the front, but this would postpone any reunion with Dallas until October.

The day after he began his work, he met the men of HMS *Kent*[1] who entertained the Allied troops in Vladivostok at a concert. On the way back to his accommodation, he noticed the sky over the harbour was a deep shade of carnelian. He joined a group of British soldiers investigating the cause and they discovered a fire at the Red Cross warehouse on the wharf close to where Emerson worked. By the time they arrived, the stores were all lost and the only thing that the fire brigade could do was isolate the flames.

The water tender was a barrel on a cart drawn by horses that supplied a hose. When pumped vigorously by hand, the jet of water reached 15, or 20 feet. However, the soldiers described the operators as a bunch of "cockatoos" for directing the nozzle at the corrugated iron sides of the warehouse and letting the precious water stream ineffectively away from the source of the blaze. A large piece of iron wall fell on the heads of the firemen, which made the scene look like something out of a *Keystone*

Cops film, but at least it drilled some sense into them as they eventually brought the conflagration under control.

★★★

Emerson remained in Vladivostok for three weeks, but Dallas did not arrive on her ship and he had no idea whether she was coming or not. It was tempting to stay on because the headquarter staff were keen to retain him. However, he discovered that one of the American Red Cross nurses had been dishonourably dismissed from the service for her relationship with a soldier and was asked to refund her expenses and return her Red Cross pin and membership card. He did not wish to put Dallas's honour at risk, so he volunteered to work for the head of the British Railway Mission, Archibald Jack,[2] who had deployed forward to Ekaterinburg.

On 8th June, Emerson was assigned to the weekly International train that took only ten days, compared with the ammunition and supply trains that took anything from three weeks to a month to reach Omsk. He described the journey in a letter to his brother:

> The *Express De Lux [sic]* has not been quite itself since the war, but they have been trying to revive it with all its old-time glory. I went down to the station on Sunday night and the train was made up with all its "buttons polished" and looking quite smart. The *wagons-lits* cars were attached and the whole had an appearance of enthusiasm and impatience to be off, as if to say "Are we really going to Moscow and am I really the re-incarnation of the once world-famous international *Express de Lux [sic]*?"
>
> We left Vladivostok and everyone had just nicely settled down to the idea of a ten-day journey when there was felt the unmistakable sensation of trouble under the wheels. We were not on a boat, neither were we on the Bay of Biscay, which heightened the suspicion that we were tumbling down the bank.
>
> I managed to crawl through the window after we had come to rest and in the clear moon-light could see the locomotive sprawled on its side across the east bound track, giving its last vaporous gasps. The baggage car was in the loving embrace of the dining car on their sides down the embankment. Two of the sleeping cars were held up by faith alone and had not gone over the precipice.
>
> A quick inspection of the track showed that the derailment had been deliberately executed by the Bolsheviks. A section of rail had been removed and the spikes pulled from another. It was at the tangent of a horse-shoe curve on a 40-foot embankment. A board of engineers could not have selected a better

place nor done their work more thoroughly. According to all theory the train should have completely disappeared and it was nothing short of a miracle that saved complete disaster.

Some members of the General Staff of Kolchak's army were aboard and a grizzled old Cossack General asked if I would mind taking orders from him. I assured him that I should be most honoured and he accordingly instructed me to guard the flank while he went back and wired for assistance. I devoted most of my time to seeing that the baggage car did not catch fire; it was the repository of my winter shirts together with about five pounds of sugar and chocolate bars. A French major joined me and we patrolled the track together. I had a Russian rifle that was made at Remington.

A company of Americans came up and took over the guard. The General dismissed me and I returned to my sleeping compartment to see what happened to the sergeant. I found him drunk, adrift on Lethe into which the tributary vodka flows. The repair gang got the car back onto the track and had it switched back to Vladivostok. The sergeant awoke in the morning and was surprised "that we should have already reached Harbin." On the whole, I imagine he considers a very pleasant time was had.

A man was captured who confessed to being one of twelve implicated in the attempt to destroy the train. Thus it is that a "neck-tie party" is not an uncommon sight along the line.

We waited three days until another train was made up. This time we started out in daylight and got well up into Chinese territory before dark. Each section of the line is guarded by one of the Allies and through Manchuria the Chinese are about as efficient as any. At one place we anchored for the night and started out again at dawn. There are several places where the bridges have been destroyed and temporary structures permit the trains to pass. The tunnels must be carefully guarded as a wreck in a tunnel would obviously be a most annoying situation. One section is patrolled by an armoured train which precedes the Express.

The Czechs are the most picturesque of the Allied armies and are credited with some of the most important services. They live in trains of box cars along the route and have their "homes" decorated with the artistic skill that is typical of the bohemian style.

One of the interpreters travelling with me was a Czech and had been a Professor of Modern Languages. He had been educated in five universities and spoke ten languages. One sees the most complicated system of nationalities and languages. The better educated people in this part of the world usually know two or three languages. Such an interchange of nationalities makes it almost imperative and French and English are usually had in addition to the native tongue. One can see everywhere people trying to learn English. I manage to blunder along with a little French and a little less Russian and when accompanied by a really first-class interpreter can talk to anybody!

Emerson was impressed by the scenery around Lake Baikal and the River Yenisei[3] that "flows rather briskly as if impatient to reach the Arctic before Christmas." Almost every day he crossed another time zone. Each day was about an hour longer[4] and there was hardly any night time due to the high latitude. He tried to set his watch at some of the stations but noticed that the clocks were equipped with two or three sets of hands all pointing to different times.

He described the fourth-class passengers as travelling in "indescribable squalor." Assorted sizes and sexes were thrown together "like the odds and ends in a bureau drawer." At every station there were "myriads of children with wild flowers for sale in the hope of earning a few kopeks." He explained that the price of butter and eggs were an index to the cost of living; they were expensive, but no more so than London in 1918, when eggs were five shillings a dozen (25 pence) and butter was unobtainable.

He was surprised that the Trans-Siberian Railway was in much better condition than the stories he had read in *The Times*. There was an enormous quantity of matériel that had been accumulated for assembly, with thousands of tons of steel rails in piles larger than the mills that rolled them. A collection of car wheels appeared high enough "to conceal a division of cavalry."

He commented on the corruption that was rife among the customs officials. The dining car company had boxes of sugar stowed under the tables as bribes to pursue their smuggling unmolested. While it was the luxury of the bureaucracy, it became a necessity for the ordinary citizen. The rouble was worth about one tenth of its gold value and there were innumerable issues of paper money, with the old Romanov notes still held in greater confidence by the public than any other. Coinage had disappeared; fractions of a rouble were paid in postage stamps.

Bales of counterfeit money passed unchallenged; a 10-year-old note would pass even though it was crisp and never folded. The Kolchak government issued their own paper money, but this was not backed by gold, rather by a promise of payment in February 1920. In England it was a common sight to see a queue at the entrance to a grocery store in the hope of obtaining provisions in return for their money but in

Siberia, the queue was at the exit of the store where people hoped to receive the correct change from the cashier.

★★★

Emerson arrived in the Siberian capital four days before the Treaty of Versailles was signed.[5] Greeted enthusiastically by the other volunteers, he began work in the British headquarters, but quickly realised that all was not well. On 4th July 1919, he wrote: "I believe the Military Mission[6] (of which our railway mission is a branch) is having a rather heart-breaking time giving advice to the new Russian Army. Of course the situation is simply that although the Mission is supplying ordnance and instruction to the new Siberian recruits, the Kolchak army have no heart in the work and don't care who rules Russia as long as they get food and clothes. As the death penalty has been eliminated from desertion, there are innumerable absentees after every parade."

Apart from the veterans of the Western Front, the British Military Mission included a group of 55 Canadian volunteers.[7] Many of these were tempted by the pay to transfer to the British Army. Emerson was given an extra half a crown a day "in view of the extra hardship and inconvenience of operations in Siberia." However, this merely compensated for the fact that British pay was issued at rates that took no account of the depreciating rouble. The grievance was felt by both officers and soldiers, who received their rouble at 6d, when it was worth only 1d in the shops.[8]

Emerson's job was to sort out the chaos on the long lines of communication and deliver the war equipment that was still arriving from Vladivostok. He found that many obstacles were put in his way by the Russian railway officials, who resented their dependency on foreigners. They were proud people and although ordinary Russians were friendly, many officials were not keen for their corrupt practices to be exposed or stopped. His experience was shared by other members of the Railway Technical Board, one of whom wrote in a letter: "The Russian Railways Service Corps, assigned as technical inspectors under the terms of the Inter-Allied Agreement, have made every effort to assist in connection with the operation of the railroad. We have been opposed in every way by the Russian Military faction and the Russian technical railroad officials, regardless of the fact that we have made every effort to assist in an advisory capacity after I was officially informed that the Omsk

Government was unable to carry out the terms of the agreement, and all suggestions made by the technical inspectors were ignored."

These bureaucrats did not represent the vast majority of Russians in Omsk who were extremely grateful to the British volunteers. Emerson met the Cossack who took control of the train derailment and discovered that he was Lieutenant General Kortzov, the former Chief of Intelligence in the Caucasus. He had commanded a division of cavalry in the army of General Anton Denikin. Emerson complemented him on his exquisite English and he explained that he was educated by an English governess as a boy. He spoke in positive terms about the help Britain was giving Russia and this inspired Emerson to write: "I feel sure that Winston should like to have him speak in the House in support of his Russian policy."

The war secretary in London had delivered many optimistic pronouncements about Siberia, but most were based on false reports from Omsk. On 7th May, he said that "we have a tremendous chance of securing the future of Russia as a civilised democratic state", but this was just after the Red Army had defeated Kolchak's left wing. Churchill would have deployed more troops if he could, but 1919 was not a year of peace. There were uprisings in Iraq and Egypt and the day before his statement, Britain declared war on Afghanistan when King Amanullah advanced across the frontier at the western end of the Khyber Pass and occupied Bagh.

Later that summer, Churchill was even more strident in recommending that the prime minister should formally recognise Kolchak's regime as the official Russian government. However, his exhortations were ignored by the British prime minister and the US president, who focused on the creation of the League of Nations to resolve international crises.

If Churchill misread the character of the Kolchak administration and was drawn into a web of deceit, it was not only due to mendacious military communications. *The Times* correspondent in Siberia, Robert Wilton, was a passionate anti-Bolshevik, who fully supported the British intervention. At one stage he compromised his position as an impartial observer by working for the military staff in the Russian headquarters. His cables and despatches were in some cases a complete fabrication of the truth and in the end he was sent back to England by Knox.

It wasn't just the military situation that was falsified. The international newspapers that eventually arrived in Omsk were scrutinised in detail by the literate population and prompted an angry outcry. Emerson commented:

"When I get the New York and London papers, the absurdity of the public attitude is apparent. They forget to think of Russia in terms of the normal state of affairs. For example, if it were published in the *London Times* that half the women in Omsk were actually barefooted it might cause a mild sensation until people were told that Russian women go barefooted through choice and would not wear shoes in summer if they could."

★★★

Emerson saw little of the British intelligence directorate, but worked closely with the training mission, providing the Hampshire battalion with the best possible support in its role with the Anglo-Russian Brigade in Ekaterinburg. In theory, this formation should have made a significant contribution to the war. It was given a boost when the Stavka issued orders that British training methods were "obligatory" in musketry, physical training and bayonet fighting. However it failed, despite personal support from Admiral Kolchak and sufficient resources, due to the pervading corruption at lower levels. There were other problems, such as language difficulties and the legal status of British soldiers, but it was the unseen staff, united in their resentment and jealousy, which ensured that "every conceivable difficulty" was put in the way of the brigade.

It did not help that London had issued strict instructions that British troops were not to enter the fray. As a result, their commander, Brigadier Blair, decided to create four battalions each of which included about seven British officers and 20 senior non-commissioned officers. They would become mentors for the remaining Russian officers and soldiers when they completed their training. However, the arrival of the first intake of 2,500 Russian recruits was greeted with dismay: "In front came the extremely smart band of the Hampshire regiment followed by the filthiest and most unkempt mass of humanity."

The first task was to scrub the recruits with paraffin and wash them in the showers because they were crawling with vermin and typhus was a very real concern. Immediately after this cleansing, the doctors checked the fitness of each recruit and this resulted in 30 per cent being discarded on medical grounds. Private Charles Shobbrock suggested that 700 of these recruits were dismissed due to venereal disease.[9] The remainder were schooled in the basics of soldiering. They were especially good at marching for miles and miles and did so cheerfully to the tune of their choir which was always placed in the middle of the column.

The British trainers set to work, despite obvious problems of communication. Everywhere there was a shortage of interpreters with only 14 available for the whole brigade. Very few British officers or soldiers could speak the Russian language sufficiently well to be of use. One who could was Captain Brian Horrocks of the Middlesex Regiment, who was assigned to the Brigade NCO School working for Captain Victor Ullman,[10] another colloquial Russian speaker.

Horrocks had spent much time as a prisoner of the Germans after being wounded at Ypres. He had acquired a colloquial knowledge of Russian having mixed with them during his incarceration and used this experience to his advantage. He instigated simple measures, such as checking the soldiers' food was cooked properly and that they received their full tobacco ration to create an *esprit de corps*.

They had to make some compromises. The Russian NCOs insisted on allowing their women and children into the barrack blocks after work, but they were always out by the time the officers arrived in the morning. The Russian NCOs were nearly all illiterate, but they were not unintelligent. According to Horrocks, they "combined a great sense of humour with considerable cunning."[11] As soon as they realised the British trainers were doing their best for them, they became very devoted to them.

In contrast, the Whites neglected their own troops and treated them with brutal severity. Captain Francis McCullagh, working in the intelligence directorate at Omsk, wrote that: "A regiment was sent from Tomsk to the front in the middle of 1919, but at Omsk the men sent a deputation to their commanding officer to say they had no boots or clothing and could go no further and as a matter of fact, they had been swindled out of their pay, rations and clothing by their own officers. The Commanding Officer had several members of this deputation shot and the remainder brutally flogged, with the result that the whole regiment passed over to the Reds a few months afterwards."[12]

Most observers categorised the White Army as an amalgamation of all sorts, but the reality was quite different. The regiments were made up of very distinct political and racial groups and there was an intense rivalry between combat arms and service corps. Even in the field of equestrianism, the Russian cavalry were often insulted by the Cossacks who considered themselves to be freemen of the forest. Ethnic and cultural differences had a detrimental effect on the efficiency of the army, but within the Anglo-Russian Brigade a sense of comradeship existed which drew envious glances from Kolchak's officers.

The brigade staff had to fight for everything they needed, even water, food and transport: "Every conceivable difficulty was put in our way." However, these obstacles made the British officers even more determined to succeed and slowly the four battalions began to take shape. The principles of fair discipline, well-organised training and sensible man-management turned the ill-kempt mob that arrived in May into a loyal and effective fighting force.

The better the brigade became the more the Russian officers criticised it. In General Knox's view, Russian officers hated to see "our fellows" make a success of what they so conspicuously failed at. Colour Sergeant Jupe suspected that although the recruits might eventually have become a respectable fighting force, the British staff had no idea whether or not these soldiers had any belief in the Kolchak cause.

When orders from the War Office directed that the experiment of the Anglo-Russian Brigade was to cease, many of the attached British officers volunteered to resign their commissions and stay on. However, their commander sensibly pointed out that if they had gone to the front they would have been needlessly sacrificed and refused the requests.

The failure of the Anglo-Russian Brigade was the final straw for the Hampshire's commanding officer, Robert Johnson. By June, he had become totally disillusioned with the White Russian Army who he described as "an incapable lot." He had been offered the job as Controller of the Royal Mint in London[13] and departed with a dozen married soldiers, travelling north along a wild and treacherous route to the Barents Sea. They were nearly marooned by the ice, but the Royal Navy managed to rescue the trapped venturers and return them to England before the remainder of the battalion in December.

Soon after Johnson left, the Red Army recaptured Perm and this opened the way to the iconic city of Ekaterinburg. The Russian officers used the British-trained soldiers as drafts for the front. News arrived that the Bolsheviks were offering 5,000 roubles for the first English soldier captured alive. Brigadier Blair met with General Gajda on 26th June and reluctantly "decided that the situation on the front was so bad that it would be necessary to move Hants back to Omsk immediately."[14]

In turn, this precipitated an exodus of international workers and Russian civilians who lost confidence in the ability of the White Army to defend the city. As the Red Army approached, Brigadier Blair reported to London that "all British officers and consul left Ekaterinburg on 12th July."[15] However, as a portent of what was to come, the British Railway Mission remained behind to organise the evacuation of the forsaken citizens.

The officer entrusted with this unenviable task was the redoubtable Archibald Jack. As the Red Army approached Ekaterinburg on 14th July, he was in his carriage, steam up, ready for a rapid departure. Through his skilful direction,[16] he managed to save the lives of thousands of British troops and Russian civilians before escaping just before the Bolsheviks recaptured the town.

Two days later, the War Office sent a telegram issuing instructions to return the British regiments to England. Churchill had delayed the order to repatriate the two battalions for four months, hoping the White Army would defeat the Bolsheviks decisively and that President Wilson would recognise Kolchak's government as the official government of Russia. However, now the Treaty of Versailles was signed and the Red Army was advancing across a broad front, he could not disobey the Cabinet decision any longer.

In the meantime, the Tigers were given menial duties to occupy them in Omsk until transport could be arranged to move them east. Entertainment was provided by the Young Men's Christian Association.[17] Unfortunately, the fifth and final member of the battalion to die in Russia drowned in the river on 30th July and Cyclist Stanley Green had to dig his grave the following morning.[18] Two days later, he was assigned to guard a train to Vladivostok and wrote in his diary: "there are five 35-ton waggons filled with bullion, also one small one full of paper money. We had an armoured train running in front of us biggest part of the time, we also had to ride on top of the train with loaded rifles. Prepared for Bolsheviks several times, but no luck."[19]

Apart from a small group of 14 volunteers, tempted by the extra pay, or attracted by the Siberian women, the Hampshire battalion had evacuated completely from western Siberia by 18th August. After they left, disenchantment set in. One of the British trainers, Lieutenant Colonel Edward Steel,[20] who built the Jaeger Artillery Regiment comprising two batteries of 18 pounders and two batteries of 4.5-inch howitzers, claimed that: "The Russians seem incapable of doing anything... Everything is 'Never mind it doesn't matter'; we call it the land of tomorrow. The departure of the Hampshire Regiment from here has been the signal for a general exodus and a stream of carts pours down to the station all day and night ... any night now the whole Russian staff may disappear without saying a word to anyone."

By then Emerson had received news from Dallas that she was working in the military hospital in Vladivostok. The Chief Surgeon, Colonel James Wilson, ensured the buildings chosen for the American hospital and headquarters each had a driven well a few hundred feet deep and their own water supply. The hospital was about eight miles from the headquarters and Dallas lived in relative comfort with the other nurses in a large detached brick building.

The American Red Cross enforced strict hospital discipline. The chief nurse completed monthly efficiency reports for each nurse, evaluating off-duty deportment as much as nursing skills. Civilian clothes could be worn only in the personal quarters, but nurses travelling in groups were requested to dress similarly. Several nurses were placed under close observation, even though their work was excellent.[21]

Dallas's disappointment at not seeing Emerson before he travelled to Omsk was noticed by her friends.[22] She did not wish to heap pressure on Emerson, but in her letter, she included a verse of Ella Wheeler Wilcox's reply to Rudyard Kipling's poem, "He who travels fastest travels alone":

> Who travels alone, without lover or friend,
> But hurries from nothing to naught at the end;
> Though great be his winnings and high be his goal,
> He is bankrupt in wisdom and beggared in soul.
> Life's one gift of value to him is denied
> Who travels alone without Love at his side.

CHAPTER 6

Trotsky or Kolchak?

There are no absolute rules of conduct, either in peace or war. Everything depends on circumstances.

LEON TROTSKY

Admiral Kolchak blamed the capture of Ekaterinburg in the north of his area on General Gajda. This young 27-year-old was a talented battlefield commander, who transferred to the White Army when the remainder of the Czech Legion refused to support the new regime. After Kolchak dismissed him on 8th July,[1] Gajda travelled back to Vladivostok, where he began plotting with the social democrats.

The seeds for the failure in the north were not sown by General Gajda, but by the generals in the south. Three months earlier, a regiment of Ukrainian troops holding Kolchak's left flank had killed their officers and transferred their allegiance to the Red Army, complete with British uniforms, weapons and equipment. They subsequently helped the Bolshevik commander-in-chief, General Ioakim Vatzetis, a former colonel in the Imperial Army, to re-capture Ufa on 9th June.

By then, the situation had become critical for the Siberian Army. General Knox believed that the three divisions which were being equipped by the British Army should have been held back until properly trained, but they were thrown to the front ill-prepared.[2] One division was sent into action at the end of a 40-mile march and 5,000 men promptly deserted to the Bolsheviks.

If Vatzetis was the operational commander of the Red Army, the strategic brain behind the Soviet campaign was the People's Commissar for Military Affairs and chief architect of the Red Army, Leon Trotsky. The Red Army was originally a guerrilla force, formed largely in factories and towns from staunch Bolshevik supporters. By the end of 1917, it numbered in the tens of thousands, but then it expanded rapidly following a decree on 22nd April 1918 that introduced compulsory military service and called for a "revolutionary war".

Although the Bolsheviks condemned the imperial past, they spent much time carefully analysing the failures of the Czar's Army, in order to preserve the good and discard the flaws. They understood something which western propaganda has always dismissed; the enduring high morale of the Russian soldier. There was ample evidence if anyone cared to look for it. During the 1915 campaign, the Russian Army, lacking in arms and equipment, met the technically superior German Army and lost more than three million soldiers. Confounding all critics, it returned six months later under General Aleksei Brusilov and won their finest victory of the war. This could not have been achieved by an army with low morale.

Trotsky reintroduced thousands of the Czar's officers into the Red Army. Although this met with opposition from Joseph Stalin and other party purists, it benefitted the Bolsheviks in the short term. The problem of loyalty was solved by the election of officers and the work of political committees. Within the ranks, communist spies reported on their fellow soldiers to the military Tcheka, known as the Osoby Otdiel which punished those who failed in their duties, or questioned authority.

However, after early failures on the battlefield, Trotsky abolished this system and promoted talented military specialists over communist commissars. This change resulted in a more effective army, but offended a large group of Bolshevik zealots. Ultimate control of the campaign was placed under the Revolutionary War Council, appointed on 2nd September 1918. It took longer than a year to mould the communist cells to its will, but by then, there were more than one and a half million men under arms.

In matters of doctrine, Trotsky took a pragmatic view and repeated a simple refrain: "this is no time for clever theories, or for bizarre Marxist doctrine. What is needed is to train an army consisting largely of illiterate peasants to shoot, to grease their boots, and to keep themselves free from vermin." However, he did approve the role of political officers vetting all orders for their validity and this dual system of command was maintained at every level in the army.[3]

The President of the Russian Soviet Federative Socialist Republic, Vladimir Ulyanov Lenin, declared: "the best army in the world is bound to be annihilated unless it is backed up by a strong, well-organised Home Front. Let every institution … treat the army as a matter of top-priority." With this attitude and a policy of giving land to the peasants, the Bolsheviks gained a clear advantage over Kolchak who, in contrast, was supported by an inefficient civil administration in Siberia.

Spending two months on the Eastern Front, Trotsky stiffened the resolve of the Red Army and prepared the counter attack that resulted in the capture of Ufa. After this victory, Trotsky and Vatzetis decided to hold the eastern advance and switch their attention to the Ukraine, where General Denikin had made significant gains. His army groups of the Don and the Caucasus and the Army of Volunteers had all advanced north. The right flank, under General Pyotr Wrangel, pushed along the River Volga, whilst the main force broke through the centre on 24th May and captured the city of Kharkov in June.

However, Lenin overruled Trotsky and insisted that the offensive against Kolchak should continue as the main effort.[4] Vatzetis was replaced by General Sergei Kamenev and his headquarters moved into the Urals. A daring outflanking march by General Tukhachevsky placed a considerable Red force in possession of the passes over the mountains and this influenced General Gajda to give up his recent gains, including Perm, at the beginning of July.

★★★

Conflicting reports emerging from Siberia and Ukraine were interpreted differently in Washington and London. In the latter, Churchill was still making misleading pronouncements,[5] based not only on the military reports of General Knox, but also Robert Wilton's despatches in *The Times*. The key issue for Churchill was to convince the American government to accredit Kolchak as the head of the official government of Russia.[6] He had plenty of supporters in the State Department and their influence resulted in a directive to General Graves to accompany the American ambassador to Japan, Roland Morris, on a fact-finding mission to Omsk.

Reluctantly, Graves set out in a first-class Trans-Siberian sleeper train on 11th July.[7] For the journey, he lived in a large wooden coach with lower and upper berths, running across the carriage, made possible by the five-foot gauge of the tracks. Both he and Ambassador Morris employed their own interpreters who were empathetic to ordinary Russian people. When the train stopped at any station, they mingled with the crowds and discovered what the locals thought of the situation.

Throughout the trip both interpreters reported that none of the men, women, or children had a good word to say for the Kolchak regime. Despite this evidence, the ambassador was under pressure to lean on Graves to provide military support to Kolchak. A conversation about government primacy revealed this tension. Morris exclaimed: "The State Department is running this, not the War Department" to which Graves declared: "The State Department is not running me."

At Omsk they were met by Consul Harris, who introduced them to the senior officers in Kolchak's Stavka. Graves suspected the military briefings were hiding the truth and was determined to discover whether Kolchak was able to make a stand against the Red Army. He had been told that General Pepeliaev held 20,000 troops on the right of the line and General Lokvitsky, in the centre, had 31,000 men under command. The largest army group of 50,000 soldiers in the south was led by General Sakharov, who had been promoted after heading up the training school in Vladivostok. There was no mention of the Red Army's recent advance across the River Ural, near Orenburg.

After playing the good guest and sitting next to Admiral Kolchak for a sunny publicity photo, Graves asked General Diterikhs for permission to view the scheduled mobilisation at Petropavlovsk.[8] The General informed Graves that it was impossible due to the "great congestion", but proposed a visit to Ishim, 160 miles north of Omsk, where he could travel by motor car with a Russian escort to see the whole thing.

Graves asked Colonel George Emerson to accompany him and had a train made up for 30 soldiers, with a flat track for his Cadillac. The start was delayed and the journey was slow. It took 32 hours to travel 160 miles and on the way west, the American guard had to respond authoritatively when a number of Kolchak's officers threatened to steal their train. They were met at Ishim by British officer, Captain Alexander Murray, who said "General, I beg of you not to go across, as the Bolsheviks will capture you, and that will spoil all we have accomplished."

The American general ignored the blatant attempt to prevent him from observing first-hand the reported mobilisation. He realised that every official representative in Omsk was hostile to his actions and this made it necessary to follow international protocol, so he called on the local Russian commander to pay his compliments. He was told by the aloof officer that there were no soldiers he could trust as a protection escort.

Graves suspected this was another deceit and decided to drive in his Cadillac to Ishim, regardless of the serious dangers suggested by Captain Murray. He set off with Colonel Emerson, Major Homer Slaughter, his interpreter, the chauffeur and a soldier with a rifle at 7p.m. on 14th August. The car had an American flag and a two-star officer's flag fastened to the radiator. They had travelled 63 miles along a rough country road when darkness descended and so they parked in an oat field to wait for daylight. Sleep was impossible, due to the mosquitoes and at about 2a.m., a Russian appeared on a horse. He told the interpreter that his village would consider it a great honour to entertain an American General, but Graves declined the invitation, explaining that he was moving on at daylight.

They arrived at a village on the banks of the Ishim River a little after sunrise. In a few moments the car was surrounded by a large group of curious men, women, and children. The Americans handed out Hershey's chocolate bars as gifts and the friendly villagers showed Graves where to cross the river on a raft pulled by a cable. After negotiating the cost of the ferry journey, they drove a further 30 miles and arrived at their destination at about 2p.m.

His arrival was a surprise to the local Russian commander who had not been notified of the visit by his headquarters. Nevertheless, he welcomed the general by grasping him in a warm bear-hug. Unfortunately, he could not divulge any useful information because he was completely unaware of any planned offensive and mobilisation and he had no troops to show the Americans. After checking the railway station to find neither "congestion, nor troops", Graves confirmed in his own mind that a blatant fraud was being practiced "in order to get money from the United States to help Kolchak destroy Bolshevism." On the way back to Omsk, he spent an hour at a priest's house, where he was hosted generously with wine and cake and discussed the concerns of the local population.

When he returned to Omsk, Graves heard about a casualty train across the river at Kolumzino. He drove over in his Cadillac with Ambassador Morris to see the condition of the soldiers, who had been evacuated from the Chelyabinsk front. They found the sick and injured had been placed in box cars with little medical support. Many were too ill to help themselves and there was only one nurse for more than 500 men. There were no arrangements for food and only a very limited quantity of water in canteens. No help was provided for the seriously sick, who needed to attend the call of nature.

In the first box car two dead men lay in the entrance. As Graves and Morris climbed in, they saw a third dying whilst a sick comrade held his head and attempted to give him a drink of water. Many of the casualties managed to crawl out of the train, but this exhausting effort left them sprawled on the ground in a destitute state.

The Americans were aghast that no official from the Stavka was present to organise the medical assistance for the helpless men, who had given their all for the White cause. Their sense of disgust increased as they walked back to their accommodation and witnessed a band playing with a thousand people dancing in the park, less than a mile from where the soldiers lay dying from neglect.

Graves left Omsk in the middle of August more certain than ever that the Kolchak government would collapse. "The trip to Omsk had not changed my views, in fact, after the trip I had more confidence in my estimate of Kolchak's strength, than I had before, because I was no longer fooled by the reports as to the attitude of the people west of Lake Baikal."

The American commander's views coincided with those of General Gajda, who stated in an interview on 10th August at Vladivostok that: "The Kolchak government cannot possibly stand and if the Allies support him they will make the greatest mistake in history. The Government is divided into two distinct parts, one issues proclamation and propaganda for foreign consumption stating that the Government favours and works for a constituent assembly, the other part secretly plans and plots a restoration of monarchy."

In contrast to the American military commander, Ambassador Morris seemed to believe that there was some hope of pacifying Siberia by helping Kolchak. However, he qualified his cautious comments to the State Department with an impossible condition; he recommended supporting Admiral Kolchak "only if the United States was willing to send 25,000 soldiers to Siberia to replace the Czechs and to provide financial assistance to Kolchak to the amount of two hundred million dollars." One can imagine the irritation this advice generated when it landed on the State Department desks in Washington.[9]

Gajda's comments were written on the same day that General Knox received a telegram from the War Office in London stating that only volunteers were to remain in Siberia and that British training was to cease.[10] Knox understood that this signalled the end of Britain's commitment. He made a plan for a staged withdrawal from the schools he was supporting, commencing with the Russian Cadets at Tomsk in September, then Colonel Morley's team at Irkutsk in October and finally Russian Island in November.

★★★

It would be an exaggeration to claim that all of the soldiers in the Red Army supported the Soviet Government in 1919. However, when faced with a choice between Trotsky or Admiral Kolchak's Government, the peasants who made up the vast majority of the battalions, preferred the Bolsheviks as can be seen by the vast number of desertions in the late summer of 1919.

An important factor in the balance of military power was the terrain. The Bolsheviks had the advantage of manoeuvring on internal lines of communication, whereas the White Russians were hampered by lengthy logistics supply lines and communication voids. Trotsky moved his armies with relative ease to reinforce crisis areas on the front, but the White Army's military leaders were able neither to coordinate attacks, nor to synchronise effort due to the enormous distances between each operational theatre. For example, on the Polish front, General Józef Pilsudski informed Major General Walter Greenly on 19th November that "I have been quite unable to get any reasonable officer to accept the task of Liaison Officer with Kolchak: the distances are too great, the isolation and separation too impossible...."[11]

The type of warfare was also a key factor in the result. It was very different from the trench warfare in Flanders. The inordinate vastness of the open plains of Siberia allowed for manoeuvre on a grand scale. Mongol and Cossack armies had perfected this type of warfare centuries before and their descendants used the same tactics to find gaps in thinly defended lines and attack enemy formations from the rear. Raiding parties captured stores and cut lines of communication, isolating troops at the front. Withdrawals could rapidly become routs, if flanks were not protected.

The geography of Siberia and Ukraine made the establishment of "defence in depth" almost impossible and led to the tactics of frontal assaults and outflanking, or turning movements. The range of machine-gun fire was the decisive factor in combat, with field artillery playing a secondary role as it had little effect on men scattered over a wide area.

Trotsky's leadership also played an important part in the campaign. His personal train of a dozen wagon-lits served as a forward headquarters, with a printing press and sophisticated signalling equipment linked to a transmitter that allowed him to maintain direct contact with Lenin in Moscow. His hand-picked officers lived and ate together in a large dining-car. Loaded with supplies of tobacco, boots and troop comforts, the train took Trotsky to whichever sector appeared most critical, where he provided "that vital shovelful of coal that keeps a dying fire alive."

Compared with Trotsky, Kolchak failed to provide the firm leadership required to boost the White Army. Depicted by General Knox as "a reed painted to look like steel",[12] he failed to master the logistics challenges of land warfare and squandered the potentially war-winning supplies provided by Britain. For example, in Ufa alone, the former found 230,000 rifles which had been awaiting distribution since January, while the recruits that were captured shared one rifle between ten men.

According to Ernest Léderrey, a Swiss Army delegate of the International Committee of the Red Cross who delivered aid in Russia during the Civil War, the uniforms captured by the Bolsheviks were "enough to clothe the entire army of Kolchak"[13] and yet his soldiers were reported by many observers to be dressed in rags. Towards the end of June 1919, Kolchak's officers felt unable to impose discipline on the starving soldiers, but the depots in Ufa at that time were crammed with 96,000 tons of wheat and 64,000 tons of oats.

It is worth considering the Siberian War as an intellectual dual between Trotsky and Kolchak. Trotsky, from an initial position of weakness, adapted the Red Army to the circumstances which he used to his advantage. Kolchak neither invested in the future, nor offered hope to his soldiers and thereby lost any advantage he gained after the Perm offensive.

Whereas Trotsky had Lenin and an industrious political machine supporting him in the rear, Kolchak appeared to have no similar political genius as a partner. At a critical time in June, when he needed to concentrate all his efforts on the military campaign, he was being pestered by the Allies to provide answers to strategic questions raised at the Paris Peace Conference that required professorships in political science, international relations and law. Shouldering this burden, it is no surprise that he was unable to achieve success in the fast and furious land campaign that decided the fate of Russia in 1919.

★★★

The Red Army consolidation in August provided the people of Omsk with a false sense of security. On 4th September, three days before the Diehards departed from Vladivostok on the SS *Empress of Japan*,[14] Emerson wrote: "We are still in Omsk and the military situation seems a little more favourable − if it may be called a 'military' situation. The Bolsheviks are retiring slightly, but I doubt if they will move far enough to permit us to get to Moscow this year. From what little thinking I am permitted to do on the subject I would say that the two sides are now almost neutralised and it may not be long before they all will compromise on a Government."

He felt sympathy for the new batch of Russian recruits heading to the front: "When one sees the Russian moujik[15] incorporated into the infantry the first thought is that the poor little fellow should be at home with his mother. The soldiers now are very young and even the older ones cannot know or care a cuss who or what they are fighting for. The time is approaching however when they will all get to be glad to go about their business and earn a living for themselves in the good old-fashioned way before the war."

Turning to his own situation, he had started to think about his return home: "I expect to return to the base before long and accompany the Hampshires back to England. The Government of Canada has invited them to cross Canada and I presume the *CPR Empress of Russia* will be on hand at Vladivostok. It is singular that all through the East, Canada is thought of in terms of the Canadian Pacific Railway Company's activities; and Canada is lucky to have such a champion."

"I should be back in Philadelphia before Christmas – unless they make me a Field Marshall [sic] with pay and allowances!"

CHAPTER 7

Remain to The Last

Everybody feels the need of a clear-cut policy in regard to Russia, and many people ask for a clear-cut policy. But it is a great deal easier to ask for a clear-cut policy, a clear, bold, wise, moderate, far-seeing, and decisive policy, in regard to Russia than it is to supply it.

WINSTON CHURCHILL IN THE HOUSE OF COMMONS,
5TH NOVEMBER 1919

It was not surprising that Emerson made the bold prediction about his return home with the Hampshire battalion. When he wrote the letter, he was unaware of the surrender of Kolchak's southern army of 20,000 soldiers, together with equipment, artillery, field hospitals and workshops in the neighbourhood of Aktyubinsk-Orsk. However, he had read about General Denikin's successes in the Ukraine, including the occupation of Odessa in August. He was also aware of the Red Army's evacuation of Kiev on 2nd September so his optimism was based on more than hope alone.

The fluctuating successes and reversals on the battlefields led many people to believe that a stalemate existed in September 1919. Military gossip in Omsk concentrated on the White Army counter-attack, delayed from when General Graves visited the front in August. This simple plan involved an advance towards the River Tobol that had been lost on 15th August.

There were two British liaison officers attached to the 1st Siberian Army on the front line. Brian Horrocks had transferred from the NCO School in Ekaterinburg with Captain Eric Hayes of the Norfolk

Regiment. They had become best friends on their journey from Vladivostok in May and served together in the Anglo-Russian Brigade until its dissolution in July. They had both fought on the Western Front and Hayes saw action in Mesopotamia where he was mentioned in despatches, before entering Southern Russia with Major General Dunsterville's irregular formation, known as Dunsterforce, that secretly was assigned to replace Russian troops in Persia after the Bolshevik revolution.[1]

Horrocks and Hayes were given a train with three wagons, or *terplushka*. One became their accommodation, another was for their Chinese workers and Russian groom and the third was for their horses. This enabled them to keep in touch with the front line by separately riding out for a week at a time. They spent nights with local communities and as the first foreigners seen by these villagers they were treated with great generosity. They were usually hosted by the village elder, sharing food and sleeping together with his family in a single room. They witnessed, at first hand, the subsistence farming that was the way of life before the Bolsheviks established the collective farms.

Horrocks also visited the nomadic Khirghiz tribe which lived in small felt huts, or yurts. They bred horses and moved intermittently to where the grazing was best. He especially enjoyed their intoxicating drink, koumiss, which was made from mare's milk fermented in casks lined with dung.

The two young British officers observed General Diterikhs advance in September and the fierce battles fought over large open spaces. The Siberian Army recovered nearly 100 miles of territory, including Tobolsk at the end of the month, but these successes did not last. Unfortunately, 15,000 Cossacks did not exploit the success of the infantry and held back on the left flank. If only they had ridden forward 60 versts[2] and held the crossings over the River Tobol, Diterikhs could have continued his advance and this in turn would have given the training schools the time they needed to complete the preparation of 44,000 new drafts, whilst the army's morale was still good.

In Omsk, General Knox wrote in frustration to Kolchak's new chief of staff, General Golovin, who had recently returned from England where he was introduced to influential peers and MPs and solicited support for the White cause.[3] In his idiosyncratic way, the British commander bluntly blamed Golovin's predecessor, Dmitry Lebedev, for the White Army's failures: "At present all seems to me to be absolute chaos and worse chaos than anything I have seen in the past 12 months. I find it impossible to obtain accurate information regarding your programme of formations and your stores of supplies of uniform and equipment and of orders placed or about to be placed abroad. The organisation changes completely every day and no one knows where he stands."[4]

When the Bolsheviks counter-attacked in October, Horrocks observed long lines of infantry advancing steadily against hastily formed defensive positions. He learned quickly that winning the firefight before the lines closed together was the critical factor. This required cool heads and accurate marksmanship, which was not always forthcoming from the White Army.

On 12th October, the two young officers representing the forward tip of the British spear in Siberia met Leonard Vining at Lebedyja. Vining had been tasked to ascertain the damage to a railway bridge that had been blown up by the Red Army. Unfortunately, the bridgehead was only 15 yards from the front line and he came under fire when he made his first attempt at photographing the site. His second attempt was in a Sopwith bi-plane, but the weather when he took off at 10a.m. was cloudy and the wind erratic during the flight. Descending to 600m, he managed to snap a few photographs, but the Bolsheviks fired at the aircraft, so the pilot could not go any lower.

He discovered that the centre of the bridge was intact, but the damage was not clear in the images, so he made a third attempt on 17th October, riding a Siberian horse with a Russian escort. They made a long approach over cultivated land and Vining took some more photographs from the cover of a doorway, with the enemy 60 yards away. He noticed that the trenches were very shallow and not much use against heavy artillery fire. The line was thinly manned and there were very few machine guns.

Picking his way back through a barbed wire entanglement, he reached his pony and crossed in front of the enemy, who did not fire at him because they believed he was a peasant working the fields. He returned to the armoured train and after the statutory drink of vodka with his escort, he departed on a hand trolley, working his way back to the station.

The next day, the Red Army broke through on both flanks. There was total chaos on the railway line as dozens of trains with supplies had been sent forwards from Omsk and these now had to return to the East filled with refugees. Vining's carriage was attached to a train with an echelon of wounded men. He always carried a medicine chest with bandages and after ten years in India, he had managed to pick up enough knowledge of First Aid "not to be dangerous." When they came to him for help, he washed the festering wounds, applied clean dressings and disinfectants, and gave them food and cigarettes.

This military breakthrough was observed by Horrocks and Hayes, who realised the game was over and felt isolated 4,000 miles from Vladivostok. They had already noticed that many of the new White battalions, wearing British clothing and equipment, had deserted and joined the swelling ranks of the Red Army. As the dam broke and the remnants of the White Army fell back in disarray, the two young British captains loaded their train and returned to the sanctuary of Omsk.

On 24th October, Tobolsk fell to the Red Army and the Bolsheviks started to assimilate the population into the Soviet system, known as the Red Terror. This was a political inquisition which involved the torture and slaughter of anyone associated with the old regime who was suspected of disobeying Soviet authority. It started after the head of the Petrograd secret police, Moisei Uritsky, was shot and killed at the end of August 1918 and became a central pillar in the country's conversion to communism.[5]

A week later, George Carvel, the *Reuters* correspondent, cabled to an unprepared world that: "The civil Government is evacuating Omsk. Admiral Kolchak's army is retreating on the whole front." Whilst Emerson helped organise a second evacuation from a major Russian city, British recriminations began to flow. *The Times* wrote: "Lacking prestige and power either as a representative government or as a dictatorship, the organisation headed by Admiral Kolchak has proved incapable either of assuring victory in the field, or of the efficient administration of the country."

General Knox's ire was directed at the wastefulness of Kolchak's Government, not its political failures. Knox claimed that 100,000 uniforms had been supplied and refused to provide anything else because this attire was being worn by the Bolsheviks. However, the majority of men wearing British clothes and equipment in the Red Army were the same soldiers to whom these uniforms were issued when they were in the White Army.

On 31st October, the Soviet High Command announced they had secured Petropavlovsk, the town General Graves had tried to visit in August. A week before they arrived, the British Liaison Officer, Captain Ronald Gillespie had departed, but two other officers were cut off and had to escape by crossing the Gobi Desert to Peking.[6] During the following days, regiments from the 11th Ural Division and 15th Siberian Division mutinied. The officers who refused to transfer loyalty to the Bolshevik cause were shot by their own soldiers, who promptly transferred their allegiance to the Red Army.

As the Siberian front folded, General Diterikhs, who had taken over as commander-in-chief, disagreed with Kolchak about defending Omsk. Diterikhs was replaced by General Constantine Sakharov, who organised a security shield around the town. By then the town was a seething mass of scared society, desperate to escape the Red tide spreading east without check.

★★★

When the Kolchak Government collapsed, the Social Revolutionaries made a final attempt to take over eastern Siberia. The military challenge came from General Gajda, who had been relieved of command by Kolchak after the ignominious defeat at Ekaterinburg. He was bitter about what Brigadier Blair[7] described as a "clique" of officers in the Stavka, who had plotted against him and he now saw an opportunity for retribution.

Since his arrival at Vladivostok on 8th August, Gajda had aligned himself to the Social Revolutionary party and provoked anger among some Whites with his political statements, such as: "Measures should be taken to restore the authority of Zemstvos and municipal Dumas,[8] and start investigation as to administrative punishments inflicted upon members. Steps must be taken to arouse the sympathy of the peasant masses and the development of agriculture."

His calculated views reflected those of the Czech soldiers, who hated both Monarchists and Bolsheviks. They believed in a parliamentary government and on 16th November, they issued a memorandum, which dramatically increased their political involvement in the crisis. The Czechs appealed to the other Allies:

> The intolerable position in which our Army is placed, forces us to address ourselves to the Allied powers to ask them for counsel as to how the Czech Army can be assured of its own security and of a free return to its own Country, which was decided with the assent of all the Allied Powers.
>
> The Army was ready to protect the railway in the sector which was assigned to it and it has fulfilled its task conscientiously. But now the presence of our Army on the railway to protect it has become impossible because the activities of the Army are contrary to its aspirations in the cause of humanity and justice.
>
> In protecting the railway and maintaining order in the country, our Army is forced to act contrary to its convictions when it supports and maintains an arbitrary, absolute power which at present rules.
>
> The burning of villages, the murder of peaceable Russian inhabitants by the hundreds, and the shooting without reason, of democratic men solely because they are suspected of holding political views are daily facts; and the responsibility for them, before the Courts of Nations of the entire world, will fall upon us because being an armed force, we have not prevented these injustices. This passiveness is the direct result of our neutrality and non-intervention in Russian internal affairs, and, thanks to our being loyal to this idea we have become, in spite of ourselves, accomplices to a crime.
>
> In communicating this fact to the representatives of the Allied Powers to whom the Czech Nation has been and will be a faithful Ally, we deem it necessary to take every measure to inform the nations of the whole world in what a moral and tragic position the Czech Army is placed and what are the causes of it.
>
> As to ourselves, we see no other way out of this situation than to evacuate immediately the sector which was given us to guard, or else to obtain the right to prevent the injustices and crimes cited above.

The Times correspondent, Robert Wilton, who had been a fierce critic of Gajda when he worked in the staff headquarters of General Diterikhs, described their announcement as "bitterly attacking Admiral Kolchak's Government and his agents." However, General Graves described this statement as an "accurate a portrayal of the real conditions" in Siberia.

That night Gajda began his move at Okeanskaya, 22 miles from Vladivostok. The coup was launched by a group using the title of the Siberian National Directorate, with the ultimate object of establishing a Constitutional Assembly. They appointed Pavel Yakhushev as the president and General Gajda as the military commander, with Colonel Krakovetsky and Mr Morovsky filling the other places in the Directorate.

The government forces were led by Lieutenant General Sergey Nikolaevich Rozanov, who had a ruthless reputation. When in charge of Krasnoyarsk, he had issued instructions to his troops dealing with partisan supporters: "The villages where the population meets our troops with arms should be burned down and all the full-grown male population should be shot; property, homes, carts, etc. should be taken for the use of the Army."

His policy was to kill ten hostages for every one of his supporters who were murdered. He knew that Gajda had been plotting, but made no move to prevent the plans. According to Rozanov, the Czech general commanded about three hundred men and by 8a.m. of 17th November, he was issuing arms to anyone who arrived at his train.

When they heard this report, the Allied Commanders held a meeting with a view to prevent murder and pillage, as well as any damage to their property. They decided to remain neutral in the contest and only provide limited protection within their allocated sections in the city. As soon as Rozanov heard this reassurance, he launched a brutal counter attack against the nascent uprising.

The *Japan Advertiser* reported: "Whether or not the revolutionaries planned a fight, they evidently underestimated the strength of the Government's troops. The training and discipline of the cadets from the Training School on Russian Island was considered the decisive factor of the fight."

In total, Rozanov had 20 officers and 600 men in the garrison, but this was reinforced by 30 officers and 500 cadets who deployed from the Training School on Russian Island run by Lieutenant Colonel John Hulton of the Royal Sussex Regiment. Their machine guns and shells, fired from the hills to the east of the station, decimated the rebels who lost over 300 in the fighting. Government casualties were relatively light with ten cadets and four from the garrison killed.

At this stage General Graves intervened, or rather his son, Sidney, did. Braving the zone of continuous fire swept by Rozanov's rifles, machine guns and artillery pieces he took a transport vehicle with Private Joseph Jerome at the wheel and rescued the women and children and other non-combatants trapped in the firefight. They, along with Major Sam Johnson, Sergeant Marv Roda, Corporal George Masury and Private First Class Bob Nickovich were all awarded the Distinguished Service Cross for exhibiting "extraordinary heroism."

By early the next morning, a forlorn Gajda was cornered in the railway station with a tattered green and white autonomous Siberian flag fluttering from his armoured train. After a short negotiation, he was forced to surrender.[9] There were 18 or 20 young Russians captured who were taken to the front of the station and offered an opportunity to join Rozanov's forces. All of them replied they would die a thousand deaths before they would join such a band of robbers. They were then marched back into the station where they were shot and killed as they descended the circular stone stairs leading to the basement. Their summary execution was carried out in front of several American soldiers who remained on duty at the station throughout the battle.

After reading their eye-witness reports, General Graves sent a telegram to Washington on 21st November. He explained that he had compiled "evidence of American Railway Service Corps which establishes the fact that Rozanov's troops refused to handle anti-Rozanov wounded, but left them for several hours in the cold snow and rain, and that they went into a warehouse where there were wounded and killed the wounded."

During the confusion, Colonel Krakovetsky and four other rebels rushed into the American headquarters and claimed asylum. Graves was put in a difficult position because he knew that if he turned them out they would be killed, but also that his headquarters was not considered to be sovereign US territory like an embassy. He let them stay whilst he conducted protracted negotiations, which included lengthy communications with Washington. Ultimately, they were smuggled to safety, but the rebels could not return to Vladivostok while Rozanov held power.

Opinions were divided within the British contingent. General Knox supported Rozanov even though he had a clear track record of war crimes. However, Brigadier Blair, who held the same substantive rank as Knox, believed the British should remain neutral in any coup. Warrant Officer Thomas Ivens, a member of the British Railway Mission also witnessed the battle. He described the situation with: "both government troops and insurgents wearing British clothing and boots and firing British ammunition out of American rifles and Canadian machine guns... There you have in a nutshell the result of Allied help to Russia."

According to *Reuters* on 18th November, a "similar movement on a smaller scale was suppressed at Irkutsk." In response, Kolchak issued a manifesto admitting the faults of the past and giving assurance of good conduct in the future. His Ministers all resigned and new ones were appointed. *The Times* correspondent cabled from Chita on 24th November that "Our chief danger lies in the ignorance of the masses and the failure of the Omsk Government to attract them. The new government will be conducted on entirely different lines."

However, it was too little, too late. Kolchak's contrition merely confirmed to many of the Allied commanders and officials that he was complicit in the brutal repression of the Siberian people during his year as Supreme Ruler. He was now stuck on the wrong side of Lake Baikal with £65,000,000 in gold bullion from the Treasury of the Imperial Russian Government, waiting for someone to organise the Siberian Railways and his train to leave the station.

★★★

Meanwhile in Omsk, the American Head of the Railway Mission gave orders for his men to withdraw with the Czechs. However, Brigadier Jack wrote in a secret telegram to General Knox: "I feel that the movements of our mission should be quite independent of what the Americans may do. Our policy has been to keep as close to the front as possible while Stevens's policy has always been to get his men out of the danger zone. I would not recommend withdrawal, feeling that if there is to be a continual evacuation movement, our men's presence will be as much appreciated by the Russians as it was previously." Emerson described the situation in a letter that he managed to send with the British consul's train on 6th November:

I have been delegated along with eight of the others to remain until the last.

The Bolsheviks are due here in about five days and there is a great panic of evacuation. We have actually hundreds of trains en route to the east on both tracks and it is pitiful to see the thousands of refugees, many of whom must die from hunger and exposure. The winter descended like a theatre curtain on the first of November and it is almost zero.

The British General Staff and all British subjects are scheduled to leave today and there will only remain a few liaison officers and railway operators to assist until the city falls.

Kolchak wants to defend Omsk but his generals think it is impossible. It will probably mean the fall of the Kolchak Government as well. The people are tired of fighting for him while the Reds have been gaining so consistently for months. They are also much annoyed that he hasn't yet divided up the land among the peasants. No doubt they will change their politics as soon as Trotsky gets his Soviet operating.

We take over the railway from the Americans as soon as it comes under military jurisdiction. They are not military railway operators although most excellent railway men.[10]

In fact, General Knox's train was delayed a further 24 hours. He left Omsk for the final time as the British prime minister spoke at the Lord Mayor's annual banquet in the Guildhall. During the course of this pivotal foreign policy speech on 8th November, Lloyd George confirmed that Great Britain had sent one hundred million pounds worth of matériel to the Whites, but that he was now pulling out all British military forces from Russia.[11] The prime minister was able to draw a close to Britain's intervention because the last formed British unit in Russia, the 1st/9th Battalion of the Hampshire Regiment, had sailed from Vladivostok on 1st November and was now steaming across the Pacific to Vancouver in the SS *Monteagle*.[12]

Since leaving Omsk in August, the Tigers had been conducting menial duties in Vladivostok, which many of the soldiers found to be dull, compared with their worthwhile work in the west. By the time they boarded their ship, they were more than ready to leave, although many had enjoyed their time in Russia. Several of the Hampshire officers were in tears as the troopship slipped its mooring. Their grief was for the adopted dogs they had to leave behind, due to the quarantine regulations imposed at the last moment. The poor hounds had to be abandoned on the dockside and they could see them sat on their haunches howling and running to and fro in distress as the ship sailed out of the harbour.[13]

They arrived off the coast of Canada in dense fog. After it cleared in the morning, they found themselves in a narrow channel surrounded by tree-covered hills a few hundred yards off Victoria, British Columbia. That evening they reached the attractive port of Vancouver, with its picturesque wooden houses. The docks were brightly lit and crowds of people welcomed the ship.

The following day, they marched to the railway station and boarded a train that crossed the Rocky Mountains overnight and stopped in Calgary for a short break. Having been used to the inefficient Trans-Siberian Railway, the soldiers were very impressed with the rapid journey across the prairie, which lay under a light covering of snow as far as Winnipeg. In Montreal they were ushered onto the SS *Tunisian* for their final leg of their journey to Southampton.

There were two reasons why the battalion did not loiter in Canada despite many invitations to stay: Bullion and Bolshevism. Their commanding officer was now working for the Royal Mint and he was keen that the British share of the Imperial Treasury[14] made a swift and secure journey to London.

The second issue was the spread of militancy in Canada. Although they received a warm welcome in Vancouver, they found a country divided by the war in Russia. Canadian soul searching over their intervention in Siberia had begun at the outset, when the Deputy Prime Minister Sir Thomas White informed Sir Robert Borden at the Paris Peace Conference: "All our colleagues are of the opinion that public opinion here will not sustain us in continuing to send troops ... now that the war is ended."[15]

Public opinion rejected the idea of a military intervention with muddled aims. Among the labouring population, there were considerable numbers of activists sympathetic to the Bolshevik cause[16] who incited the mutiny of the 259th Battalion in 1918. There was a real worry about the spread of Bolshevism across the Western world.[17] Canada was at the forefront of the Red Scare with the Winnipeg General Strike in June 1919 supported widely by sympathy strikes.[18] Drastic action was taken by the Government with the Royal North Western Mounted Police used as strike breakers and rebranded as the Royal Canadian Mounted Police to act throughout the country.

The Hampshire battalion was protected from militant politics during their rapid crossing and embarkation. In any case, the soldiers just wanted to return to their families in England after nearly four years abroad. The trusty troopship[19] provided them with a comfortable final passage and they arrived at Southampton on 5th December, exactly five weeks after leaving Vladivostok. The teasing coast line sparkled brightly and flashed brilliant beams from light houses as far as the eye could reach. An early morning mist greeted them at breakfast, but once it cleared, they berthed and received a rapturous welcome home.[20] As they disembarked from the ship, they had no idea of the chaos they had left behind in Omsk.

CHAPTER 8

Dash for Freedom

We cannot of course, afford to continue so costly an intervention in an interminable civil war.

PRIME MINISTER DAVID LLOYD GEORGE AT
THE GUILDHALL ON 8TH NOVEMBER 1920[1]

On the day Emerson was ordered to "remain until the last", winter drew a curtain across the autumn vista as the snow settled on the streets and horse-drawn sleighs replaced wheeled traffic in Omsk. Leonard Vining was given the unenviable task of directing the evacuation of more than half a million desperate people. His group of nine swelled with the arrival of four soldiers from the headquarters, including the military intelligence officer, Francis McCullagh, who volunteered to replace the cipher officer who was taken ill.

The pandemonium spreading through the city stemmed from the station yard. The situation was compounded by Bolshevik saboteurs and workers, who refused to handle traffic and stores because they had not been paid for two months. Emerson spent his time frantically trying to solve this chaos:

> Day and night the incessant flood of transport swept through the streets: horses, oxen, sleighs, wagons, camels, motor lorries with their cargoes of all imaginable merchandise for transportation to the railway.
>
> The scenes in the railway yards were indescribable. Thousands of refugees with their scanty possessions were huddled together in small freight cars where many of them must perish of cold, starvation and disease. Gradually the various allied missions withdrew from Omsk with the exception of the remnant of the British Railway mission to which I belonged, detailed to assist in the evacuation of the city.

Vining secured two wagons on which he painted the Union Jack. These became magnets for many dispossessed people claiming British nationality. This curious collection included men, women and children who had not been able, or willing, to travel before November and famished families, who had fled from the Red Terror in European Russia.

These refugees represented the broad multicultural diaspora of the Empire and included Persians and Indians who could speak only a few words of English, as well as Russians married to English consorts. Vining took pity on the migrants and agreed they could stay in his overloaded carriages, but this meant that the British soldiers had to double bunk and sleep on the floor in the corridor to allow the women and children to have some privacy. On 6th November, the day after the Soviet forces entered Ishim, 160 miles north of Omsk, Vining wrote:

> General Knox's echelon pulled out last night. Two officers of this mission still to come into Omsk. They have missed the General's train and will have to come on with us.

The two officers were Brian Horrocks and Eric Hayes who were stuck among 200 trains waiting to enter the city from the west. However, the muddled Russian authorities were unable to control the schedule because the railway workers refused to help. They needed to dispatch 30 trains each day, but consistently missed their target.

By 10th November, the young captains had joined the Vining's group, but the situation had not improved:

> We got out only 11 trains during the last 24 hours, the situation is hopeless, and no one, not even the ministers, seem to have any power.

The next day, Vining helped the authorities dispatch another 18 trains. However, after McCullagh was warned by his Russian contacts that the game was up, Vining wrote:

> We must hustle along now, things are looking very bleak, and the Reds are expected at any moment. It is not the regular Red Army which is feared so much as the local Bolsheviks in Omsk who are very numerous and strong and they are expected to rise and take the town at any time. No one is allowed to be out after six o'clock at night.

On 12th November, work ground to a halt and according to the *Manchester Guardian*: "all the political prisoners in the Omsk prison were shot."[2] Vining and the Regimental Sergeant Major, Fred Walters, spent the whole night shunting carriages, so their train could depart the following day. They were frequently challenged by armed Russians and had to shout "*Angliyskiy*" to avoid being arrested.

At 2p.m. on 13th November, Emerson and his compatriots pulled out of Omsk in the last train to escape before the fearful city was captured. That night, after crossing the frozen river, the Red Army cut off the railway line from the south at point 753. They surrounded the metropolis and seized a huge amount of military matériel in the process, including 300,000 British artillery shells.

Vining's wagons bearing the Union Jack were attached to a train full of Polish soldiers and since the Poles controlled the line to Tayga, they were allowed to ride on the track usually reserved for westward trains. At the beginning, their locomotive made good progress, overtaking ribbons of trains on the east bound track. Emerson wasn't sure how long their journey would take, but he knew that it would be more than the *Express De Lux* and that they might be forced to live together for some while.

As he settled into his seat in the crowded compartment, Emerson sized up the other soldiers in the group. He knew his commander well and enjoyed his company even though Vining had described him as a lovesick "gloomy prawn" on their long voyage to Vladivostok. The major was a slim, athletic officer who had lived in India for many years as a bachelor. He had developed a razor-sharp wit and "Puck"-like sense of humour at a tough boarding school in Flintshire, but was very resourceful and cared for the soldiers under his command. His orderly, 21-year-old Sapper Smith, lived near to the Windmill at Willesborough in Kent and was a talented chef. Very graciously, he volunteered to cook for the 14 other British soldiers and make the most of the meagre rations on the dirty stove that acted as both heater and cooker for the companions.

Warrant Officer Fred Walters was known as "Uncle Charlie" because he was by far the oldest of the group. Born in Birmingham in 1870, he had emigrated with his wife, Emily, to Canada where he had eight children before he enlisted in 1916. Despite reaching a half century in years, he was incredibly fit for his age and his "ramrod straight" bearing ensured that his responsibilities for discipline were never undermined. Officers and privates necessarily mixed on terms of equality, but perfect discipline prevailed and they all worked harmoniously together for the common good.

The two infantry captains, nicknamed "Jorrocks" and "Georgik"[3] were like peas in a pod. Everyone was relieved they were with the group because their combat credentials were second to none and Horrocks spoke excellent Russian. Emerson's vocabulary had improved during the past five months, but it was useful to have more colloquial speakers, including Francis McCullagh, a 45-year-old captain in the Royal Irish Fusiliers from County Down,[4] who had served with distinction in the Dardanelles in 1915, working for military intelligence. In Siberia, he was also accredited as a journalist and had rebuilt the Russian propaganda office in Omsk, earning him a reputation as "an officer of unbounded industry and thorough knowledge of Russia and Russians."[5]

Vining's collective included four officers who wore the Royal Army Service Corps'[6] cap badge. Captain Herbert Prickett was born in Tottenham, Middlesex, but had emigrated to New York where he was a telegraph operator when he enlisted in the Canadian Army in July 1918. He became Vining's adjutant, but more importantly he could play the banjo as well as any Tennessee hillbilly. Prickett had transferred from General Elmsley's Brigade in the summer along with 24-year-old Edward Stephens from Bristol and the fresh-faced 20-year-old Bernard Eyford of Prince Albert, Saskatchewan.[7]

The Canadian serving the longest time in the British Army was Lieutenant William Dempster. He was a 30-year-old, heralding from York County, Toronto and the only married officer in the group. He had joined up as a private on the Western Front early in the War and rose rapidly through the ranks. Receiving a field commission in June 1916, he was awarded the Military Cross for saving an ammunition train two years later.[8] After the Armistice, he volunteered to serve in Russia, rather than leave the Army. Despite his undoubted courage, Dempster could be quite abrasive and Emerson was worried that he might upset some of the civilians in the carriage.

Sergeant Frank Illingworth was the tallest soldier in the group and was known as "Illy" to everyone. He was good friends with Sergeant Joseph Rooney because both had been privates in the Royal Fusiliers before transferring to the Royal Engineers on promotion. Rooney was a loquacious Irishman, who spoke Italian, French, and German as well as he spoke English. He was "was well-known in the theatrical world of London"[9] and was an accomplished musician who had entertained rapturous audiences in the cafes and bars of Omsk during the summer months.

Finally, there were two Hampshire soldiers, Sergeant George Robert Lillington, known as Bob, and Private Percy James. Twenty-four-year-old Bob[10] had been with the battalion from the start of the war and learned to speak Russian very well. However, he was renounced by his regiment when he married a 22-year-old Russian girl, Ludmilla Martinova, on 31st August. He gave up his place on the voyage home for his new wife and volunteered for the stay behind party in Omsk. Percy was born in Somerset in 1893 and joined his father working at the coal mines near Bath as a carting boy, before joining his local regiment, the Somerset Light Infantry. After transferring to the Hampshire Regiment, he endured sun stroke in India and various ailments in Siberia which meant that he was left behind when the battalion withdrew to Vladivostok.

★★★

Initially, the British carriage maintained good spirits with the talented Sergeant Rooney singing rag time tunes, accompanied by Herbert Prickett with his banjo. It was only when they looked out of the windows and saw the plight of others that reality intervened. As they arrived at a halt, or a replenishment station, there was a real worry that their locomotive would be stolen by desperate officers, whose engines had broken down. To prevent any assault, Vining organised a tight regime whereby one of the officers and a soldier would guard the front of the train whilst the others stood alert inside their carriage with loaded weapons. At dawn and at dusk, they stood to arms, when the ladies in the carriage were asked to lie flat on the ground.

Once they picked up speed, the chatter resumed with stories from the front. Horrocks regaled everyone with the time when he provoked a duel between a cavalry officer and a Cossack during an overnight stop in Manchuli and then defused the situation by claiming his faulty Russian had been the cause of the misunderstanding. However, these yarns could not distract the passengers from the view outside as they passed queues of human misery on the tracks that ran parallel to the railway.

The despairing sight of civilians, who they knew would die within the hour without help, was very stressful. There was a constant discussion about giving humanitarian assistance, but knowing that time was not on their side and that they already had taken on board more than a fair share of migrants, they just had to think about their own survival. As the days passed, they became immune to the despairing cries of help, but at night the ghosts of the dead invaded their minds and prevented them from the deep sleep they yearned.

Keeping the engine running was a constant worry. Francis McCullagh wrote:

> We found great difficulty in getting water and fuel for our engine owing to the fact that there was no firewood at the stations and that nearly all the water towers had run dry or got frozen...
>
> All our energies were concentrated on satisfying our locomotive's insatiable cravings. The struggle for water on these occasions was a nightmare as half a dozen engines sometimes contended for the privilege of filling their boilers first, and as the commandants of rival echelons almost came to blows.

Sometimes they watered their engine from a wayside well, but this was not easy because there was always a long line of men from other trains doing the same thing. The wells looked like holes made in a frozen river with the sides encased in a thick waxy coating of polished ice. There were no railings and the risk of falling into the well was considerable. If one did tumble down, there was little chance of a swift death by drowning because the overflow had frozen and the faller would have been wedged tight in the narrow part above the water.

At 10a.m. on 16th November, they arrived at Barabinski. There appeared to be a hopeless muddle ahead and Vining went forward on foot with a few others to find out what was happening. As they approached the station, 15 corpses were suddenly flung out of the hospital train in front. These bodies were all frozen stiff in contorted positions. It was horrific, but by then they were already inured to the sight of dead bodies and "no one paid the slightest attention to it."

They were held at Barabinski for four days before they were allowed to continue to Novo-Nikolaevsk. Now their progress slowed significantly. When they halted at a station, they met other British soldiers who had departed before them from Omsk, but who were stuck on the westerly track. These desperadoes realised that they might be stuck forever, so started to "train-jump", rather than waiting at the back of a ribbon of trains. Some of them became very adept at this game and as soon as they arrived at a halt, they would walk forward to the leading train that was due to depart from the station and persuade the stern commandant to give them a lift to the next station, where they repeated the trick. Only two or three were able to do this at a time because the trains were so overcrowded, but all of them eventually succeeded in escaping the clutches of the Red Army.

Vining's band was more of a cohesive unit and felt obliged to look after the British women in their care, so they did not separate. They all took their turns to stand guard at night. The redundant water towers at the stations "loomed skywards like huge Paschal candles with streams of congealed wax." In the freezing cold silence, they looked out on the dark forests "which continued for thousands of miles to the northward, till they dwindled to stunted shrubs and finally disappeared altogether in the frozen tundra of the Polar Sea."[11]

On 30th November, they arrived at Novo-Nikolaevsk,[12] 550 miles from Omsk and felt pleased with their progress. Emerson calculated that at their present rate, they would take eight weeks and reach Vladivostok. However, they were now held up and in the long periods of inactivity, his mind turned to Dallas and these thoughts made him feel depressed.

Whilst he was in Omsk, working 18-hour days, he was not reminded of her very much, but on this long journey, he wondered whether he would ever see her again. Meanwhile, Dallas was still in Vladivostok. When she was off-duty, she would attend some of the cultural concerts with other nurses and hear about the progress of the American soldiers from Omsk. However, there was very little news about the British and she often worried how far Emerson had progressed on his 2,500-mile journey.

★★★

When the final bitter month of the year arrived, the Siberian Army's retreat rapidly degenerated into a rout, with the Red Army advancing 20 versts each day. As Kolchak's empire crumbled, he replaced General Sakharov with the popular General Kappel.[13] However, more White

regiments made their peace with the Soviets and this encouraged the
Red Army to press forward, which in turn increased the cycle of fear
and panic further down the railway line.

After five wasted days, the last British echelon slowly pulled out of
Novo-Nikolaevsk on the east bound track at 1.30p.m. The weight of
their train was so heavy that a banking engine had to push them up the
hill. There was a dramatic shortage of fuel and water. Many engines were
now breaking down in the freezing weather and blocking the line. This
meant that the trains behind were halted for hours at a time and had to
be conserved carefully, otherwise they too would seize. Emerson and
the others regularly had to leave their carriage and form a human chain,
passing baskets of snow forward, in order to maintain steam pressure in
their locomotive.

On 7th December, they only moved a few versts to the next crossing
station, or *raziast*, where they made another attempt to get out of the
hopeless ribbon of trains onto the west bound track. The next day
at Oiash, the station commander informed Vining that there were
five echelons to transfer before his. In the evening, when it came
their turn, a train full of so-called ministers gazumped them and they
discovered that it had five British carriages with it, including Brigadier
Jack's deputy, Lieutenant Colonel Eric Johnston. They left on the west
bound track and Vining followed them a few hours later on the east
bound track.

Within Emerson's carriage the stress became tangible. Francis
McCullagh's sense of helplessness made him feel as if he was "manacled
in a rudderless boat shooting down towards the falls of Niagara." They
all suffered from nightmares as they "counted the gradually diminishing
number of versts which separated us from our relentless pursuers."

At Tayga, the Czechs, Poles and Russians fought for control of the
locomotives after they repulsed two enemy attacks six miles west of the
town. Here, Vining received a message from Johnston: "If the situation
seems to warrant it, do not hesitate to take complete control." The British
contingent found this perversely amusing and agreed that it would have
taken a whole division of 10,000 British soldiers to solve their current
problems. They still felt optimistic that they would reach Lake Baikal

before the Red Army, but as the temperature dropped further and the snow deepened, their progress slowed to a few miles each day.

There were only two ways of escaping from the Red tide; by train, or by sleigh along the track that ran parallel to the railway. The British noticed that the steady stream of ponies pulling pathetic burdens of women and children was increasing. They caught glimpses of the fear and sorrow in their faces, with many of them starving and ill, somehow clinging to the top of their possessions on the cart. The sick that fell down and died were soon covered with snow, or trampled underfoot.

The conditions were described on 12th December by *The Times* correspondent:[14] "The terrible sufferings of the refugees during the railway journey eastward are indescribable. Whole trains were burned by the half-frozen passengers, who were compelled to trudge, and many succumbed to cold." The walls of the stations were covered with pitiable messages: "To Dominica Ivanovna Glyebova – We cannot get any further and are staying here in Bolotnaya in the Square opposite the Church. Dom Rykachev No 8. Vanna is sick of typhus – Sergius and Natash."

Francis McCullagh was touched by the confidence shown by the writers that there must be a secure haven of refuge somewhere. "At Novo-Nikolaevsk, Tomsk was the abiding city; at Tayga it was Mariansk; at Achinsk it was Krasnoyarsk. The British had the same illusion, but there was something symbolic in the futile hunt for security, there is no abiding city...."

Inside many of these stations there was an area converted into an emergency hospital. Outside, the pile of naked corpses increased by the hour, made up of those who had succumbed to typhus, or cold injuries. The snow affected everything. It whitened young men's beards and eyebrows; it encased rifles in glittering frost and made the railway station look like an Eskimo's igloo. The carriages wore fantastic wreaths of soft snow on their roofs, window sills and steps.

Two days later, Admiral Kolchak reached Mariansk, 665 miles from Omsk, as the Red Army captured Novo-Nikolaevsk, only 250 miles behind him. Here, the Soviet haul included 10,000 prisoners, 200 motor cars, two armoured trains and 20,000 wagons half-loaded with various kinds of military stores. The chaos as the town's citizens fled east was exacerbated by the running battles between sledges, reminiscent of chariot fights in ancient Rome.

The next day was one of the worst for Emerson. Halted at the small station of Bolotnaya, only 118 versts from Novo-Nikolaevsk, he was called forward for his technical opinion and had the sad duty to inform everyone that their engine had finally given up. Horrocks went to the office of the besieged station master to negotiate for a new locomotive, but there were dozens of train commanders complaining about the unfair assignment of the engines, so he was unable to acquire a replacement from the poor man.

Reporting back to Vining, they discussed what to do. It would have been impossible to hire local sleighs, but by a piece of good fortune an officer from the Jaeger artillery regiment that Edward Steel mentored who spoke fluent English gave them a letter to his colonel asking him to provide them with a sleigh. Vining and the others set off to find the battery and by another stroke of fortune they met a driver who knew where it was camped. When they arrived at the battery, they saw that each gun had a small Union Jack painted on it and the horses were large Canadian animals. Graciously, the officer in charge of the battery agreed to give a lift and instructed them to jump onto the transport sleighs as they passed later that evening.

In the meantime, Horrocks arranged for the 24 ladies and unfit men to be transferred to a Polish train. They piled as much luggage into the one car which contained eight coupés and stuffed boxes of canned stuff and other food into it. The men then thrust a few personal items into kitbags and burned their classified documents and code books. The scene was desperate, surrounded by a large crowd; it was like evacuating a home that they had lived in for seven months in half an hour.

At 5p.m. the artillery regiment arrived and the British soldiers jumped on board their sleighs "passing like bats out of a cave" on the track parallel to the railway line. It was bitterly cold. Many of them had not slept for 72 hours and they were not prepared for a night on the sleighs perched on top of the baggage. It was almost dark when they set off in horrendous conditions, with the mercury rapidly dropping below 20 degrees Celsius.

At about midnight, they stopped in a small town, where they sheltered in the council house. Vining paid liberally with roubles, canned food and rum to rent the main chamber. They spread a blanket on the floor and very soon a medley of snores filled the room. Unfortunately, Private James, who still wore the boots issued to British troops that were about as useful "as a sick headache," had frozen feet. Vining wrapped them in a blanket and applied goose fat to the enormous blisters on the first and second toes and on his heel. He also bought a pair of felt boots, or *pymwy*, which probably saved Percy James from losing his foot to gangrene.

Breakfast the next morning, 16th December, was baked potatoes and butter. They thanked the artillery commander effusively for their rescue and hired two private droshkies and three ponies for 1500 roubles. Sitting on top of their possessions, they clung on to what they could, but the tracks were rutted with many obstacles and the treacherous going caused them many problems.

After a couple of hours, Emerson, who sat on "a camel hump of saddlery", fell asleep and suddenly found himself in the snow, having lost his precarious grip of the side of the sleigh. His spectacles fell off his nose and he floundered about, desperately searching for them with numb hands. As other sleighs passed by, he was hit by a horse's perilous hooves, but he eventually retrieved his glasses and jumped aboard another cart that looked as if it had some space. Unfortunately, it was a partisan's sleigh and the driver headed off the main route into the forest before the other passengers threw their English stowaway overboard.

Lost in a desert of snow, Emerson started to retrace the tracks towards the main route, wading through the deep drifts. Just as he was about to give up hope, he saw a man on a pony and shouted out in his best Russian. The kindly horseman helped him up and agreed to take him to the next station in the easterly direction. They rode on for about thirty minutes and then as they descended into a gully, a queue of sleighs blocked their way. Emerson suddenly saw his comrades up ahead and breathed a huge sigh of relief!

He realised that he had been incredibly fortunate. If he had not been helped by the Jaeger, he would soon have become one of the hundreds of corpses that marked the side of the track. It was now so cold that everyone took turns to "run beside the sleigh for a mile or two" to keep their blood circulating. Fortunately, Emerson had also invested in a pair of *pymwy*, which protected him from frost bite. At last they arrived at a sizeable village and knocked on the door of a house belonging to a woman with five children. That night, 18 of them had to crowd into a room that was twelve foot by ten. They lay down head to toe on the floor and were so exhausted that sleep came quickly, but in the morning the putrid smell in the room was unforgiving.

They were not alone invading the peasants' houses along the route. These poor individuals had their possessions, food and animals commandeered by Kolchak's soldiers and endured much suffering as a result. On one occasion, a homeowner politely asked the Russian soldiers to leave his hut, so that his wife could give birth. When they returned a short time later, the mother of the newborn baby was making tea at the stove.

Most of the group tumbled off the sledge at one time or another. Francis McCullagh was fortunate to be hoisted aboard another sleigh by a Canadian riding behind the British after falling for the first time. On another occasion he became separated from Emerson's group at night, but made his way to the next village where he tried to find a house for shelter. He forced himself into one room full of Russian officers, some of whom were sleeping whilst sitting up in the chairs. Suddenly, he realised that the man next to him was in fact dead and had probably expired from typhus, so he made a rapid exit and found a more welcoming nest.

The fellowship set off at 4a.m. to beat the rush hour. As they left the villages in the dark, they watched the flames of the huge fires in the pine forests where Russian soldiers, who had not been able to find a room in a village, had made themselves as comfortable as possible. When the wind increased, it acted like a whip across their faces and visibility dropped to a few feet. Icicles formed on their mufflers and even with their layers of clothes and fur overcoats, the cold penetrated their bones, so they had to pause every two or three hours to warm themselves in livestock barns before they collapsed from the cold. Incredibly, they all survived intact apart from Private James, whose frost-bitten heel turned black.

Despite their hardships, Vining's cohort felt they had made a sensible decision to take to the sleighs. The queues of trains they passed were so bad that on 16th December the commander-in-chief of the Czech forces, General Syrovi, issued an order to uncouple all the engines conveying Russians and to use these locomotives to hasten the evacuation of the Czech Legion. He justified this order on the grounds that the Russians had not fulfilled their oft repeated promise to provide sufficient engines and fuel for the eastward move of his forces.

The general's orders resulted in Kolchak's personal trains being stopped outside Krasnoyarsk on 17th December. His entourage included the remnants of the Imperial Gold Reserve, although one quarter of this had been exchanged for war credits.[15] Despite his protests, the Czech in charge of the station refused to let the train move any further. After furious telegrams were passed between Kolchak and the French head of the Allied forces, he was eventually allowed to move on, but this turned out to be a critical delay for the Supreme Leader.

Meanwhile, Emerson and his group battled through the weather for five days. The sleighs and their occupants were a sorry sight. The wiry ponies were exhausted with their heavy burdens. The long hair on their heaving flanks was frozen in patches where the sweat had turned to ice. They frequently slipped into the deep snow and had to be fished out. Jets of vapour extended from their icicle framed nostrils and drooping muzzles into the frosty air.

Progress was very slow, but after covering 90 miles they reached Tayga, where the Polish commandant explained that the line ahead was clear. Suddenly, one of them saw the carriage with their women and children standing in the yard. The spontaneous greeting as they knocked on the carriage door was highly emotional. The women begged the men to stay with them, so they all crowded into the carriage, which was intended for only 16 passengers.

That day, Kolchak's rear-guard evacuated Tomsk, 100 miles east of Novo-Nikolaevsk as the Red Army approached. Their rapid speed magnified the fear further down the line and three days later, on 23rd December, the White Army fought its final battle in Siberia. Reporting on this comprehensive defeat, the *Manchester Guardian*[16] commented that: "the shattered remains of Kolchak's army scattered and all stores, munitions and practically all artillery were lost." General Kappel issued orders to make for Krasnoyarsk as the next major defensive line. However, this proved impossible as 45 echelons of the White Army were held up on the railway line with frozen engines, stuck between Bogotol and Kozulka.

The next evening, the British made the most of their situation. There was a babble of noise as 40 people, squeezed into one carriage, ate their

Christmas Eve supper of soup, rice and vodka. A whisky bottle was shared around and they held an impromptu sing song until 11.30p.m. with a magnificent rendition of "Helen of Troy" and "Give me the Moonlight".

The following day, Vining walked into Mariansk Station and found that it was completely blocked. A sense of gloom descended on the British carriages as the news extinguished the fleeting hopes of the past few days. Vining and Walters managed to attach the ladies' carriage to a Polish Red Cross train, which pulled out at 9p.m. However, the men's departure was delayed and progress during the following week was turgid, with the length of the halts increasing between their short moves. With mournful humour, Horrocks exclaimed, "It's no bally good, boys. We shan't get away. I'm with you. I'm the Jonah, all right. We'll get pinched."

After another long wait outside Achinsk, the British entered the town on 31st December to find a scene of utter desolation. They discovered that the station was completely destroyed because three days earlier, a freight train carrying dynamite had exploded in the centre of a dozen refugee trains standing on parallel tracks. Five hundred people were killed instantly and thousands injured; many of them women, children and babies. Emerson observed: "the dead were piled up like cordwood. There were hundreds of them, but they were luckier than the injured who still lived and who could not possibly receive medical attention." In ordinary times this would rank as a global disaster, but here it was just another unfortunate episode in the unfolding tragedy of the retreat from Omsk.

The British carriage was now attached to the rear of another train full of the Polish Rifle Division and began to make good progress. However, on 3rd January, the bumps and thumps from the worn tracks became so bad that they could not lay the tables with crockery at meal times. Every time they went up a slope, Francis McCullagh's heart was in his mouth "as it used to be when I heard the long-drawn wail of approaching Turkish shells in Gallipoli. Never till then had I realised that there were so many nasty inclines on that section of the Trans-Siberian which, when I traversed it formerly in swift and well-appointed trains, had always seemed to me as flat as a pancake."

The constant churn resulted in one of the couplings shearing and another becoming so damaged that they had to attach a wooden splint to avoid it fracturing. Vining assigned a permanent sentry to watch over it and, if the injured connection looked like breaking on an incline, to throw a log of wood under the wheels to avoid the carriage rolling backwards. It became so bad that Vining went forward to the Polish leader. Initially, he was unresponsive, but after bribing him with more roubles, he found some spare couplings and placed the British carriage next to the engine.

At this stage, a large number of sleighs crossed onto the railway line and travelled along the rails to increase their speed. In doing so, they threw so much snow over the lines that sometimes the rails were four or five inches under the surface. This greatly hampered the train, as the driving wheels did not grip the rails and simply flew round, while the engine coughed as if it was speeding at 30 miles an hour. The angry Poles tried to stop the sleighs from travelling along the line, but this was similar to King Canute ordering the incoming tide to retreat.

As they approached Krasnoyarsk they were told that their ladies passed the same point three days earlier and this raised their morale. However, there was another long halt at Meneno on 6th January, which they put down to the fact that the locals were celebrating Russian Christmas Eve.[17] In the afternoon, they were waiting to move forward in a queue of trains ascending to a plateau to their left. Emerson watched a mounted courier ride to the head of the column. Suddenly, the locomotive in front blew its whistle and their train replied, but it did not move forward. Sergeant Rooney struck up on the banjo and sang "Take me back to dear old Blighty".

Then someone in the train remarked, "A Russian officer has just thrown his sword over the bank." Several more followed his example; all around, they saw White Army soldiers throwing down their rifles and pistols. They had travelled only 350 miles in the seven weeks since they departed from Novo-Nikolaevsk, but now they realised this was the end of their forlorn dash for freedom and the beginning of their captivity at the hands of the Russian Soviet Federative Socialist Republic.

Omsk Cathedral: the funeral of the last British officer to die in Siberia, Lieutenant Colonel Edward Steel DSO, was held here. Steel died on Friday 17th October of influenza, complicated by the severe chest wounds he had suffered at the Somme in 1916. He was buried with full military honour in the Cossack cemetery alongside Private Taylor of the Hampshire Regiment, who drowned in the Omsk lake on 31st July. (Courtesy of Angus MacMillan)

The rebuilt station at Novosibirsk, where Emerson and his compatriots were held up in December 1919 during their mad dash for freedom. While waiting for the line ahead to clear, some of the group purchased amethyst, turquoise, beryl and alexandrite stones from the Urals, which were readily available in the market outside the station. (Courtesy of Patrick Gilday, 2017)

PART 2

Razed Russia

CHAPTER 9

Captured in Krasnoyarsk

Further presence of Allies in Siberia can serve no useful purpose; it is indeed actively
harmful in that it retards natural development of Russian people…

SECRET CYPHER FROM MILES LAMPSON[1] AT
CHITA ON 13TH JANUARY 1920

After Emerson and the others watched the White Army soldiers throw
down their rifles and pistols, they decided to eat early. As their gallant
chef prepared the food, a soldier wearing a fur cap with a red plume,
similar to a British fusilier's hackle, entered their carriage. A few minutes
later, his commander climbed in and promptly asked whether he could
join them for supper.

The visitors explained that Krasnoyarsk had been seized by partisans
from Minusinsk, a safe haven for political revolutionaries exiled from
European Russia in the 19th century.[2] Kolchak's so-called volunteer
movement had failed to defend the rear areas and the Red Army's
advance had been unhindered for several days. They instructed everyone
to rid themselves of weapons and wait for Trotsky's Fifth Army, which
was due to arrive any day. Then he bade farewell and set off towards
the town station.

Vining quietly discussed the options with his "pow-wow team" away
from the civilians in the carriage. They spoke about escaping by sleigh,
or trekking north through the snow to the shores of the frozen sea, or
south to the Chinese frontier across the Gobi Desert.[3] It is the duty of
every officer to support any escape attempt, so Vining could not prevent
anyone from going. However, he did point out that the journey, which

would have been difficult in the summer, would be virtually impossible in mid-winter. The sleigh journey from Bolotnaya to Tayga provided them with a realistic idea of the challenges of travelling in deep snow. There were some, such as Private James with his frostbitten feet, who were medically incapable of embarking on an escape journey.

They knew that the northern route passed through impenetrable and uninhabited forests that stretched for thousands of miles until they gave way to the Arctic tundra. In the south, the terrain was less hazardous, but the Bolsheviks held most of the villages from there to the Chinese frontier, 500 miles away and the Himalayas were impassable at this time of the year.

The situation was recorded by Vining on the day after their capture: "It is difficult to know what to do. It is absolutely and utterly impossible to escape into the forest as the snow is too deep and there is nowhere to go to … perhaps there won't be a tomorrow – damnation take it … anything would be better than sitting here and waiting for goodness only knows what … anything but this suspense."

Meanwhile, the White Russians in the carriage overwhelmed the British soldiers with abuse. After two months together, there was no love lost between the two groups. During the first days of the journey, the Russians demanded that Sapper Smith should cook for them, but Vining rejected their authority. There were many other irritating habits that alienated them from their rescuers, such as wasting precious drinking water when washing their clothes.

Their attitude was typical of many White Russians who wanted to employ the British Army in a way that would have caused mutiny in the ranks. Among them, was a young Russian officer who, even when fleeing from the battlefield under a foreign flag, could not restrain himself from criticising England for the unfolding calamity. McCullagh placed him in the category of those who had "no backbone", blaming everyone else for their unfortunate situation. Vining had enough of his bad language and so he told him and the others to leave the carriage and make their way into town.

Once the ingrates departed, the British waited for instructions from their captors, but they were left alone for two days. When they realised that they would have to fend for themselves, Horrocks walked to the station and met a forlorn British refugee, William Yates, who was fluent in Russian and had been travelling on a different train.

Yates was born in Ekaterinburg to English parents and he was attempting to escape the mayhem with his pregnant wife Lydia and son, Ernest. His uncle was a famous explorer of the northern forests in Siberia and was now the congregational minister in Tiverton,[4] where William was trying to lead his family. Horrocks invited him to join together in their attempts to find accommodation, much to the relief of the stranded family.

Krasnoyarsk was bursting to the seams with displaced people, but Yates and Horrocks found a couple of rooms to rent in the Zemski Soyuz, government building, close to the centre. Retrieving their baggage proved to be a very difficult task. Their train was stuck four miles out of town and the cabdrivers refused to leave Krasnoyarsk for fear of being commandeered by the Red Army. A further complication was caused by the Soviet Government declaring that Kolchak's currency was void and Vining had practically no other roubles, so he could not pay for transportation. Yates managed to secure the services of a couple of cab drivers, or *izvoshchiks,* by promising to pay them with clothes, blankets, soap, and other commodities.

However, there was more trouble to overcome when they loaded their sleighs. A number of villainous-looking men gathered round and started pushing the British soldiers and grabbing their possessions, evidently with the intention of picking a quarrel and then looting their belongings. Fortunately, the Red commander who joined Vining for supper was at hand. He addressed the strangers "with a sternness and dignity worthy of a Roman Tribune" and asked them by what right they were acting. When they failed to provide any such authority, they slunk away and the British were all able to transport their luggage to their quarters without further mishap.

★★★

On 10th January there were in Krasnoyarsk 4,575 senior officers of the White Army. All these men queued in an orderly file outside the commandant's office to register with the new authorities. A couple of days later, Horrocks and Hayes joined this mass of humanity, which had not moved forward very far because the office only remained open between 9a.m. and 4p.m. and the process of registration was so slow. They returned in the afternoon to the remainder of the group with grim news. If they did not register in two days' time, they ran the risk of being shot and would be unable to buy food or fuel, nor pay for medical treatment.

The next day, they decided to take drastic measures. Polishing the buttons on their best uniforms, they marched to the front of the queue, which was already about a quarter of a mile long at 7a.m. They announced that a British delegation was there to see the commissars. Whilst they waited, a Red soldier pushed his way through the guards to greet the two captains and thank them for the "wonderful times they had together at Ekaterinburg." Horrocks noticed that one of the British mission's interpreters, Makarov, was working in the office and he helped their cause by handing over the all-important ration cards.

Although the threat of being shot had receded, their pangs of hunger had not. No trader would take their Kolchak paper money, so they spent most of their day waiting in long queues waiting for the food commissars to give them bread tickets and other concessions. There was never enough to feed everyone in the group, so they desperately had to find ways of earning money for meals.

Half a dozen of the party were able to secure teaching jobs at local schools for the equivalent of about ten shillings (50 pence) a week and a hot lunch. Francis McCullagh worked for one of the officials, who only paid four roubles an hour, a fraction of a halfpenny, plus one meal per day and a place to sleep on the floor, in the corner of the drawing-room after everybody had gone to bed. When he pointed out that a packet of ten cigarettes cost 24 roubles, the commissar's young wife just laughed and said that the German prisoners received much less.

Most of the group found a way of bringing in some contribution each day for the common fund. Sergeant Rooney was the most successful; not only teaching Italian, but also playing the piano in a cafe. Eyford and Stephens took spare clothes to market to barter for food, but they were frustrated and returned with little to show for their efforts, other than a bag of nuts and a pair of skates.

A week after they were captured, Francis McCullagh began to plot his own escape.[5] The freezing weather that week reached a new low and on 16th January, it was 74 degrees below freezing. The metal on his glasses burned the bridge of his nose like red-hot irons and the glass was constantly frosted when he was outside. However, this did not prevent him from observing that hundreds of Siberian horses were dying in the streets and the dogs were feeding on their carcasses.

All livestock had been made the property of the state, but the Bolsheviks did not care about their animals. Thousands of horses were abandoned for want of fodder and wandered loose on the streets and all over the surrounding countryside. Some were smart cavalry horses and others heavy transport horses, but most of them were the shaggy Siberian ponies taken without payment from poor farmers during the retreat. They were as tame as pets and tried to follow other horses which had bridles and masters and a recognised place in society, but the stable doors were always shut in their faces.

These lost souls looking for shelter even walked into the cafes, but they were shooed away by the irate owners. Eventually, their heads drooped and they lay down with filmy eyes, dying from neglect. Their frozen carcasses dotted the side of the roads with some taken away to be cut up and sold at the market. Finally, the Bolsheviks took action and they transported the remainder into a field by the railway station. There the pitiable animals were skinned and had their tails cut off before they were deposited in huge contorted piles to rot.

Another uncomfortable sight for the soldiers was the large number of British uniforms worn in the street. A great quantity of Red Cross supplies, including woollen comforters and balaclava hats had also found their way into the hands of the Bolsheviks. Many were sourced from White Army recruits, who had been given these clothes when they joined the ranks. If the day was warm, they would part with all the winter outfits for a glass of vodka, or a few roubles. A week later, when it was cold, they complained bitterly to their officers that the English had neglected to supply them with suitable clothing.

Some Red Army soldiers wore the complete British uniform, but even those who did not had some token such as a pair of British putties, a British warm, or prized above all, a haversack and web pattern belt. Once, when Horrocks was being lectured truculently about the supplies his country had provided for the White Army, he transformed the commissar's dark scowl into a pleasant smile by simply remarking, "Well, it seems that you have got most of it!"

When given the opportunity, he asked about their repatriation to Vladivostok. The officials merely offered their apologies. They excused the delay with pleas about the poor state of the railways and the fighting between Russians and Japanese in eastern Siberia that prevented any movement.

Accommodation was at a premium and the British were constantly under threat of being turned out of their rooms. They had great difficulty acquiring a written order from the Quartering Committee, due to the huge number of people who were trying to get one at the same time. Their lodgings were checked by officious inspectors regularly, but each time the authorities realised that they could squeeze no more people into the British rooms.

On 17th January, Vining bought a small cooking stove, which improved the feeding situation greatly. Their daily menu was fairly repetitive; lunch was stew and supper was baked potatoes, or *kasha*, a porridge made of barley or rice. Fortunately, they still had plenty of butter from their train and this small luxury made the dry staple food more palatable.

That day, he met the Danish consul[6] and a group of downbeat Scandinavian staff. The Dane was the last senior diplomat left in Krasnoyarsk and informed Vining that he was allowed to send telegrams to the outside world and that the American Red Cross was still in town. The next day he sent a Czech officer under an assumed name to Vining. This desperate man, accompanied by his wife, had been the commandant of Ekaterinburg and knew that if he was caught by the Bolsheviks he would be put in jail and executed. His wife somehow believed the British could assist them to escape, but Vining's rooms were already packed with British families, so he could not help.

Even now, the military members of the group were weighing up the prospect of escape, but they did not feel they could abandon the vulnerable members of their curious collective. According to Horrocks who spent the most time waiting in queues, the cold of the Siberian winter was "almost unbelievable". The continuous mental and physical strain on everyone since the beginning of November was beginning to have an effect. Emerson's letters changed from the confident tones, written on the official paper from Omsk, to the stressed handwriting on cheap Canadian YMCA paper at Krasnoyarsk.

Krasnoyarsk, Siberia January 25 1920

Dear Allie,

Before this reaches you there shall, no doubt, have been news of my capture by the Bolsheviks on January 6th. This letter will be only a "shot in the dark" as it is hoped that we may have a chance to communicate with the outside world within the next few days.

As yet we have no news of when we may be permitted to leave the country. We are assured that we are not Prisoners of War. Nonetheless we are under detention. The difference is that Prisoners of War are accorded rations and accommodation, whereas we have to supply our own as aliens, here in sufferance. At present we are as comfortable as might be expected and feel confident that we will be able to arrange to go home in a few months. The Danish Consul is trying to communicate with the British Government.

You must appreciate that I cannot begin to give details of the most fascinating weeks that preceded our capture. I will send that account later. The Soviet Government has declared all money void with the exception of their own and you can imagine it takes some skilled financing on our part to earn a living. There are sixteen in our party and we feel certain that several other isolated parties are also captured.

We abandoned our trains at Bolotnaya and did about 90 miles on sleighs before joining the Poles at Ta[y]ga. It is feared that the colonel, one major and two captains were killed at Ta[y]ga. From all evidence at hand I feel confident that we are safe from violence although we may yet suffer considerable inconvenience.

I shall leave the next page blank until the opportunity develops to send this. The city is under the most rigid military rule and the death penalty is enforced for drunkenness, theft, assault and other minor offences.

Sincerely,

Emerson

Vining did a remarkable job keeping everyone cheerful. It helped that he was able to pull out his guitar and hold regular concerts in the evenings, with "Tipperary" being the usual encore requested by the civilians. The key was to maintain that strange British blend of leadership, combining a sense of humour, with formal discipline and a compassionate approach to human problems.

Two days later, the commissars told Vining about an Anglo-Russian prisoner agreement being negotiated in Copenhagen and that the Allies' blockade had been lifted. This news seemed to cheer the Bolsheviks and the next day, they gave Vining 10,000 roubles and allowed him to write a telegram to the War Office. The message was vetted by the leading communist personality, Veniamin Sverdlov whose brother, Yakov, had signed the Czar's death warrant when he was the chairman of the Central Executive Committee before his own death in 1919. The influential deputy minister for transportation objected to the word "detained" in the telegram that simply stated:

> Following British Personnel detained in Krasnoyarsk by Soviet Government urgently in need of money please arrange credit.
> Major Vining. Captains Horrocks, Hayes, MacCullagh, Prickett. Lieutenants RJ Stephens, Dempster, Eyford. RSM Walters, SM MacMillan, Sergeants Rooney, Illingworth, Lillington, Private James, Sapper Smith also British Civilians RA Purvis British Corporation. William Yates, Ernest Yates, Lydia Yates Tiverton Parsonage.

Vining made a subtle change to Francis McCullagh's surname because he had taken off his uniform and reinvented himself as an Irish journalist sympathetic to the Bolshevik cause. Since he had been registered as an officer in the Irish Guards when they arrived, a substitute was needed to make it appear to the Soviet authorities that the group was still intact. The Czech officer from Ekaterinburg was very grateful for this opportunity to suddenly become a naturalised Irishman.

They had heard from four separate sources that Eric Johnston and his party[7] had been killed at Tayga, but now Sverdlov told Vining that in fact, he had been returned to Omsk. He also told Vining that the Fifth Army was expected in Krasnoyarsk within the next few days and this might mean they would be thrown out of their quarters.

Meeting the commissars was a challenge due to the long queues. A whole day could be wasted in the freezing cold, standing outside their door for a two-minute rebuff. All the local communists had been imprisoned at one time or another by Kolchak's Government. One official was suffering from a cruel scourging that had been inflicted on him by White soldiers. His back was still in bandages and Horrocks was astonished that, under the circumstances, he was not even ruder to the British. They tried to persuade the British to support their cause, by showing them pictures of alleged war crimes, but the photographs were inconclusive and the general feeling was that the atrocities were "six of one and half a dozen of the other."

They needed all their tact and charm when dealing with the officials, who regularly made gruesome threats. After the local government changed, they met a woman commissar, tougher than any of the men who previously held sway. She had a cigarette constantly in her mouth and a large revolver in her belt, which she was not afraid to use. Another threatened to conduct a "raid" for belts and binoculars, which would probably result in them losing all their precious items that made life bearable. Yet another said to Vining: "As you are prisoners of war your proper place is in the concentration camp. You can go there at once if you like." These words chilled them to the bone because they knew this was the equivalent of a death sentence.

One year before, in February 1919, a military team led by Lieutenant Colonel Francis Harvey[8] had visited Krasnoyarsk to investigate the possibility of establishing a British training team there. He had found a barracks five miles out of town, which was fully occupied by 13,000 Austrian and German prisoners of war, 4,000 of whom were officers. He moved on to Tomsk, leaving Krasnoyarsk to the Italians who stationed a battalion in the town. Nothing was done about the camp, or *laager*, and the conditions became desperate as the civil war continued. Now it was a death trap with 30,000 men living in the overcrowded barracks, blighted by corpses stacked high in the sheds, waiting for burial. It was the last place the British wished to be sent.

On 30th January, *The Times* printed the headline "Siberia All Red" and this coincided with the arrival of the Fifth Army in Krasnoyarsk. Now Vining and his hardy band began to see the reality of the Soviet System at work. Many of the officers who had served in the White Army had been coerced to fight for the Red Army because their families were being held hostage. Some of them appeared to be sympathetic to the British. However, the key decision-makers were three political officers, who vetted every order and sat humourlessly together in a large room in the military headquarters.

The new Red governor was a tall, spare man, with a straggling beard and the thin face of a fanatic. He had been a chemist before the revolution. Vining had a stormy first interview with him and realised that he was dealing with a state of affairs of which he had had no previous conception. The stern official professed to be a servant of the people, and referred to the British officers as lower in rank than their soldiers. Everything was settled according to the "proletariat conscience", rather than legal or international conventions.

Outside the governor's office, the Red Army discipline appeared to be run on a friendship principle; if you knew someone important, you were allowed entrance. No officer was allowed to wear epaulettes, which made the British even more determined to stand apart and to wear theirs. Another order abolished titles. If one wrote the word "Mr" before a man's name on a letter, it was likely that the recipient would be arrested. Only "tovarish", or "comrade", was allowed and in this respect, the British played the game to avoid the spotlight falling on their friends.

The Soviets were unwilling to maintain the British in what they saw as a state of idleness and demanded that they work for their rations. Vining refused point blank and asked why they did not send them back to England: "We are no good here. Only two or three of us speak Russian." The caustic reply came back, "In order to shovel snow, one did not need to know much of any language." The deputy minister attempted to bribe and coerce Vining to work for the Bolsheviks, but the stoical Royal Engineer never wavered. This resulted in hunger for all, but everyone backed the decision, despite the threat of the prisoner of war camp, where men were dying at 200 a day.

The British were constantly lectured about the open war being waged throughout the world between capitalists and the proletariat. Sverdlov told Vining that the British group would not be allowed to return home unless they gave satisfactory assurances of taking the proletariat side in the great struggle. Mixed with this Bolshevik ideology, the commissars cited more pragmatic motives for detaining them: "We must keep you as hostages. We may wish to exchange you for Russian communists detained in England." They did not realise that if they had freed the British immediately after their capture, they would have departed under a favourable impression of the Bolshevik regime.

On 31st January, the typhus epidemic was raging throughout the city. Vining was keen to leave their rooms because a large group of people had moved next door and they were worried about the spread of disease. Hordes of body lice were coming through the wooden partitions and as fast as they could beat them off, others filled their ranks. The terror of the voiceless, creeping insects, whose bite led to sickness, unconsciousness, physical collapse, and sometimes death, gave everyone in the room nightmares.

The next day, Francis McCullagh moved out of the British room. Vining decided to spend a small amount of their money buying everyone lunch in a cafe. On the black market, he sold some Japanese currency at one yen to 60 roubles and some dollars at a rate of one to 100 roubles.

On 5th February, Vining met the commissars with the Danish consul present and asked again when they would be sent home. The next day, they learned that part of the Fifth Army was moving east, but their cable to the War Office had not yet been sent. Finally, after a month of uncertainty, there was some news about their move. The governor told them that the Americans, French, British and Italians would all be sent to Moscow. He gave Vining an order for the station commander to provide a 4th-Class carriage with three tiers of wooden bunks divided by small partitions.

The prospect of going to Moscow did not enthral them. "East, East, East" had been their cry for the past month. The Soviet capital was perceived as the heart of the mayhem and a place to be avoided at all cost. The amount of space they were given in the carriage was also a problem. It was supposed to sleep 20 people. However, Vining's group included 26 men, women and children, including Yates and a British Corporation engineer named Prentice, who had been in Russia for many years and married local women. When they included their baggage, the wood for cooking and heating and their provisions, plus two French and two Italian soldiers, they realised that they would have to double bunk, as they had on the journey from Omsk.

★★★

Whilst Emerson was packing his kit, the fate of the Supreme Leader was decided in Irkutsk. One of the seven British officers, who arrived in Omsk with Horrocks and Hayes on 17th May 1919, was Captain

Norman Stilling of the Duke of Wellington's Regiment.[9] He was now working as an intelligence officer,[10] attached to Admiral Kolchak's retinue, which comprised a headquarters train and another transporting the Imperial Treasury, valued at £65,000,000.[11] His personal guard boasted a thousand officers and soldiers.

Their prolonged halt in December proved critical. On 27th December[12] Kolchak's train arrived in Nizhne Udinsk, still 280 miles from Irkutsk, which by then had been taken over by the Socialist-Revolutionary party. The new leaders were particularly incensed with the White forces because General Cechov had taken away 31 political prisoners as hostages when he left the city and brutally murdered them all.

Kolchak's guard had had enough. They laid down their weapons, tore off their epaulettes and abandoned the train. The *Manchester Guardian* described the situation in which Kolchak's men "donned red rosettes and played every night at the local Revolutionary Club."[13] His train was protected by the Czech troops, but they were unwilling to fight for the old regime.

The problem was caused by the fact that there was authority for only one carriage to go east. This would mean that a number of Kolchak's retinue would be left behind, but the Admiral would not hand over loyal subordinates to the mercies of the Bolsheviks and decided to share their fate, however terrible it might be.[14]

Kolchak sent frantic telegrams to the Allied High Commissioners who were still in Irkutsk and on 4th January, he agreed to hand over supreme power of the whole of Russia to General Denikin, the commander-in-chief of the armed forces in the south. Eventually, the Allied commander, General Janin guaranteed the safe conduct of the Admiral. On 8th January, the day after Russian Christmas Day, his carriages were coupled to the train of the 6th Czech Regiment and left for Irkutsk. If he could just reach Lake Baikal, he believed he would be safe because the line from there to Vladivostok was still controlled by the Japanese and Americans, who would guarantee his safe passage.

However, the train took seven days to reach Irkutsk and the Czechs were challenged at many stations to hand over the Admiral. Finally, on 15th January, they arrived at Irkutsk and the carriages were surrounded by a hundred revolutionary soldiers with machine guns. That night

Admiral Kolchak spent his first night in captivity, although he must have felt he had been a prisoner for much of the previous month. He did not know that his so-called Allies were opening trade talks with the Soviet Union that same day in Paris.[15] The Irkutsk authorities were directed by Moscow to send Kolchak to the capital for trial by a special court, but the railway lines were so congested this would not be possible for several months.[16]

General Syrovi attempted to negotiate on behalf of the Allies, but the authorities were insistent and the powerless General Janin reneged on his earlier guarantee.[17] On the morning of 31st January, Norman Stilling was visited by Tovarish Hornstein, the Foreign Commissar of the Irkutsk Military Revolutionary Committee. He then attended a mediation conference with General Syrovi and Dr Blargosh, the representative of Czechoslovak Republic, when they were still hopeful for Kolchak's release.

Stilling received information from what he described as "a reliable source" that a White officers' organisation, which had been secretly formed for the purpose of rescuing Kolchak, had bribed a guard to gain access to "His Excellency" and inform him of a plan to secure his release. However, the Admiral seemed resigned to his fate and reaffirmed that he "would rather undergo whatever was before him, than attempt to escape at the expense of the lives of many of his adherents."[18]

On 5th February, General Voitsekhovski attempted to rescue Kolchak with 8,000 loyalists. They captured the town of Polovina 80 miles west of Irkutsk, but as they threatened to advance, the Revolutionary Committee decided, with the approval of the Fifth Red Army, to execute Kolchak and his prime minister.[19] The Extraordinary Investigating Committee, led by Tchudnovsky, interviewed the Supreme Leader for the last time to establish just cause and evidence.[20] At the previous eight hearings he had to answer an average of 24 questions, but on this final day, there were nearly 150 demands, with a particular emphasis on the brutal repression of the Kolumzino rising in 1918.

The order for Kolchak's execution was signed by Shiriamov, President of the Military Revolutionary Committee, together with three other commissars.[21] In the early hours of 7th February, a firing squad arrived by lorry at the prison. General Pepeliaev had to be dragged out of his cell, but Kolchak remained calm. He was offered a bandage for his eyes, but he refused and Stilling reported that after smoking a cigarette, the Admiral offered the diamond encrusted case, presented to him by the Czar in recognition of his naval victories, to a member of the firing squad with the words "I shall have no pockets in my shroud."

Very soon afterwards the Czech Legion handed over the remaining gold bullion estimated to be worth £65,000,000. As a result, the Soviet Government guaranteed their safe withdrawal to Vladivostok.[22] The Soviets claimed to have been cheated out of some 90,000,000 roubles, but no one ever admitted to the theft.

★★★

Before his imprisonment, Kolchak passed command in eastern Siberia to Ataman Semeonov, who remained firmly in control of the Trans-Baikal. In contrast, General Rozanov's position in Vladivostok had become untenable. On 26th January partisans entered Nikolsk and some of the garrison troops rebelled against their officers; however, loyalists still held sway and transferred the rebels to Russian Island. Two days later, Rozanov put the city under martial law, but the momentum had shifted permanently. In rapid succession, the surrounding towns fell into the hands of the social democrats, so the White general appealed to the Japanese, who gave him safe passage to Tokyo.

Political power in the *Primorskaya Oblast*, or Maritime Province, passed to the Zemstvo party on 31st January. The Bolsheviks wished to extend their revolution, but they realised they had to compromise because they could not defeat the Japanese, who still had several thousand troops based near the port. The Zemstvo head of the government, Aleksandr Medvedev, was accepted by the Allies, who continued to provide most of the economic and medical support in Vladivostok. The majority of the population did not wish to see the Americans or British depart.

In February, the American Red Cross Siberian Commission's committee decided to concentrate on civilian assistance.[23] Dallas joined one of the relief trains sent from Vladivostok to hand out supplies along the railway and hopefully reach Emerson.[24] Setting off with her friend Beverley on the day after Admiral Kolchak was executed, she reached Changchun, but the fighting around Lake Baikal prevented the train from continuing to Irkutsk and after a "mad and merry journey in Manchuria," she failed to get any closer to the British prisoners still detained in Krasnoyarsk.

Whilst Dallas made this attempt, Vining moved everyone to the railway station. On 9th February, they found the 4th-class wagons were in a dreadful state and this situation was made worse by a horrific stench. Apart from the rotting horses nearby, thousands of refugees living in box cars had used the railway yards as public latrines. Polish prisoners had been set to work cleaning the area and digging the frozen filth with pick axes. The muck was loaded into trucks and taken out of town, where it was dumped. However, much of it remained and Emerson hated to think what it would be like after the thaw.

Yet again, they had to make do and mend. They stuffed wood for cooking and heating under the seats and hung their coats in the narrow corridor, which soon became blocked. They brought two wash basins from their rooms, but these were barely sufficient for washing and shaving. Blankets were rigged up for the married couples, but it was impossible to observe all the rules of etiquette.

For three days, they found themselves waiting for the locomotive whistle to blow. Then on 12th February, Vining recorded in his diary that Captain Horrocks looked "seedy today." Suddenly, their worst nightmare arrived in the form of a six-legged enemy, *Pediculus humanus corporis*, the much-feared body louse.

The Bolshevik Commissars allowed Major Vining to send one telegram from Krasnoyarsk to the War Office in London listing the names of the British prisoners and asking for money, but he received no response. Commissar Sverdlov demanded that Vining replace the word "detained". (Courtesy of Leonard Vining, St Catherine Press)

CHAPTER 10

Downing Street Dilemma

Without previous reference here, no negotiations which might be construed as recognizing the Bolshevik Government are on any account to be entered into. Any exchange of prisoners must be purely local arrangements between commanders on the spot....

WINSTON CHURCHILL, 10TH APRIL 1919[1]

Long before Vining's group was captured, the British Government began negotiations with the Soviet Government about the exchange of prisoners in Russia. During the summer of 1919, discreet communications were established through wireless messages between the respective capital cities. However, the Soviet Government refused to continue these exchanges and demanded a formal meeting with a British representative.

Two weeks after David Lloyd George spoke about the end of the British military intervention at the Guildhall, a secret assignment was set up in Copenhagen. The prime minister asked the Labour MP for Leeds South East, Mr Jim O'Grady, to meet the Soviet Government's Assistant Commissar for Foreign Affairs, Maxim Litvinov. O'Grady's task was to secure the repatriation of the British prisoners of war in Russia and the release of the British civilians detained by the Bolsheviks, or otherwise prevented from leaving the country.

Litvinov was a 43-year-old revolutionary who had been arrested by the British Government in 1918, on a charge of speaking at public gatherings opposed to the government's intervention in Russia. He was exchanged later that year for Britain's agent in Russia, Robert Bruce Lockhart, who had been imprisoned on 31st August after the assassination attempt on

Lenin that sparked the Red Terror. Litvinov worked as an assistant to the Soviet Commissar for Foreign Affairs, Georgy Chicherin. He became a trusted roving diplomat, helping to broker multilateral agreements with a range of combatants, including the United States of America, Great Britain and France.

The Soviet ambition was to achieve some form of official recognition of the Russian Revolutionary Government by the signatories to the agreement. The dialogue was established outside the framework of the newly-formed League of Nations, although the commissioner to repatriate war prisoners, Fridtjof Nansen, had already started his work on refugees in Russia that earned for him the 1922 Nobel Peace Prize.[2]

Jim O'Grady was a 53-year-old Labour politician and former president of the Trades Union Congress, who had been an MP since 1906.[3] In April 1917, he had been part of the Franco-British socialist delegation which visited the Russian Provisional Government after the abdication of the Czar. Along with Will Thorne, the MP for West Ham and William Sanders, he attempted to persuade the Russians to continue fighting along the Eastern Front, but their efforts failed.[4]

Despite being a staunch trade unionist, O'Grady supported Lloyd George's policies and spoke often in the House of Commons about British Foreign Policy. In the December 1918 elections, he was returned in one of the new constituencies formed from part of his previous electorate. He was the ideal man to meet Litvinov and travelled to Denmark on a steam ship that he boarded at Harwich.

The capital of Denmark was the most suitable choice for the meeting with its position halfway between Britain and Russia. During the war, the Danes maintained their precarious neutrality through the diplomacy of their astute Foreign Minister, Erik Scavenius.[5] Germany had called up 30,000 men from Northern Schleswig to fight in Flanders and placed tremendous pressure on Denmark to join the axis powers. However, the Danes were more closely aligned to Scandinavian countries at the time and the country was attempting to grow a tradition of peacemaking.

There was another good reason for the meeting to be arranged in Copenhagen. The Danish Red Cross remained as the only foreign mission in Soviet Moscow after the Americans left in September 1918.

Even when it was forced to withdraw in 1919, some of its diplomats continued to work as individuals on behalf of war prisoners and looked after the interests of western countries in Russia, including Vining's cohort in Krasnoyarsk.[6]

An air of deep suspicion hung over the first meeting between the two envoys in the lush setting of the Hotel Angleterre on 25th November 1919. As soon as the initial statements were read, it became clear that the wily Soviet official would not be satisfied with a mere exchange of Russians in England and British in Russia. His outlandish opening gambit caught O'Grady by surprise.

Litvinov's suggestion widened the scope of the exchange not just to other parts of the British Empire, but also to Germany and the neutral countries of Europe. He asked for guarantees that all obstacles were removed to ease the return of any Soviet Russian nationals and dissidents, but he admitted that he was indifferent about the so-called White Russians.

O'Grady promptly adjourned the meeting and cabled London for instructions. The Foreign Office sent a rapid response telling their representative to reject any arrangement by which the repatriation of the British in Russia should be made dependent on Russians in countries outside British jurisdiction. As a result, the honourable Member for Leeds South East broke off the negotiations.

However, the Soviets understood the power of the media and Litvinov immediately issued a press communiqué, which was worded to give the impression that he would be content with less than he had first required. When the foreign secretary in London was made aware of this statement, he gave instructions for Mr O'Grady to make "further attempts to find a satisfactory solution." A frustrated MP returned to the meeting room. It must have seemed to him as if he was playing chess, blindfolded, with regular instructions cabled by Curzon from London to adjust his position.[7]

Progress was so slow that French diplomats suspected the British Legation of discussing wider political questions. However, O'Grady did not stray out of the "lane" prescribed by the foreign secretary in his letter of appointment and subsequent directions. Even though no agreement was reached by Christmas, the two envoys promised to meet again in the New Year.

When he returned to London, O'Grady gave the Soviet list of demands to the Foreign Office, where industrious civil servants set to work on the technical and legal challenges they faced. After contacting the British representatives in other countries, they established exactly how close they were to meeting Moscow's requirements. The result was compiled into a draft agreement for the exchange of prisoners which was circulated to Cabinet Members by Lord Hardinge of Penshurst.[8]

The covering note[9] informed the prime minister that the government had made very considerable concessions. There were two outstanding points; one theoretical and one practical. The first issue played to the Soviet ambition to be recognised as the official government of Russia. It centred on a request to have a representative on the proposed "International Commission for the Repatriation of Russian Prisoners of War in Germany". The second point of contention was the release of certain Soviet prisoners in the hands of the Archangel Government.[10]

For the first proposal, Hardinge was unable to do more than support the Soviet contention should a commission materialise, which he believed was doubtful. With regard to the second point, he denied that the United Kingdom held any jurisdiction, whether the prisoners were originally captured by British troops or not. However, the Foreign Office had approached the Archangel Government and discovered that its leader, General Yevgeny Miller, "was willing to release certain of these prisoners, as soon as they could be identified, provided that they wished to return to Soviet Russia. In turn, he required the release of certain White prisoners in the hands of the Soviet Government."

This was a legitimate point of contention. When General Miller had previously attempted to arrange an exchange, the Soviet Government refused to "negotiate with rebels." However, at Copenhagen, Litvinov had told O'Grady that it was entirely a matter between the Reds and the Whites. Hardinge claimed indignantly that: "If the Soviet Government refuses to negotiate with Archangel and expects His Majesty's Government to obtain the release of the Soviet adherents in the hands of General Miller, it is impossible for us to entertain the suggestion that we have no *locus standi* in the matter of the White officers. If on the other hand, the Soviet Government are prepared to effect an exchange with Archangel they should say so, and conduct separate negotiations for this purpose, a course of action which would be welcomed by His Majesty's Government as narrowing the scope of Mr O'Grady's discussions."

★★★

Russia was one of six major international challenges facing the British Government at the start of 1920, but it took up the most time.[11] Apart from the O'Grady negotiations, there was a lengthy foreign policy report presented on the situation in South Russia by Sir Halford Mackinder[12] together with comments from the General Staff circulated by Winston Churchill. Mackinder had left England on 4th December for Paris to meet four members of All Russian Council.[13] His exhaustive fact-finding mission, which encouraged further anti-Bolshevik military operations, included a visit to Warsaw where he had been briefed by Sir Horace Rumbold and the head of the British Military Mission, General Carton de Wiart.

There was also a memorandum from Admiral Sir David Beatty on "Russian Prisoners of War in Germany" and another on the blockade of Soviet Russia with observations by the First Lord of the Admiralty. Added to the 39th secret "Report of Revolutionary Organisations in the United Kingdom" circulated by the home secretary and an intelligence department memorandum on Bolshevik influence on Moslems,[14] there were many different views presented to the prime minister. Unfortunately, this allowed members of the Cabinet to read what they wanted into the papers and reinforce their bias, rather than change their beliefs.

There had been several bruising encounters in the House of Commons during the previous year, with virulent anti-Bolsheviks, led by the war secretary, preventing any official recognition of Lenin's government. Those who wished to normalise relations and allow Russia "to stew in the juice of Bolshevism"[15] were equally entrenched. One of the reasons for the chasm in opinions was the shortage of accurate advice in London after the departure of British officials from Moscow and St Petersburg.

Lloyd George was acutely aware that his government had become ensnared in the Siberian war by choice, rather than by accident. The entanglement was not comparable to a beautiful spider's web, designed and built by a brilliant strategist working patiently at the centre. It was similar to the coils of barbed wire after angry artillery bombardments had twisted the cold steel into an inescapable morass.

Now there was another heated debate as the established differences of opinion played out in the discussions over the O'Grady agreement. The key issue was what to do if the Soviets did not accept the British concessions, but there was no question of further military intervention because Britain was facing its own hardships, with high unemployment and rising social costs. Lloyd George was also aware from an informant who returned from Russia on 9th January that Lenin and the other Bolshevik leaders were quite willing to hand over the development of Russian industrial and commercial enterprises to foreign experts, provided that there was no interference in the system of government by Soviets.[16]

In the end, the Cabinet agreed to the aim of securing the repatriation of the British in Russia as the overriding priority. O'Grady was asked to meet with Litvinov in Copenhagen again and his departure on a ship from Harwich was recorded with hopeful headlines in the media.

Litvinov did his best to convince his British counterpart of the Bolshevik cause, but O'Grady rebutted all approaches, which led the Soviet envoy to describe him as a "Trade Unionist Philistine who is nearer to English Liberalism than Socialism."[17] O'Grady occasionally stumped his opponent with his pragmatic wisdom, such as when he told the Soviet envoy that "the worst thing that could happen to Russia was a revolution in any of the great manufacturing countries."[18]

On 20th January, O'Grady reported that he had reached an agreement with regard to sending British subjects in Russia certain supplies for their support.[19] It had been arranged that for each ton of such supplies, Russia should receive a ton of medical and other necessities. However, this premature press announcement did not mark the end of the negotiations. A clause was inserted which allowed the respective governments to retain those prisoners "who have committed grave offences"[20] and this concession, together with confirmation that Admiral Kolchak had been executed in Irkutsk, induced the Minister Plenipotentiary of the National Commissariat for Foreign Affairs to sign the agreement on 12th February 1920.[21]

After three months of intense negotiations, O'Grady returned to England and left the 23-year-old Foreign Office official, Lionel Gall, to manage the implementation of the agreement. Lord Curzon wished to thank O'Grady for his successful venture, but since he was a Labour politician felt it inappropriate to award him a King's honour. On 18th March, the foreign secretary suggested that the MP for Leeds South was given a piece of silver plate and asked the Lords Commissioners at His Majesty's Treasury for 40 pounds.[22] The curt response was in two parts. The first reminded Lord Curzon that "no differentiation should be made in his case on the grounds of his being a Labour member." The second explained that the Treasury was "unable to authorise the offer of a gift of plate to a Member of Parliament for Public Services rendered."[23]

The prime minister personally congratulated Jim O'Grady, believing that the agreement would draw a line under the issue. However, little did Lloyd George know that this was the merely beginning of a process, not the end and that the problem of the British prisoners of war in Siberia would inconvenience him for the remainder of the year.

CHAPTER II

An Irish Spy Escapes

All over Russia the remainder of the British spy networks that Cromie had so patiently built up closed down as agents either fled the country or went underground.[1]

HARRY FERGUSON, 2008

Francis McCullagh took off his uniform and moved into a room at the heart of the Soviet institution. He still saw his compatriots, but he did not give them his address because he was suspicious about some of the interpreters, who now worked for the Bolsheviks and occasionally visited the British quarters.

At first, he had difficulty explaining his position as a journalist to the commissars. However, he was helped by the general chaos and by a scrapbook that he had maintained for many years. This was full of newspaper cuttings in which he was styled as a "celebrated war correspondent". It helped that some of his published articles criticised the Czar's government at the time of the 1905 revolution.[2]

He could not use his passport because it revealed his employment as a British army officer, so he used the cutting from *Who's Who*, which described him as a journalist and another editorial from the *New York World* containing a portrait, which was much better than a passport. He had also written about the brutality of the Italian occupation of Libya[3] and this struck a chord with the Bolsheviks, who credited him as an active supporter of the proletariat.

McCullagh soon realised that he could still wear British uniform as long as there were no badges of rank, or unit identification on the garments. The vast majority of Russian men living in Krasnoyarsk wore some piece of British uniform. The fact that the buttons bore a British coat of arms did not seem to worry the Bolsheviks, but the secret was never to brighten them with polish. He did exchange his military overcoat for a sheepskin, but he quickly regretted this trade because the British coat was much more effective at keeping out the cold.

When he arrived in the third largest city in Siberia, McCullagh had the sense to register on the commissar's list as a civilian journalist. However, he had also been included as an officer in the Irish Guards on the list that Brian Horrocks submitted to the military authorities. He thus acquired a dual personality and Vining had to substitute a double for him when he moved out of their rooms at the Soyuz building.[4] The British group was obliged to report once a week to the town commandant, but since he had never met McCullagh, the ruse appeared to work. Nevertheless, it was always a worry for everyone, in case the officials discovered the deception.

For most of the previous year, McCullagh had worked for British military intelligence in Omsk. General Knox had brokered a deal for him to regenerate Kolchak's propaganda offices and this provided him with unique insights into the workings of the Stavka. It was an incredible risk that he now took to convince his new masters that he was, and always had been, sympathetic to their cause. If they had discovered his writings about the "monstrous and irresistible force" of the Red Army, or his comparison of Bolsheviks to the "Masked Tuaregs of North Africa," he would have fallen into great trouble.

McCullagh felt the risk would be worthwhile, if he could secure an early escape and so he changed colour like a chameleon. In his new guise, he wrote about the great happiness in Krasnoyarsk when the red flag of the revolution hung out of every house, with red ribbons flying from the soldiers' caps. As a Northern Irishman, he knew how colour could inflame tempers in a split community. However, in the first weeks after the Reds took over, he observed very little disturbance on the streets, despite the shortage of food.

Once he settled into his new accommodation and work, he set about securing permission to leave the town. There were four changes of governorship in Krasnoyarsk in January. The ensuing chaos helped his impersonation, but delayed his departure. During this turbulent month, he managed to ingratiate himself with the influential commissars[5] by presenting them with presents of clothing, gold sovereigns and a typewriter.

McCullagh knew that if he asked Tovarish Sverdlov for permission to go east to Vladivostok, his suspicions would have been aroused. The fact that the railway was severed at some of the rivers and tunnels, plus the fierce fighting between the "Kappel'evsky"[6] trying to rescue Admiral Kolchak and the Japanese hold of Trans-Baikal meant there was little hope of reaching the maritime province. He therefore asked to go to Ekaterinburg in order to witness Trotsky's great scheme for converting the Red Army into an efficient labour force by compelling a hundred thousand soldiers to "beat their swords into ploughshares."

He had already visited Ekaterinburg three times, but this seemed to be an important stepping stone for reaching Moscow, where escape would be much easier to plan. Without notice, he was offered a place on a train of technical experts leaving in a few hours. Foregoing any farewells to the other British soldiers, he grabbed his small bag of personal belongings and made a dash for the station. He just managed to arrive before the locomotive pulled out of town. Stowing his bag on the upper bunk that he was assigned, he sat down in the carriage and looked out of the window as the engine headed west.

The cold on the journey was the worst he had experienced. Even inside the heated carriages the chill caused the windows to be coated with sheets of ice, half an inch wide at the top and two inches thick at the bottom. All the brass-work was covered with hoar frost and whenever a door was opened, the cold air rushed in and made him huddle into his sheepskin coat.

The head of the expedition was a Ukrainian named Dovgolvsky, who had been educated in Belgium and worked in France as an electrical engineer. Like most Bolsheviks in authority, he was a tireless worker, a good organiser and a strong Socialist. At every large station a telephone connection was made with the town and the expedition leader set to the task of bringing order out of the chaos left by the great retreat.

Food was frugal; a hot drink and a little black bread greeted McCullagh in the morning. At about 6a.m. he was given a bowl of porridge and more *ersatz* coffee. Supper of imitation coffee and black bread was fixed for 10p.m.; but the tables were sometimes covered with papers and the dining-car full of local railwaymen until two in the morning, so occasionally this did not arrive until after midnight.

On 3rd February, McCullagh passed Novo-Nikolaevsk and crossed the River Ob. He noted that it took him less than 48 hours to cover the same distance that took seven weeks when he was heading east. One of his fellow passengers was a physician, who told him that 50 doctors had died in the town during the past six weeks from typhus and that more than 20,000 bodies lay unburied in the snow. Many of the railway stations had been converted into typhus hospitals, but most of the cases lay on the bare floor without blankets. There were huge piles of unidentified corpses and in one of the hospitals, exhausted surgeons were busily engaged in amputating gangrened limbs caused by severe frostbite.

McCullagh adapted to the Bolshevik regime through his journalistic training. He was able to "follow their train of thought and to enter their frame of mind" even though he disagreed with their ideology. Inevitably, he was involved in lengthy conversations with fanatics when he had to sympathise with their goals, if not the ways and means of achieving them.

He was constantly worried about the discovery of incriminating evidence. By coincidence, one of the carriages on their train was numbered 1,167; the British soldiers had occupied this wagon at one time on their failed escape journey. In a cavity under the floor, McCullagh had deposited several letters with his name written on the outside of each envelope.

Fortunately, this carriage was kept so full of people and baggage that the secret receptacle was never opened. Eventually, he managed to burn the letters and destroy most of the clues that pointed to his connection with the British Army. However, on several later occasions, he came across a bank receipt or some other paper which exposed his military rank.

On 19th February, his train arrived at Ekaterinburg. When he was there with the Hampshire battalion, it was a boisterous city of good cheer, overcrowded with prancing horses, philanthropy, sin and religious fervour. Now it was grey and dull. The station was deserted apart from the secret police. The only things that could be seen in the public buildings were a few grim soldiers and the propaganda posters flattering workmen, condemning capitalists and exhorting the Red Army's diligence.

In the capital of the Urals, he managed to interview the haunted murderer of the Czar, Yakov Yurovsky, who now suffered from cancer.[7]

The 41-year-old assassin described the events in the cellar of Dom Ipatiev house in July 1918 which were still fresh in his mind. It was a unique experience that made McCullagh dislike the Soviet system even more than before.

At Omsk, he kept a low profile because he had lived there for six months and knew many people who might disclose the fact that he had worked for Kolchak. The Stavka was now a divisional headquarters with the higher one established at Tomsk. The building that housed the British Military Mission had been converted into a hospital.

He began to notice the desperate state of the food markets. He knew there were thousands of tons of frozen fish at Tobolsk, but they were left to rot there because the government had no time to distribute them, and because no individual would do so. Stall holders sold their goods in a fearful state in case they were accused by the Extraordinary Commission[8] of being a speculator. At one such market, a boy pointed at him and called him "*Anglichanin*".[9] This caused him to beat a hasty retreat to his train carriage because he knew that if the vindictive Tcheka arrested him, it would be impossible for Dovgolvsky to protect him.

This fear nagged at him throughout the journey west and made him extremely tense when he was told that the secret police would check the train on its way to Moscow. The searchers consisted of three men. Their leader was a virulent communist sent from Petrograd to show the Siberian workmen how all those with bourgeois tendencies should be treated. The object of their inspection was to prevent anyone exporting food out of Siberia for the purposes of "speculation". However, when they saw the state of McCullagh, their leader was favourably impressed by his impoverished appearance and the fact he carried no tobacco, or food. He simply said "You are a foreign comrade" before passing on to the next man.

The Irish journalist arrived in Moscow on 8th March[10] and any inherent sympathies that he had for the Bolshevik system soon evaporated. For the first fortnight, he lived in a railway carriage without official papers, money, or food. He trudged round Moscow, creeping along the sides of buildings to avoid the deep slush which caused him to suffer from trench foot. He could not shave and his hair grew long.

McCullagh compared the scene to his experiences at the front line. "When the night advanced and the darkness increased, there was not a gleam of light in the streets, other than moonlight for there were no street lamps and no shop-windows. There were also no trams for passengers, but, once an hour or so, a solitary tramcar rushed madly uptown, flashing fire from the electric wires overhead as it tore onwards".[11] These occasions reminded him of the deserted villages of No Man's Land with "corpses lying in the streets and enemies hidden in the cellars."

The silence during these bitterly cold nights was broken only by the sound of these rickety tramcars lurching unsteadily over the ill-fitting tracks, or the distant hoots of a far-away engine and the unexpected crack of a pistol shot in the dark. When he met an occasional contact, who he had worked with during his two previous visits to Moscow, they gave him a small amount of money, but did not encourage further assignments as they looked at him with deep suspicion. These funds enabled him to buy an occasional cup of porridge for 100 roubles from a pop-up stall near to the Kremlin and kept him from starving, but by associating with hundreds of famished Russians without food tickets, he came to see the true consequences of the Soviet system.

The dishevelled journalist relished his disguise and wrote: "The best testimonial I ever received to the perfection of my make-up was the undisguised incredulity with which that excellent clergyman, the Reverend Frank North received me in Moscow. 'You mean to tell *me* that *you* are a British officer!' he cried three times...."[12] He knew the city well, so he was able to steer clear of the officials and distinguish the many changes caused by Bolshevism. He noticed how control of food gave unprecedented power to the government and made everyone completely dependent on the State. Those citizens who were disenfranchised were all cowed and dispirited, with their time taken up finding food and fuel and solving the innumerable daily difficulties of life.

McCullagh also made it his business to interview many of the senior advocates of Bolshevism. He realised that their agitation led them to reject anything from the old regime. At the same time, he discovered from his meetings with Trotsky and Chicherin more about the leadership's industry and austerity. Trotsky shovelled snow and expected his entourage to do the same. The portly foreign minister personally read every news telegram that left Moscow and granted interviews to international journalists after midnight.

McCullagh survived as an independent correspondent for two weeks, before he was caught in the Ministry of Foreign Affairs trying to find the address of another foreign journalist. A commissar recognised him and demanded to know why he had not reported his arrival in the city. His name was immediately registered on the official list and he was moved into one of the guest-houses on Mala Khartonovskaya Street, near the Red Gate, whilst his credentials were checked.

In the final week of March, he was transferred to the notorious Savoy Hotel, where he was introduced to the "Underworld of the Third International", an institution which planned the overthrow of every government in Europe, Asia, and America. Other "guests" included overseas journalists, who had been released from prison only after promising to work against their own countries. There was also a Korean committee planning independence from Japanese rule.

Two months after leaving Krasnoyarsk, on the night of Good Friday, 2nd April 1920, McCullagh was arrested by the Tcheka. Half a dozen armed soldiers entered his room in the middle of the night and conducted a thorough search of his possessions. He was relieved that he had just removed the photograph of himself with "Director of Military Intelligence" stamped on the back, from the lining of his coat because their thorough search checked every possible hiding place. They were looking for incriminating papers and collected all the documents into one package, which they tied together with string.

He was taken across Lubjanka Square to the secret police headquarters that had been built by the insurance company Rossia. The dehumanising process of three intensive body searches, together with harsh accusations for owning anything other than basic necessities was followed by a tiresome transition to the infamous prison, hidden within the outside building.

McCullagh's cell contained no furniture other than a wooden bed. A wrenching smell of urine and excreta, left behind by the previous occupant, infused the air. Prisoners were only allowed to visit the latrines once a day, but due to the unhealthy food, several visits were necessary.

His solitary confinement meant that he was without books, or pencil and paper. His jailors were masters at psychological tricks, such as using lights and noise to interrupt sleeping patterns and withdrawing food to wreck an individual's nerves. It was designed to create morbid ideas

in the tortured minds of the inmates.[13] Once they were on the verge
of mental collapse the inquisition commenced, with the interrogators
hoping that the prisoners would incriminate themselves. Women were
treated in exactly the same way.

McCullagh's response to the softening-up treatment was to walk up
and down the cell singing songs and rehearsing speeches. As a man of
faith, he also turned to prayer. After 70 hours of confined isolation,
he was brought to the committee for examination on Easter Sunday
morning. He felt calm and self-possessed as he answered the questions
of Comrades Xenofontov and Mogilevsky.[14]

The interrogation was a classic case of one official offering moral support, whilst the other pressed aggressively for inconsistencies. McCullagh
knew that some indications of his army service still existed, such as the
rank and number written on his kit bag. However, they had clearly not
found any incriminating evidence and after several hours, they switched
tack and tried to recruit him into the Soviet intelligence network.

This was the hardest part of the examination for McCullagh. Through
his astute answers, he was able to rebuff their advances without making
them suspicious about his commitment to the proletariat. Finally, they
eased up and told him that he would be released later that day.

His freedom was secured with a chit signed by the chief of the Tcheka,
Felix Dzerzhinsky. After his exit from prison, he was granted permission to
leave Russia with the other 123 British prisoners of war, who were repatriated
under the O'Grady-Litvinov exchange agreement, including Lieutenant
Colonel Eric Johnston, who had been sent from Tomsk to Moscow.[15]

McCullagh could have remained as a correspondent in Moscow on
very favourable terms, but the risks of the Bolsheviks discovering his role
in British military intelligence were high. He approached the Reverend
Frank North, who added his name to the list of British prisoners to be
exchanged as part of the O'Grady-Litvinov Agreement. The Irishman
accompanied North as they travelled through Finland and returned to
England on the SS *Dongola*. Arriving in London, he was debriefed by
MI6 in the War Office and interviewed by the Foreign Office Committee
to Collect Information on Russia.[16] Subsequently, he worked behind
the scenes to secure the release of Vining and his other compatriots still
held in Siberia.[17]

CHAPTER 12

Typhus Torment

They put me in dirty rooms and filled me up with lice; I could show you the marks on my back now.

HENRY BENJAMIN JEFFERS, 15TH JUNE 1920[1]

Brian Horrocks was really ill. The fever and burning thirst were bad enough, but it was the constant retching that made him feel so feeble. The others in the party looked at him with dread in their eyes. Since he was laid low with a temperature of 101 degrees, they prepared for the worst. Sure enough, the arrival of a rash on his chest the following day confirmed that he had *sifnoi teiff*.[2]

In Krasnoyarsk, there were 30,000 cases of this pernicious disease reported during February 1920. The mortality rate in Siberia increased from 7 per cent in 1918 to 11 per cent in 1920. The large hospitals where these poor people went to die were crammed full with patients lying in their own vomit and excreta.[3]

Vining visited one where the stench was so overpowering that he had to leave before he retched. The prospects for Horrocks looked bleak, but fortunately, the district medical authorities remembered the generous donation of Captain O'Driscoll and the relief work of the British humanitarian, Mrs Campbell-Clark, who distributed Red Cross comforts to hospital patients in Krasnoyarsk.

They pointed the British in the direction of a private infirmary that was located in a converted school. Vining put the patient into a tight coat and buttoned him to the neck before carrying him to a sleigh with

Prickett. Georgik Hayes then escorted the semi-conscious Horrocks to the small hospital, which only had 125 patients.

In the meantime, the Bolsheviks brought enough food to last a month to the British train. Emerson and Sapper Smith created a small cold store, where they hung three carcasses and stacked the flour, rice and butter. However, there was no sugar in town and they were desperately short of eggs, vegetables and fresh fruit, as well as any jam, or confectionary.

At least they now knew they would not starve. There was also a large supply of *makhorka,* a harsh, cheap tobacco made of bark that could either be smoked in a pipe, or in hand-rolled cigarettes. The British had been without good tobacco since Omsk and had to make do with the eponymous T and B cigarettes which caught the throat.[4] Vining paraphrased William Shakespeare in his diary, when he wrote wistfully: "Our kingdom for good tobacco."

On 15th February, they washed down and disinfected their carriage in an effort to reduce the number of lice residing between the floorboards.[5] Meanwhile, they continued to visit the delirious Horrocks, who failed to recognise any of his compatriots. He fell in and out of consciousness for ten days; however, with the care of a dedicated Russian nurse and treatment by a visiting doctor from the American Red Cross, his situation slowly stabilised.

There was a view that a man with a stout heart had "every chance of getting through and a person with a weak one goes under." By definition, Horrocks had the characteristics to survive the ordeal, so everyone remained hopeful; but he could not do it alone and his friend Hayes paid him many visits wrapped up in a raincoat and hat, regularly staying through the night to help him regain his strength with the extra food he brought from the station.

On 25th February, the British prisoners were told once more that they would leave for Moscow, but yet again their hopes were dashed. Day after day, the same story played out with their requests for information turned down. They occasionally picked up bits of old news; for example, Vining heard about the Czech peace agreement three weeks after it was signed on 7th February.[6]

That night, Horrocks's fever broke and in the morning his temperature returned to normal. Everyone was hugely relieved, but unfortunately

Sergeant Illingworth now had a temperature of 103 degrees. Illy suffered from the odd bout of malaria, so Vining hoped for the best and gave him nine grains of quinine. However, three days later, a rash appeared and the doctor confirmed that he also had contracted typhus, so Vining took him to the hospital where Horrocks was recovering.

Another week passed without their departure and they wondered whether the Soviet authorities were waiting for Horrocks to return, before releasing them. In fact, the Bolsheviks had more pressing matters. On 1st March, after hearing rumours of an uprising, the secret police arrested 4,000 former White officers and placed some into the *laager* and the most important, into prison.

The next day, Emerson met the American medics who had instructions to leave for Vladivostok. Disappointingly, they told him that they had heard the British would be sent to Moscow. With this unwelcome news, the Americans donated some porridge and dried apples to the British group. Feeling deflated, Vining immediately went to see the commissars and waited four hours in a queue to be told nothing.

Meanwhile, Emerson wrote a couple of brief letters, which he asked the Americans to post when they reached the maritime province. He wasn't certain whether Dallas was still in Vladivostok. The Americans said that the hospital where she worked had not closed and the American Red Cross was still active in eastern Siberia, so he was hopeful his message would reach her:

> We do not know whether we shall go East or West, but presume we are held as hostages, pending negotiations. They asked us to go to work to help straighten up the railways but we refused. The Americans volunteered to go to work, but were not accepted. In our party are all the other foreign missions – French, Italians – but we are entirely in the dark as and what will become of us.[7]

It had become clear for some time that Lydia Yates would not be able to travel with the group due to her pregnancy. William had found new rooms for his family and their departure reduced the crowding in the carriage. The French and Italian officers, together with the orderlies, had bailed out with permission from the commissars, so the congestion had reduced considerably. When the Chinese workers heard that the destination was Moscow, they too asked not to travel and so the British employed two Hungarians and a German who had been prisoners of war, for their cooking and carrying duties.

On 5th March, the patients returned from hospital and Vining "inflated the goose" to play "Cock o'the North" on his bagpipes. That day, a mini-thaw melted much of the snow in town. The streets quickly became ankle deep in mud with an accompanying stench. Vining used some of his precious money to buy two mattresses for Horrocks and Illy, who were both passed fit to travel.

Vining was becoming extremely frustrated by the lack of any official communications from London or the British diplomats in eastern Siberia. The only information he received was from second-hand messages passed by the other Allied prisoners and humanitarian workers. This was probably just as well because the British group would have been livid to be told that the War Office had demoted Vining and some of the other British officers from their temporary ranks on 13th March.[8]

★★★

Whilst the British battled the typhus menace, Trotsky launched his own "war" against the hated parasite. He understood that the American Red Cross was much more successful at defeating typhus than the Russian medical system. The American facilities that the Bolsheviks took over in places such as Petropavlovsk, Ekaterinburg and Novo-Nikolaevsk had excellent records for curing patients suffering the symptoms of the disease due to their strict regimes whereby they disinfected all the clothes and bed linen every day. Trotsky would not give the Americans credit, but insisted on importing their ideas and standards of hygiene throughout the country.

On 19th February, he summoned the chief of the District Medical Services in Ekaterinburg and listened to his plea that there was no chance of the typhus epidemic decreasing until April. The Red Army leader then responded with a scathing attack that made the apathetic doctor jump out of his wits. "I am no doctor, but I understand from you that typhus is communicated by lice. Now it must be possible to destroy these lice by delousing apparatus and by a certain degree of heat, which could, if necessary, be produced in some of our public baths. Several of the baths are very nearly hot enough for the purpose as it is...."[9]

After setting the doctor to work on the technical aspects, Trotsky then turned his attention to educating the people. He imposed a fine of one hundred roubles on anyone who shook hands or offered to do so. He switched the full might of his printing press over to the problem and soon the capital of the Urals was covered with placards preaching cleanliness and denouncing dirt. There were representations of a louse as large as a house and exhortations to treat it as a more hateful enemy than the "Supreme Leader".

These pictures were designed to convince the illiterate, as well as those who could read, to change their ways. There were images of washerwomen killing enormous lice with a smoothing iron. There were depictions of death stealing unwashed children. One of the commonest posters dealt with the nomadic lifestyle of thousands of Russians who slept together, huddled in communal groups on the floor of railway stations.[10] This animated poster demanded: "Don't lie down wherever you happen to find yourself at nightfall until you first make sure that the place is free from lice."

Francis McCullagh likened this propaganda to a mixture of medieval church frescoes, where the fear of sin was taught by means of horrific representations of hell, and "the most up-to-date American advertising." However, the slick messages were not the scripts of swindling "quack doctors", for the people could see the huge piles of infested corpses everywhere they went by train.

In Siberia, there was only one doctor for every one hundred typhus cases. In the district between Omsk and Krasnoyarsk practically all the medical men had been attacked by typhus, and 50 per cent of them had died. One surviving doctor observed counterintuitively that the mortality rate was lowest among young illiterate peasants and highest among middle-aged intellectuals.

McCullagh saw this terror at first hand on his travels with ordinary Russians. He dreaded the "infinitesimal" bite of a body louse more than the bite of a rabid dog. He was horrified that some women in his carriage could not shake the folds of their dresses without sprinkling lice on everybody in their immediate vicinity.[11] His worst experience was in Moscow, where a man fell ill in his compartment, with all the symptoms of typhus. He fled in horror and spent most of the journey in the corridor, but he could not keep his eyes off his belongings piled close to the patient. Instead of generating sympathy towards the sick, he believed that the epidemic made the healthy hate typhus patients as if they were brigands or "murderers".[12]

★★★

Despite the burgeoning epidemic, Vining's attempts at eradicating the lice from his carriage proved effective and no one else in the British group was struck down by the disease. At last, everyone was fit and well and the daily forecast of their Russian escort that they "would leave tomorrow" proved to be truthful. On 18th March, a locomotive attached to their carriage and they finally left Krasnoyarsk. To their delight, the train headed east towards Irkutsk.

Once Trotsky defeated Kolchak, he turned his attention to "a new white peril" the dreaded typhus-bearing body louse that killed millions of Russians during the Civil War. His propaganda team covered Siberia with posters designed to convince illiterate peasants, as well as those who could read, to change their ways. (Courtesy of the Wellcome Trust)

The British prisoners captured in Krasnoyarsk in March 1920. The future Lieutenant General Sir Brian Horrocks is sixth from the right. (Courtesy of Leonard Vining, St Catherine Press)

Many of the British soldiers serving in Siberia held Russian women of all classes in awe. (Courtesy of Angus MacMillan)

CHAPTER 13

Deceived in Irkutsk

*Although we were informed by M. Litvino[v] that steps were being taken to move
[British prisoners of war in Siberia] to Moscow with a view to repatriation, we have
not been able to ascertain what happened to them. Information has just reached us
from an escaped Dane that there are 150 of these at Irkutsk.*[1]

CURZON OF KEDLESTON FOREIGN OFFICE,
27TH MAY 1920

Emerson's train departed from Krasnoyarsk on 18th March at 8a.m and
headed for Irkutsk. Travelling east, they were led to believe that their
destination was Vladivostok and this may well have been the Bolsheviks'
intention after they reached their agreement with the Czech Legion.
However, the Japanese still held firm east of Lake Baikal and their puppet
ruler, Semeonov, was proving to be a tough opponent, so the British
were not certain about their journey's end.

They made much better progress than their previous train ride, with
the engine travelling at 31 versts per hour, compared with 21 per day
in December. At one of their first halts, Emerson caught a glimpse of
the sharp steel of female protest against Bolshevik authority. A peasant
girl, perhaps 19 or 20 years old, stood near the rails and stared intently
at the strangers. She was neither pretty nor prepossessing in her looks,
but there was a purposefulness in her face that commanded the attention
of all the British soldiers.

One of the train guards saw her and advanced with his sword drawn
from its sheath. He ordered her to move away. A slow flush rose in the
girl's cheeks for the guard's words were slimy and disgusting. She sprang

toward him and the guard, sword and all, recoiled. A magnificent storm of words spewed from her mouth; Emerson could not understand every word, but he knew that she was "burning him up." She didn't say anything that might not be repeated in a court of law, but her retorts made the guard cringe and he retreated to the train, whilst the girl resumed her inspection of the British group.

Horrocks asked, "Were you not afraid he might strike you with his sword?"

She replied, "Bah, the son of a swine has no heart; none of them have."

She might have been referring to the hapless attitude epitomised by the often-repeated response, *Nichevo*. This was on the lips of every man who suffered the slightest annoyance, but was afraid to do anything about it. It bubbled up through the mud into which these same people had been trampled face down, by the blind feet of their Red brethren. It means, "Oh never mind" and is whispered by the man in his mud sepulchre with his last breath, whilst those above shout back in agreement, *Nichevo*!

★★★

During the first day of this journey, Frank Illingworth suffered severe gastric problems and Vining was concerned that he needed specialist medical care. When they reached Kunak-Eniseiski,[2] 225 versts from Krasnoyarsk, they heard that there was a good hospital and decided to take him there during the scheduled two-hour tea-time halt. Edward Stephens volunteered to stay with him and together with Vining and Prickett, they hired a droshky to carry Illy to the infirmary. Unfortunately, the transfer took slightly longer than anticipated and when the escort returned from the hospital to the station, they saw their locomotive steaming away in the distance.

The station master apologised for misleading them about the time of the halt and told them that another train heading east was expected later that day. They were worried because they had no documents or escort, so when they joined the afternoon train, they slipped into the crowded rear carriage, where the other passengers looked at them suspiciously.

Vining was much relieved to catch up with his companions 25 miles down the line at Ilanskaya[3] and decided to have a "camp bath". It just so happened that this was the moment the secret police arrived to search the British carriage for weapons. The British knew from their time in Krasnoyarsk that the Tcheka was the most feared part of the Soviet system. They could arbitrarily condemn people to death with no appeal process and were already responsible for the torture and execution of hundreds of thousands of Russians.[4] Vining interviewed them from his canvas bucket.

The hardened Bolsheviks found the outlandish commune of British soldiers and civilian families making the most of their overcrowded conditions and maintaining a peculiar lifestyle. Yet again, Vining's extraordinary ability to defuse tension with his sense of humour won them over. After a cursory check of their papers, the head of the police departed on friendly terms, saying farewell to "my good English comrades."

The following day, they remained at Ilanskaya and the warm sunshine and clean air improved the mood of the party. The background of snow-covered hills and forests seemed to be straight out of a postcard and almost made them feel as if they were at a retreat in the Engadine valley.[5] When the train resumed its eastward journey that evening, the soldiers all slept well apart from the orderly officer, who had to stay up all night stoking the stove, to maintain some warmth in the carriage.

After three days, there was another extended halt on the River Uda at the large depot of Nizhne Udinsk, where they made use of the skates, which had been exchanged for Horrocks's shirt. Their spirits were up and whilst some of them waited for their turn on the ice, they occupied themselves with a snowball match. In the chilly market, they swapped a few reels of cotton with an old woman for a large number of eggs, so that everyone had two for tea. Sergeant Rooney tried to buy a comb, but after a lengthy mime performance, the shopkeeper offered him nit powder.

On 25th March, their train stopped abruptly and Vining discovered that the railway line was cut and a bridge crossing one of the Anghara tributaries was destroyed.[6] Their escort told them that they would have to travel by sleigh for a short distance and this was a great inconvenience because they had to give up some of the precious items that had made their journey less harsh. They loaded up the five carts, or *tipolska*, that were provided and nine of them set off in the first shuttle run, whilst the remainder waited their turn.

Fortunately, the weather was clear for the ride across the ice and once they boarded the new train they headed on the final stretch along the left bank of the River Anghara. As they contoured the river, they could see Irkutsk on the southern bank with its fine cathedral in a commanding position over the city. Arriving during the afternoon on Friday 26th March, they were too late to visit the commissars in charge of affairs, so they made themselves comfortable at the Glaskov station across the river. The night was bitterly cold as there was no cloud cover. The polar star was directly above Emerson as he stared up at the sky and admired the Great Bear constellation, which in Siberia lays upside-down. In the morning, screeching gulls woke the party before dawn and they shivered from the cold. There was an orange halo around the sun as it rose in the east. Suddenly a yellow streamer shot vertically into the sky and the heat of the sun made them all feel better.

After breakfast, Vining and Horrocks walked across the frozen river and made their way to the administrative centre. They managed to find the head of the Revolutionary Committee, who had signed the orders to execute Admiral Kolchak.[7] All arguments about onward travel to Vladivostok were useless, as they were told that they would have to remain in Irkutsk until the authorities in Moscow sent instructions one way or the other.

Each day, the Irkutsk commissars repeated the same story; nothing heard from Moscow. Vining's frustration at the delay and lack of communications was tempered by the improved conditions. In Krasnoyarsk, the group had felt threatened the whole time they were outside their accommodation and were often questioned and searched in the streets. Now they were afforded some recognition and so Vining agreed that everyone could put up their epaulettes again. Occasionally these caused trouble with some of the fanatical soldiers of the Red Army,[8] but they maintained their composure and knew when to give way to their "hosts".

Despite the evidence of street battles on the blackened walls, the town was more distinguished than Krasnoyarsk. The British were given some money by the commissars and they took the opportunity to visit the ballet, theatre and opera in the evenings. They enjoyed performances by some of the leading actors and actresses from Petrograd and noticed that the boxes were full of workmen and soldiers, whilst the stalls were occupied by ladies and officers of the old regime, wearing very plain clothes. The reversal of fortunes in this topsy-turvy world made no difference to the audience, who appreciated the clowns in *Pagliacci* and the water sprite in *Rusalka*, but the highlight of their visits was the performance of Verdi's *La Traviata*.

Emerson became friendly with the owner of the meat packing plant that had been nationalised by the Bolsheviks. He was a social democrat, so he survived the initial cull of the hated capitalists and bourgeoisie. A committee was formed from his employees and they confiscated dozens of items from his house and took over the executive roles at the works. Things went from bad to worse and the whole plant was destroyed, together with a ranch of 50,000 cattle within four months of the seizure. Soon afterwards, he gathered his family together and fled to Manchuria.

The British group found some of their travelling companions from Omsk, who had separated from them in January. A Persian family now worked as shoe repairers in the town and seemed to be making the best of their situation. It appeared to the British that the only other diligent people were the German and Austrian prisoners of war, who had adapted to the harsh conditions. Emerson had no qualms about buying some tooth powder made by these industrious inmates, which was packaged in a cardboard box made by other prisoners and decorated with ink made by yet more captives.

★★★

As they were now close to the Trans-Baikal, they heard snippets of news about the fighting between Japanese troops and the Fifth Red Army, which prevented their onward travel. However, there was little information from Vladivostok, where the social democrat, Medvedev, remained in power. His Zemstvo party had become increasingly beholden to local Bolsheviks with the first commissar, Vilensky, arriving on 10th March. Two weeks later, they began to follow Moscow's directives and these instructed Medvedev to add more communists to the government's ranks. General Graves had some inkling of this new development, but he did not believe the Japanese would allow it to happen after he departed from Russia.[9]

Sure enough, General Oi Shigemoto launched an offensive three days after the American Expeditionary Forces left. The attack on Easter Sunday, 4th April, was well-timed and the Japanese met very little opposition. By the early hours of the next day, "all major governmental institutions and means of communications had been seized, all Russian forces remaining in the city had been disarmed, and many Russians, including government and Party leaders, had been arrested."[10]

The Zemstvo Government had been popular in the city, and the Japanese encountered significant non-military resistance. None of the international community was harmed, but the Red Cross personnel found themselves in more real peril than at any time since they arrived in 1918. Apart from looking after eight hundred children in Vladivostok, they had plans to continue their programme of taking medical supplies by train to their hospitals in captured territory. However, after the Japanese offensive, the State Department changed its policy and Washington directed that American citizens should no longer travel into Soviet Russia. This put paid to any further thoughts that Dallas had about holding on for Emerson and so she travelled to England on the SS *Carmarthenshire* to wait for his hoped-for return.

★★★

Emerson and the others were delighted when Stephens and Illy re-joined the group a few days after their arrival. Now they were reunited, the Soviet authorities allowed Vining to send a cable to the British headquarters at Peking,[11] requesting supplies. Two days later a train from the East arrived at 2p.m. with the rear carriage flying a Union Jack. Their morale soared when out stepped Captain Rex Carthew, who handed them a packet of English cigarettes and a dram of "luscious" whisky.[12]

Carthew apologised for not bringing more supplies of clothes, underwear, boots and food, but told them another train was being prepared with these items. He gave them the encouraging news that officers of the Inter-Allied Railway Agreement were still controlling the railway from Manchuria through the Trans-Baikal. He also said that he would wait with them whilst their fate was decided.

After more tense negotiations, the Soviets allowed the civilians in Vining's group to leave with the British delegation, but prevented

Emerson and the others from boarding this train. They were so near and yet so far and hugely frustrated by this staggering decision. Nevertheless, when the families departed on 11th April, all the British soldiers turned out to wave farewell and cheer them on their way.

The problem was caused by the Japanese army's offensive campaign. The British prisoners in Irkutsk were not the only ones affected by these operations. On 14th April, the international railway board complained about security breaches and subsequently, the representatives from China, France, Great Britain, the United States and Czechoslovakia sent a protest cable to their capital cities, stating: "The Japanese Military authorities have ... usurped functions, by right belonging to the Technical and Transportation Boards and have used them in such a manner as to add to the confusion on the railway, and actually to delay the progress of the Czechs."[13]

Horrocks's and Hayes's thoughts turned again to the possibility of escaping through Mongolia when the weather improved in May. It was a real quandary for them because some of the soldiers, such as Illy and Percy, were not fit to make the journey. They all knew that if one escaped, those left behind would most probably be sent to rot in prison.

Emerson was fit enough to make the journey to Manchuria, but he was more worried about Dallas's situation than his own. The only compatriot who he could confide in about his betrothed was Sergeant Bob Lillington. Bob was in a similar quandary because he did not know whether his new wife, Ludmilla, had managed to reach Vladivostok.[14] He often thought what might have been if he had not stayed behind in Omsk when his battalion left in August.

Bob was one of many Hampshire soldiers encouraged to meet local girls by the commanding officer, when he organised ballroom dancing lessons in their barracks. After meeting Ludmilla's family, the relationship flourished and Bob decided to volunteer to stay behind with the British Military Mission when the battalion departed in August. Seventeen days before his 24th birthday, he solemnized their union with a short marriage ceremony in Omsk.

Many of the British soldiers held Russian women in awe. Those who saw the magnificent work of the nurses could not fail to be impressed. Their diligence was replicated by tireless females of all classes, who were the mainstays of family life. Brian Horrocks noted their vital role when he saw them in the training school at Ekaterinburg and Vining observed: "The women of Russia are totally different from the men. In character, conduct and pluck, they leave the Russian male standing."[15] Phelps Hodges agreed with this sentiment when he wrote: "I got very fed up with the Russian officer, but acquired a great liking for his womenfolk. They were far braver and more intelligent."[16]

The central role played by women was recorded by Lieutenant Colonel Harvey when he wrote about Russian character in Siberia: "There is never any necessity to hurry over anything; tomorrow is better than today and the day after tomorrow is better than either. He doesn't appear to be able to exist without his womenfolk and feasts and holiday making are just as important during the war as they are in peace."[17]

There was another side to this character. Russian women realised that marrying a soldier in a foreign army was one way of escaping from the warring factions and many attempted to ensnare a husband. The Allied commanders dealt with these proposals according to their domestic laws and national policies. In the case of the American Expeditionary Force, General Graves knew that US law would not allow immoral women to enter the country and felt that some steps should be taken to ensure that standards were maintained.

However, he also believed it was "un-American" to tell a soldier he may not get married, so he issued orders stating that if any soldier married, without the consent of his immediate commanding officer, he would not give his wife transportation to the United States of America. At the same time he instructed all his commanding officers to investigate the background of the women who their soldiers asked to marry. If she proved of good moral character, they were allowed to marry, but if she had an immoral character they were refused. This pragmatic policy worked well until the Red Cross complained and Graves was ordered to give transportation "to a most dissolute woman, who had married a soldier."[18]

The British Army relied on peer pressure and fear of venereal disease to "test" these relationships to breaking point. Most of them foundered on the choice between "pals, or pulls", but Bob was adamant that his marriage was for the long term and intended on settling in Russia with his new wife. However, when it became clear that Kolchak's government would fall, he turned his attention to Ludmilla's journey to England.

The Portsmouth sergeant knew that if his wife could reach Vladivostok in time, she might be able to take his place on the battalion's return journey to England. Alternatively, as Ludmilla now held a right to British citizenship, she could take one of the transports evacuating civilians from the eastern port. With a heavy heart, he said farewell, "*Dosvidaniya*", to his new wife as she set off on her first trip to the maritime province.

The Omsk bride felt anxious about leaving her husband and the uncertainty of what would happen when she reached Vladivostok. However, she prepared well for her journey and made herself as comfortable as possible. She managed to secure a middle tier bunk in the carriage because the top level was always too hot and the lower bed was cold. Bob had given her plenty of money, so she was able to buy food on the way and enjoyed the odd delicacy such as snipe and the hard biscuit flavoured with ginger, known as *pryaniki*. At each station, she made use of the *kipyatok,* boiling water, to make tea.

Ludmilla's 180-mile journey round the southern shore of the Holy Sea of Baikal was memorable for the stark contrast between the elegant view of the lake and the grime in the 38 tunnels. She felt a sense of relief when the train reached Verkhne Udinsk, where the train meets the caravan route that heads south across the Mongolian desert for 40 days to Kalgan. There, she was comforted by the sight of the American troops of 27th Infantry Regiment, who still guarded the line from brigands and insurgents.

After a long halt, her train negotiated the sparsely populated Trans-Baikal plateau, where frost is evident in every month of the year apart from July. At Chita, the central base for Semeonov's operations, the population of 75,000 people had doubled with the influx of refugees. Near Karimskaya, the train stopped at the junction with the All-Siberian railway line that runs north-east to Habarovsk and thence south to Vladivostok. However, Ludmilla took the line to Manchuria, which was shorter and safer.

At the frontier station, the Trans–Baikal branch turned into the Chinese Eastern line. This junction was another thriving hub for caravans made up of horses and Bactrian camels. It was almost 600 miles from Harbin, the principal town in western Manchuria lying astride the Sungari River. Harbin was significantly warmer than the plains and Ludmilla was grateful for the overnight halt, so she could wash some of her clothes. The final stage of her rail journey covered the 480 miles, via the customs post at Progranichnaya, to Vladivostok. As she approached the port, she began to feel very nervous and worried about what would happen when she arrived, but in the end, the American Red Cross helped her to find a passage to England, via the Suez Canal.

★★★

In Irkutsk, a pall of gloom hung over the British soldiers after they were left behind by the civilians. They were so near and yet so far from freedom. An early thaw cut off the station, where they lived in a cold carriage, from the rest of the city centre. They now needed to take a ferry across the river to visit the market or the commissars. Vining became worried about morale and to pull them out of their despondency, he invited some of the opera singers to tea. This was a huge success. Sergeant Rooney surprised the Russians with the range and versatility of his voice and at the conclusion, they held a "thunderous" sing off, which raised everyone's spirits for a while.

They made the acquaintance of an American business man who was establishing contacts with the Soviet Government. Hector J. Boon had arrived with Rex Carthew and was held in much credit by the Bolsheviks because he had been arrested and beaten in the Trans-Baikal by Ataman Semeonov for challenging the theft of his goods. In Irkutsk, he rented a lavish apartment and was very generous with his invitations to dinner.

Unfortunately, when Vining and the others left Boon's parties at night, they occasionally became embroiled in the regular shooting incidents that took place in the darkened back streets of the city. They found that the best approach was to walk calmly into the middle of the road, shouting *Angliyskiy* and then stand in the moonlight, where they could be searched by the authorities and allowed to pass through the Bolshevik cordon.

★★★

Back in London, Winston Churchill and the other members of the Cabinet presumed the group in Siberia was being released at the same time as those under the care of the Reverend Frank North in Moscow. The prime minister now hoped that the issue of British prisoners of war in Russia would soon be over. As he travelled to the San Remo conference at the end of April, Lloyd George had in his mind the MI6 report from a Soviet informer,[19] who stated that Lenin's economic policy had changed. He understood that the Russian Government was now anxious for peace and recognised that their main challenge was to address the inadequacies of the transport facilities, since these were reducing the value of their victories over Kolchak and Denikin.

In the light of this information, the prime minister was keen to re-establish trade, in order to help British business. He knew that whilst British prisoners of war continued to be detained in Russia, there was little chance of the anti-Bolshevik members of the British Cabinet agreeing to a compromise. However, there was a dearth of information about the prisoners because the military intelligence network in Russia had collapsed and the Admiralty's Weekly Intelligence Summaries[20] did not extend beyond the littoral, merely reporting: "there is a certain number of civilian and military prisoners of war of which the number and whereabouts are unknown."[21]

The San Remo conference was chaired by the prime minister of Italy and attended by the prime minister of France, as well as American Ambassador Robert Johnson and Japanese Ambassador Keishirō Matsui. They addressed some of the outstanding issues from the main Paris Peace Conference, including: the treaty with Turkey; the mandates for the League of Nations in the Middle East; Germany's financial obligations; as well as the situation in Russia. Lloyd George was delighted that, despite some reservations, they all agreed on 25th April to adopt a resolution to restore trade with the Russian Soviet Federative Socialist Republic.[22]

★★★

Given the acknowledged problems of the Soviet transport system, it was not long before the authorities in Irkutsk attempted to "turn" Emerson and the other members of the British Railway Mission. During May, Vining's group received "extraordinarily good treatment". They were issued with plenty of food and allowed greater freedoms than ever before.

Vining was also introduced to a "survivor" from the train of death, which had held 12,000 Bolshevik prisoners for 13 months until all but 60 died. The British prisoners were shown photographs of alleged war crimes, but some of these had previously been used by the White Government to expose Bolshevik atrocities.[23] All efforts to generate some empathy with the Soviet system failed. There was too much evidence of the misery caused by the overthrow of the old regime and the corruption of the new ruling class. For example, an acquaintance of Emerson was imprisoned for three weeks at Irkutsk for playing cards.[24] When he was released, the prison governor discovered he had a gold watch that had escaped the eyes of the guards. This official promptly pocketed the valuable time piece and gave the man an order empowering him to steal the first good watch that he fancied.

On another occasion, Emerson witnessed a Red Guard scatter a peasant woman's small supply of foods that she had brought to the market. The few rounds of butter, milk churn and half a dozen eggs were strewn across the road. Through her tears, she cursed and reviled the despicable man, his ancestors and his children because her livelihood had been destroyed. The Red Guard made no apology and just moved on to his next victim.

Despite their problems with some of the Bolsheviks, the British forged strong relationships with the ordinary Russians in Irkutsk and were invited to join the local football league. There were four teams in Irkutsk and Vining, who was a capable soccer player, organised matches with all of them in order to lift morale.[25]

Their first match was against Irkutsk Athletic. Vining had some difficulty raising a team due to the illness of some of his group and the fact that several had never played soccer before. There were also a couple of rugby players, who were enthusiastic, but lacked skill. However, a very large number of spectators attended the match, which helped their cause and raised their popularity. Although the Russians won 5–0, the spectators cheered whenever a player was flattened and so the British rugby players claimed a win on the "clapometer".

For the next match, Vining recruited a Sikh, Jiht Singh, who had lived in Irkutsk for eight years and claimed British citizenship. Although he did not speak much English, Vining had passable Urdu so they were able to communicate on the pitch. Singh was an excellent sportsman and although the British lost again, at least he scored a goal to make the result respectable. The third match was against the German, Austrian and Hungarian prisoners of war. This was a surprisingly friendly affair, but the British were irritated to lose 2–4. The final match was against the best team in Irkutsk, but by then, the British had improved considerably and although they lost 3–5, the result was in doubt until the very end.

During these matches, they discovered much more about the Central Powers' prisoners of war in Siberia. Following their transportation from the front line, they were allowed some liberties to work. After five years, those captured in the first years of the war had more or less been assimilated into the local community. As a result, Emerson reckoned that seven out of eight of the Red Army guards who formed their escort, were either German, or Austrian.

Vining was deeply frustrated that apart from the train from Manchuria, his group had received no communications from the British authorities since their capture. In Emerson's case he had received no international post since June 1919. Delegates from other nations traveling through Irkutsk had told them what news they could glean about the outside world, but they had been given neither messages, nor mail and the promised British train with supplies never arrived.

Approaching the end of May, Vining wrote in his diary: "There have been opportunities for getting word through to us, and we have absolute proof of this; yet nothing has been sent us and no telegram or letter has reached us... Our mail, an accumulation of some ten months, is at Vladivostok, this could have been sent through ten times over, but doubtless for excellent reasons unknown to us jail-birds, no steps have been taken to send letters or any communication to us."[26]

He did not know that whilst he wrote this in Irkutsk, the prime minister and foreign secretary were about to meet with the People's Commissar for Foreign Trade, Leonid Krassin. The Cabinet Secretary, Sir Maurice Hankey, described the Russian delegates as having "the appearance of men who have lived for long under great strain."[27] As an exiled Bolshevik, Krassin had become a millionaire in business and an accomplished engineer, before he returned to Russia after the revolution to assume a senior appointment in the government. According to Hankey, he was "an intelligent looking alert man of between 50 and 60 with a close-cut beard, rather a good eye and with a slightly defiant look."[28]

The most important item on the prime minister's agenda was "the question of British prisoners." In a preparatory note,[29] Lord Curzon described the main categories of concern as: civilians imprisoned in Moscow, Petrograd and Vologda (possibly excluded from the O'Grady-Litvinov agreement); British prisoners of war in Siberia; and British Naval mechanics recently captured in the Azerbaijan capital, Baku. After a second interview on 7th June, when Krassin "revealed a somewhat truculent attitude,"[30] the Russian delegation returned to Moscow with the British demands.

Whilst the prime minister "grasped the hairy paw of the baboon,"[31] Vining sent another cable to the military attaché in Peking, but he received no response. Since they were running out of money, Hector Boon loaned them a significant sum to buy clothes and tide them over. Two weeks later, a solemn and dejected group, who had spent six frustrating weeks in Irkutsk, were given orders to travel 3,500 miles to Moscow. It was with heavy hearts that they boarded their train and began to retrace the route from whence they came.

CHAPTER 14

Three-Legged Teddy

May I ask whether the question of British prisoners in Russia is not of much more concern to us?

CHARLES PALMER MP, HOUSE OF COMMONS DEBATE,
14 JUNE 1920[1]

On 12th June at 2p.m. the remnants of the British Railway Mission left Irkutsk in a train heading west. The dejected company passed familiar stations with a sense of resignation as they travelled along the Siberian railway for interminable miles. The landscape was very different without its thick covering of snow. The distant mountains to the south seemed closer in their summer colours than their winter white. When the train passed through the immense spacious prairie, they looked north and imagined escaping to the frozen tundra with its prehistoric fossils, reindeer and Sami people.

The soldiers did not know that two days after their departure from Irkutsk, David Lloyd George was being embarrassed in a parliamentary debate that highlighted the plight of British prisoners of war in Russia. The first question was posed by the Liberal MP, Lieutenant Commander Kenworthy,[2] who asked the prime minister about Russian prisoners, held in Britain and by His Majesty's forces.

Lloyd George replied, "I am not aware that we have any Russian prisoners abroad."

This was immediately challenged by the famous backbencher, Colonel Josiah Wedgwood,[3] who had been sent to Siberia on a military intelligence mission in 1918 and knew about a group of Russians, held in Khorasan. He exclaimed, "Is it not a fact that you include among those who are awaiting deportation some prisoners taken by our troops in Russia?"

This was embarrassing enough, but then the Independent MP, Charles Palmer[4] intervened with his question about British prisoners of war, to which the prime minister could only provide the lame response, "We are doing our very best to get them out."

The parliamentary debate was the start of a torrid month for the government when the deep divisions about Russia were exposed. Churchill, as the leader of the anti-Bolshevik faction, was livid that the prime minister was negotiating a trade agreement with the Bolsheviks. The chief of the General Staff, who was intent on assisting General Wrangel in the Crimea[5] and Marshal Pilsudski in Poland, believed that Lloyd George was a traitor for agreeing to the Soviet Trade delegation visit in May.

Churchill forwarded a secret memorandum[6] to all members of the Cabinet on 11th June setting out his demands, which effectively required the Soviet Army to surrender and disarm. He included as one of the specific requirements that "All British prisoners of war captured in Siberia and elsewhere are to be returned forthwith alive and well" and made the "immediate acceptance of [this] the *sine quâ non* of further negotiations."[7] However, it was clear from the memorandum that the War Office did not know the exact whereabouts of the British soldiers.

Parliament was dismayed that the government had lost track of the prisoners of war five months after they were captured in Krasnoyarsk. Backbenchers continued to put pressure on the government. In July, the well-informed and insistent Wedgwood pressed the prime minister to "lay Papers in connection with the intervention and operations in Siberia from the date when our fleet entered Vladivostok in January 1918, till the evacuation of the British military mission in this year."[8]

Churchill was under the media spotlight as well. The *Daily Herald*, which was being funded and fed by the Soviet Government,[9] exposed the Secretary of State for misleading the House of Commons and this was pursued by *The Nation*.[10] The issue centred on the publication of an account of a conversation between Churchill and one of Kolchak's agents, General Golovin, which provided clear evidence that the war

secretary had wilfully deceived both Parliament and the electorate by
attempting covertly to force a new offensive into being on the pretext of
covering the withdrawal of British troops from North Russia. The *Daily
Herald* demanded Churchill's impeachment and *The Nation* denounced
the war secretary.[11]

★★★

Back in Russia, each day was practically the same as the last for the
British prisoners heading west on the Trans-Siberian Railway; the only
difference was that the Russian guards in Irkutsk had been replaced
with Hungarians. The dismal situation affected the younger officers
and soldiers more than the mature members of the group. Without
money, mail or newspapers from Britain, they began to argue among
themselves and tiny irritants were blown out of proportion. At the
station halts, the dull stares of the dirty population began to make them
feel as if they were zoo animals. The foul smell, soot and plague of
flies all added to the sense of despair. Even Sergeant Rooney felt the
brooding disquiet and became less inclined to sing his inexhaustible
supply of songs.

Unlike many of the other members of the group, Emerson saw a
positive side to the journey. He knew that he had a good job waiting
for him in Philadelphia and that the expedition to Moscow would
provide him with a unique insight into the Soviet Government,
which had been in power for nearly three years. As the quartermaster,
he did his best to raise morale by purchasing some extra food and
a quantity of muslin that they rigged over the bunks to prevent the
flies disturbing their sleep. However, these were pinpricks of light in
the pervasive gloom.

After Krasnoyarsk, they became slightly more active. At Achinsk, the
snow had melted so they could see the full extent of the devastation
caused by the explosion in December. When the train passed through the
ancient coniferous *taiga*,[12] they were reminded of their sleigh journey and
how close some of them had come to death. Listening to the villagers at
the short halts, they heard that provisions in Omsk were scarce, so they
stocked up with a good supply of curds, butter and bologna sausages
where these were sold.

Ten days later they arrived in Omsk expecting to move straight through, but the President of the Siberian Revolutionary Committee, Podlovsky, decided to hold them for a few days. For the third time, they were told to take off their epaulettes or to wear civilian clothes; but they ignored this instruction. Again, they refused to work for the Bolshevik authorities, so they were only given food tickets for half a pound of bread for each man per day. They became reliant on the money loaned by Hector Boon and the store of supplies Emerson had purchased on the journey from Krasnoyarsk.

Podlovsky refused to provide them with passes to walk freely through the city. To circumvent this, Emerson typed a chit for everyone and added the British Railway Mission official stamp and a red seal from a cigarette tin. Since few of the Red Guards could read, this allowed them to leave their carriage at the station and move unmolested from street to street.

Apart from bathing in the river and drinking koumiss, there was very little to occupy them in Omsk. They met some Danish relief workers and two American reporters, but steered clear of Russian acquaintances because there was a tyrannical purge whilst they were there and they did not wish to implicate their friends by association. The bazaar in Market Square that thrived in 1919 was now a place of fear and suspicion, frequently raided by soldiers with the object of catching speculators and arresting people without proper paperwork.

It was here that Emerson met another example of "womanhood" and the resistant spirit that seemed to be lacking in Russian men. A Red Army officer stopped him and angrily demanded the removal of his epaulettes. "Take them off" ordered the officer, pointing to the hated marks of authority. Emerson refused and the tyrant threatened. They were in the midst of an argument which Emerson was about to lose, when a slight teenage girl, with the delicate oval face and wide eyes of a dreamer, appeared suddenly crying in English: "Do not obey him!"

She turned to the officer and showing by her choice of words that she was educated, said: "He is an Englishman, a gentleman too and not the mud under horses' hooves like you." He replied by cursing her and again ordering Emerson to remove the marks of rank.

The fearless girl responded magnificently. Measuring the officer from heel to head, she dissected him with the skill of a surgeon working with a glistening scalpel. The officer's waving sword seemed to mean no more than a straw to her as she traced his ancestry to: "a grey ape that died from starvation because it had not intelligence enough to distinguish its ear from its mouth." Emerson gained courage and when she stopped for breath, he made his case. The routed officer walked away, but not because the British protest defeated him. He was afraid of the young woman, who turned to Emerson and said: "Don't ever take them off," before she too vanished into the dusk.

Something else happened at Omsk that lifted British spirits out of their slough of despondency and gave them fortitude and inspiration. It was a moment such as Robert the Bruce experienced with his famous spider. Whilst they assembled outside their carriage one morning to walk into town, a small Siberian puppy crossed the railway line ahead of them.

Unfortunately, a locomotive engine was passing at the same time and the little mongrel became caught in its wheels. Herbert Prickett ran over and rescued the injured dog whose hind leg was hanging by a flap of skin and tail was reduced to a stump. The adept Prickett completed a quick amputation behind the knee and bound the two wounds with bandages from their carriage. All the others in the group gathered around and made a fuss of the fluffy hound, feeding him a few morsels from their thin larder.

They decided to adopt their diminutive new companion and named him Teddy. He rapidly learned to scamper around on three legs, dissipating melancholy moods by his cheerfulness and unbounded faithfulness. Any of the group who became too self-absorbed was soon shaken out of his gloom when Teddy came to play.

★★★

As the British prisoners in Omsk tightened their belts at the end of June, the British Government telegraphed a memorandum to Moscow incorporating their conditions for the Anglo-Soviet trade agreement.[13] The cable was sent to the aristocratic People's Commissar for Foreign Affairs, Georgy Chicherin,[14] following David Lloyd George's first meetings with the trade envoy Leonid Krassin on 31st May. Churchill's demands for disarmament were watered down, but the issue of prisoners of war remained paramount.[15] Chicherin accepted these principles in a telegram of 7th July.

Apart from the Siberian cohort, there was a group of 31 Royal Navy officers, petty officers and ratings, who had unwisely strayed into the hands of the Azerbaijan Bolsheviks at the end of April. They were due to take a ship from Baku to Enzeli, but were held up at the railway station and failed to make their way to the port. After four days at the station, they were taken to Bailloff Prison on 1st May, where they were allocated three cells.[16]

In contrast to Churchill's secret prisoners of war in Siberia, the Baku prisoners received wide publicity.[17] In the House of Commons, the MP for Battersea, Viscount Francis Curzon,[18] who had served as a Royal Navy commanding officer during the war, highlighted their plight by asking the prime minister on 1st July: "what is the latest news of the officers and men captured and reported to be held as slaves and undergoing torture at the hands of the Soviet forces at Baku?"[19] Their cause was taken up by the *Daily Mail*, which described them later that month as being in the "Black Hole of Baku".

It is not clear why these Royal Navy technicians received greater attention in Parliament and the press than the soldiers in Siberia, who suffered a far harsher ordeal. One might conclude that the Royal Navy was a more caring employer than the Army and her officers in the Admiralty were better advocates than their counterparts in the War Office. It certainly plays to a national theme that the British Army is respected by society, whereas the Royal Navy is loved by the public.

★★★

Emerson and his 13 companions in Omsk knew nothing about the British Government's attempts to have them released because they had received no messages from the outside world, nor any British newspapers, for eight months. They managed to read the Bolshevik papers, but they treated these with a strong degree of scepticism because there were so many implausible stories about revolution in England. They had no understanding that their onward travel was being delayed by the British troops in Georgia, assisting the remnants of the White Army.[20] The Bolsheviks did not wish to allow any chance of rescue or escape, but with the departure of Brigadier Percy's mission from Sevastopol on 29th June and the British evacuation from Batum on 10th July, the way was opened for Vining's group to leave Omsk.

Four days later, the British carriage was attached to a locomotive that steamed out of Kolchak's former capital on the next stage of their journey. In many ways, this was the most fascinating period because it revealed the Soviet system in its dysfunctional state. They quickly realised that it was not the clash of arms that caused the desolation they witnessed along the railway line. It was the experiment of Bolshevism that was doing the damage. The nationalisation of everything of value from women to brains, together with the confiscation of all assets and resources, from farm animals to foreign capital, brought civilisation to a complete stand still.

Inertia and stagnation were evident wherever Emerson looked. In the Urals, he saw mines and factories closed down; since the mines did not produce coal, the locomotives had to burn wood, but there wasn't enough of it to maintain a regular schedule. At every railway terminal, they saw scores of abandoned engines and wagons that had been side tracked for want of minor repairs. They discovered that two thirds of the locomotive fleet was inoperative and the rate of scrappage was 200 per month. Emerson was told that in Turkestan, officials were attempting to transport 8,000,000 *poods*[21] of cotton to the factories in Moscow at a rate of two trains per month.

They also noticed that food was less readily available than in the east. At one station, Emerson tried to buy some eggs. However, the *babushka*[22] with gnarled hands and a wrinkled face refused to take his money. Her long locks escaped from the shawl that covered her head and straggled down to veil her rheumy eyes that were fixed intently on the basket at her feet. For paper money she had no use, but she did ask for food for her chickens because without it, they would not lay their eggs tomorrow. Abolishing Omsk money had resulted in the peasants losing their trust in paper banknotes, which were now being thrown by the tonne into pulping machines.

In some of the towns, they came across the Bolshevik propaganda trains that toured the country with a film projector and printing press. At each new village, they would raise a screen, put on a film show and present special dramas about the revolution. The villain was always a bourgeoisie capitalist and the hero a poor down-trodden member of the proletariat.

The British soldiers could see in the towns that this representation was not universally accurate. The two largest buildings in a Russian *gorat*[23] were the prison and the vodka refinery. The production of vodka was nationalised and the Russian peasant, who thrived on it was aghast. The reality was that the "poor down-trodden hero" would rather queue for vodka than for bread.

The peasants were in a state of confusion. They had been harried, robbed, and flogged, first by one side, then by the other. Their horses, carts, sleighs, sons, and food were requisitioned without compensation. Many honest workmen were trying to study and better themselves, but their stomachs were empty and their heads filled with misty notions and impossible expectations. The greatest tragedy was the generation of children, who lost their innocence and became accustomed to the most awful sights and haunted by the vision of Death.

A fallacious rumour spread along the railway, which gave false hope to the people. They were told by the commissars that the end of hostilities and the lifting of the European blockade would alleviate the crisis they faced and the shortage of raw materials. However, anyone who thought about it realised that the opening of trade would make greater demands on Russia's natural resources because these were the sole products that the government could exchange for goods in Europe.

Russian women continued to give the British soldiers cause for hope. Apart from witnessing spirited girls and courageous nurses, they knew that Russian females had saved the church during the war. Without their support, every vestige of religion would have been stamped out by the Reds because the priesthood of the Orthodox Church had been placed at the end of the list in the allotment of food, with no provision made for the upkeep of the church.

The personal sacrifice of many women allowed Russia to keep its church and to restore a deeper worship amongst communities. Their needs were more primitive than the former ritualistic observance and the clerics had to respond to the troubled lives of millions of ordinary Russians. As a result, the church became a source of comfort and a place of refuge, enabling the women of Russia to confront their daily fears.

Just before the British soldiers arrived at Irkutsk, the Red Army seized the Archbishop of Siberia and ordered him to turn over holy vessels and icons to them. The aged priest refused and was promptly incarcerated in the prison. As the Easter feast and day of thanksgiving approached, the women of the city marched to the commandant's headquarters and demanded the Archbishop's release so that he might celebrate Easter Mass. The female protesters were so insistent that the Bolshevik's haughty bluster faltered and he liberated their beloved cleric.

★★★

The mid-summer twilights in the shadow of the mountains were glorious as the British prisoners approached the Urals. In that northern latitude the light lasted almost all night and for Emerson, there was something mystical about the sight of the mountains with their hidden wealth of emeralds, amethysts, platinum and gold. However, this all changed as they crossed the line that divided Asia from Europe and entered a land that had been razed to the ground.

The evidence of the famine that they saw from the train reminded the young officers of Francis McCullagh's cautionary advice in December: "the more one knows about the system, the more one dread[s] it." For miles on either side of the railway, there stretched fields that once had been golden with ripening grain, but which for the last three harvests had been barren because the Bolshevik commissars had commandeered all the crops, including the farmers' last seed. They could not disguise this disaster, for it was a common sight to see grass growing on the railway tracks at the entrance to the rusting grain elevators.

The images impressed on Emerson's mind were shocking. He described the scenes in his diary: "A peasant's cart dragging wearily under a burning sun; flat lands cracked open by heat and drought with dead grain stalks withered in the sun; emaciated bodies lying by the roadside; black wings circling in the brassy sky overhead. More carts, many, many more carts at a river bank at sundown. What need of campfires when there is no food?"

He saw an abandoned village that was utterly cleared out. The streets were littered with broken jars, bottles, rags, and rubbish. Dead people lay in doorways; the wave of hunger driving the villagers to fight for their food stores. Those not dead had been blown away like dry leaves in a hot wind. Multiply these scenes by a thousand more on roads and in villages, until they covered an area as great as all the United States east of the Mississippi.

The wide River Volga marked another significant watershed. They had to shut all their windows and carriage doors as their train crossed the magnificent waterway. Looking to the west, there were more bodies lying crumpled by the side of the railway line, some cholera smitten. Looking to the east and north-east, they saw columns of carts crawling across the dead land, with expectant wings hovering over the slow procession. There was nowhere to go and yet, they must go somewhere. Along the Volga, 12 divisions of infantry and two of cavalry were positioned to shoot down the hunger-driven as they approached the crossing points. Will there be cartridges enough? Will the sabres grow so dull that they will become mere bludgeons?

One of the best examples that Emerson recorded about the commercial workings of Bolshevism was in the handling of the salt mines. At Omsk, there were millions of pounds of salt; mountains of it, and yet across the Ural Mountains in European Russia there was none. Under the communist theory, no one was allowed to traffic in a commodity. To reinforce the ruling, the death penalty was imposed on any Russian caught carrying the crystalline mineral from the apparently limitless supply in Siberia to Moscow, where it was worth the same as gold, grain for grain.

Emerson was secretly advised to smuggle salt into European Russia and stowed about 40 pounds in a kit bag. Within 50 miles of Omsk, at a little village where their train stopped, they were surrounded by a crowd of women and children. When the guard stepped away from the carriage, a woman in rags stepped close and whispered *Salee*. A handful of salt was traded for a pound of prized butter and the woman seemed to think she had the best of the deal.

These peasant women, who hated but did not cringe at the Bolsheviks, took the greatest pains to ensure that the Reds did not suspect the British of smuggling contraband. For the next 1,300 miles Emerson kept the group supplied with milk, cheese, and other foods, scarce even in the farming districts, but still obtainable in exchange for salt. At one station a little peasant girl had wild strawberries for sale. She had the sad eyes that had become so common in Russia. The British gave her a cup of tea. She remembered having tasted it before, but was not so sure about sugar.

As their train rumbled along the maze of tracks leading towards Moscow, the remnants of the British Railway Mission were aghast at what they witnessed. There were literally tens of thousands of wagon cars falling to pieces, painted with the initials of the Russian Soviet Federative Socialist Republic as if the new nation was proud of this deserted pile of scrap. Giant locomotives, made by Baldwins in Philadelphia, were being transformed into heaps of rust. Engines that had a slightly leaky valve were shoved into a siding and left to fall to pieces for want of maintenance. A hot box, easily repairable in normal times, was sufficient cause for a carriage to be scrapped.

On their final evening before they reached Moscow, Emerson reflected on what he had seen. For six weeks, with many stops and starts, they had trundled along the railway line for 3,500 miles. The journey condensed to the images of a peasant dying in a withered field with a vulture wheeling overhead and a steam engine wilfully abandoned, whilst a fanatic studied a map in Moscow, dreaming about the red fires of world revolution.

Squalor and high-sounding words; starvation and glowing promises; disease and artful phrases; death and *Nichevo*; this was the Russia that the prisoners of war experienced in July 1920 after nearly three years of Bolshevik rule. Little did they know that everything before this moment would be considered luxury when compared with what awaited them in the Soviet capital.

CHAPTER 15

Moscow Monastery

*This evil spirit of Tartary, that once was the curse of Tsarism, is indulging today
in an orgy of blood the like of which has never been seen.*

GEORGE POPOFF[1]

From the dismal ante-chamber of the railway graveyard, the British
group entered the outskirts of Moscow on Wednesday 21st July. Against
the skyline, smokeless chimneys of redundant factories appeared like the
straggly teeth of an enormous dinosaur about to swallow the city. The
scene of desolation continued as they passed the residential areas. Closer
to the centre, the streets were alive with human beings, invariably clad
in greenish-grey army uniforms.

The crowds moved as hurriedly as a colony of ants disturbed by
the thrust of a cane. Where were they going and why? The shops
were boarded up or looted, the factories were idle and all places of
public assembly were closed. It appeared to be a city of mental disorder,
which sometimes broke out with the wild shouts of a delirious man
and sometimes dwindled away to the plain whimpering of a starving
child.

The unfinished central station looked like a shipwreck with its rusty
rigging. The ancient scaffolding had been erected before the start of the
war, but the interior of the waiting room had never been finished. The
British prisoners were ushered into this large hall and as with every other
halt on their 3,500-mile journey, they were initially told that there would
be no hold up en route to the next destination, Petrograd.

However, when Vining approached the authorities to discover the timings of their departure, it became clear that they would neither be allowed to catch a train to Petrograd, nor to roam freely in the Bolshevik capital. He was very worried about some of the incriminating papers that he carried and whilst they were assembled in a gaggle, he whispered to the American journalists, who had been their travelling companions since Omsk. These reporters held special dispensation to travel via another route and one of them, named King, had offered to take Vining's diary out of the country. Herbert Prickett caused a distraction with Teddy and this allowed Vining to hand over the precious documents in a paper bag.

Apart from the 14 British soldiers, there were two Hungarian cooks and one German porter under Vining's care. Although they had felt threatened on several occasions during the past six months, they had always been treated by the authorities as prisoners-of war, rather than felons. This changed in Moscow and for the first time they felt like criminals, when an officious man in uniform segregated them from the civilian passengers and instructed them to wait for orders.

They spent an uncertain night at the station and it wasn't until the following afternoon that a lorry arrived to take them into the city centre. The truck carried them in shifts for a 15-minute journey to a set of formidable gates that guarded the headquarters of the Extraordinary Commission in Lubjanka Square.

They were fortunate because they were delivered to the All Russian Vserossiskaja, or V-Tcheka at Lubjanka 2, rather than to the Moscow, or M-Tcheka at Lubjanka 14. George Popoff distinguished these two secret police headquarters when he wrote: "If there was any difference between them, Lubjanka 14 had the reputation of being a mediaeval torture chamber and the scene of mass murders in an even higher degree than Lubjanka 2".[2]

As they climbed down and stood in the courtyard, Emerson noticed many faces watching them from behind barred windows and suddenly recognised a woman he knew from Irkutsk. She shook her head and made a sign of a rope around her neck and over a beam. When he attempted to speak to her, a guard shouted at him and pointed his bayoneted rifle into his midriff. It was clear that he was not allowed to move from the spot where he was standing.

After two hours of waiting, the five senior officers were ordered to follow a sentry into an office where they were searched thoroughly. All money and papers were confiscated. The inspectors demanded Vining's razor and cigarette case but he refused to hand them over. The chief of the Tcheka was consulted and the British commander was allowed to keep these prized items.

Horrocks managed to read a piece of paper on the desk that was written by the vindictive Head of the Omsk secret police, Comrade Podlovsky. The note stated that the British had enormous sums of money and had never been searched. This did not auger well for them and, sure enough, Vining was told that whilst they waited for their onward travel to Petrograd, they would be held in a special *laager*.

The search of their belongings took five hours. Many precious items were taken from them, before they were all herded into a single room for their first night in the infamous penitentiary. However, in response, Vining did what the Russians least expected. He pulled out the banjo and, together with Rooney and Prickett, led a rousing "sing-song" to celebrate their situation.

★★★

At 10a.m. the next morning, the British group were ordered to take what they could carry and be ready to march to another prison. Vining demanded a cart so they could take the pile of possessions in the centre of the courtyard, but this caused another argument. Their heap contained stoves with chimneys for cooking, as well as pots and pans of every description, wash basins and all their winter clothes and equipment.

Eventually, a cart arrived and they rapidly loaded it because they did not wish to stay for a minute longer. They marched out of Lubjanka as a squad behind this cart, surrounded by Red Guards. Sergeant Bob Lillington had the honour of carrying Teddy. They all put on their smartest uniform and the officers wore their Sam Browne belts, so they created a mild sensation as they passed through Lubjanka Square, heading south towards the river.

After 20 minutes, they arrived at the notorious Ivanovsky monastery, which had been converted by the Bolsheviks into a political prison. They shivered at the sight of the barbed wire round the top of the walled perimeter. Entering through the gates, they were immediately pushed through a disinfection and quarantine process and were made to take stand-up baths in the laundry room. After their names were registered in the commandant's office, they were put into three cubicles, each about twelve feet by eight. Vining divided them into two groups of five and one of seven and put himself in the largest cell with six others.

There were 457 prisoners in the monastery, of whom 45 were women. Many were held as hostages. There was no hope here and some of the inmates had gone quite mad.

Whilst the rules were exceedingly strict, they were allowed to walk and talk with other prisoners in the courtyard during the daytime. There was an extraordinary collection of individuals. Princes and barons, generals and admirals, ladies-in-waiting, members of the Imperial Duma and lord mayors, professors and adventurers from "almost every country on the globe," as well as thieves and prostitutes all mixed together.

There were a number of former industrial magnates; the cobbler who repaired the prisoners' boots had been one of the wealthiest shoe manufacturers in Russia. Another of the unfortunates was an American aviator, who was captured when serving as a soldier of fortune with the Polish army. Most of the inmates spoke at least two languages, and many of them four, or five. It appeared that the Bolsheviks hesitated to kill them due either to their prominence, or their usefulness as surety.

A series of bells regulated the day. The morning routine started at 8a.m. but the British refused to work and did not rise until 11a.m. An hour and a half later, the 12.30 bell sounded for lunch. At 2p.m. another bell signalled the start of the afternoon shift until 5p.m. At 7p.m. there was a roll call in the corridor which was controlled by the *Staristor*, or "prisoner prefect."

They quickly realised that the daily food issue was below starvation levels. The staple was dried herring, which reminded them of strips of shrivelled shoe leather, but smelt worse. Three quarters of a pound of black bread was issued in the morning; some unpalatable boiled grain arrived at midday and a watery "grey eyes" soup was the sum of the evening menu. Emerson began to feel like Oliver Twist when he asked for "more".[3]

At night when the lights were extinguished, battalions of biting creatures emerged from their hiding places in the crevices of the walls and the cracks between the planks of the wooden beds. They soon devised a plan to eliminate this contagion.[4] On the word "go", everyone lit their candles and killed as many as possible before the bugs beat a hasty retreat.

One evening, soon after their arrival, they heard the fire alarm and were released from their cells to help put it out. The fire was in the book binding room and whilst some of them burst open the door, others fetched water from the cesspool. After about 20 minutes the blaze was extinguished, but unfortunately, there was so much smoke that one of the officers had a bucket of liquid flung over him by mistake. Vining suggested that he sleep elsewhere, so bad was the smell and the next day he had to send his clothes to the wash.

★★★

Hundreds of prisoners were shot whilst the British were in prison. In 1918, the head of the Tcheka, Felix Dzerzhinsky, developed a technique known as *Nackenschuss*, which became the favoured method in Ivanovsky because it caused instant death and avoided the loss of much blood. The prisoner was ordered to descend some steps and was shot in the nape of the neck as his head bent forward. The executioner then went back for another victim whilst the guards removed the body.[5]

Sometimes a squabble or a fit of depression descended on the British group, but a few minutes later Teddy came to the rescue and lifted morale again. Everyone gave him some scraps of their food, so he did not lose much weight, but they did worry about his safety. There was a man who they knew had eaten two dogs, but they quietly "had words with him" so he realised if anything happened to their canine companion, they would come after him.

Sunday was the visiting day. The British inmates watched the sad procession of weeping wives and anxious acquaintants enter the gates to comfort the Russian prisoners. This was when friends and relatives passed secretly smuggled items across to the wretched inmates. Respectable old gentlemen then bartered these illicit goods on a recognised exchange mechanism. For example, a herring and a half could purchase a *pika*, or tablespoonful of sugar.

A strange comedy played out in the place of work. Many of the nobility wore morning coats to do menial tasks such as sweeping a yard. One of the most distinguished gentlemen was in charge of the wash rooms. The only way to use the facilities was to click one's heels, salute and ask "Your most highest. May I have the privilege of using the lavatories today?" A thunderous voice replied: "Permission granted!"

There was a small library operated in connection with the prison. On making an inquiry in Russian for a certain book, Emerson was pleased to be answered in English. The librarian proved to be the ex-Adjutant to Grand Duke Nicholas and his assistant was Prince Gorchakov.

Emerson spoke with many prisoners and the majority had been in jail ever since the Bolshevik Government came to power in 1917. Few of them had had trials and were, in effect, detained indefinitely. One man introduced himself as Count Kotzebue and asked what had become of the Czar. Even in 1920, many Russians still believed that their former ruler was living in England.

He learned many new things about the Soviet system. For example, no mother was allowed to keep her child by the fireside at night in Moscow. They had to hand them over to Bolshevik "clubs" where the children were indoctrinated and in some cases sent home to spy on their parents.

The British soldiers were visited by the French Red Cross, which in Moscow was run by Madame Charpentier. She and her two daughters arrived at Ivanovsky with food twice a week. These supplements prevented the foreigners from starving; potatoes were most welcome, but the real treat was when they were brought an egg, or a portion of sugar. They were also grateful to her for bringing in an occasional bone for Teddy.

In spite of the desperate situation, the discipline of the group remained intact, with Uncle Charlie ensuring that all the soldiers paid complements to the officers by saluting on parade each day and on formal occasions. Sapper Smith continued to do most of the cooking, with the two Hungarians sous chefs and Hummel, the German, fetching water and scrubbing the room twice a week.

★★★

Unbeknownst to them, a crisis about Poland flared up between the Allies and the Soviet Government soon after they arrived in Moscow. On 6th August, *The Times* declared that the situation was "tragically serious." As Churchill belligerently raised the prospect of British troops fighting in Russia again, the Labour Party held anti-war meetings. Meanwhile in the House of Commons, the prime minister had to explain the British policy of supporting Poland at the same time as hosting a second Soviet trade delegation, whilst the British prisoners of war languished in jail.[6]

The situation had been coming to a head since Russia offered a peace treaty with Poland under generous terms. This had included handing over parts of Byelorussia and Western Ukraine, but Poland's leader, Marshal Pilsudski, encouraged by the Allies and remembering the "Time of Troubles", when Polish Kings had been invited to rule Russia, demanded the restitution of their pre-1772 frontier.

The Soviets were shocked at this ingratitude and unsurprisingly refused. This provided the Poles with an excuse to invade Ukraine in January 1920 when they captured Starokonstantinov. They pursued a dual strategy of coercive negotiations and military advances throughout the spring, forcing the Russian troops to evacuate Kiev on 7th May. However, the Polish occupation was short lived because the Red Army counter attacked on the northern route from the River Dvina to the River Dnieper. Meanwhile, the Polish line of communications was sabotaged and they had to fall back to avoid being surrounded.

Winston Churchill circulated a secret memorandum to the Cabinet raising questions about the British attitude towards the Poles and the spectre of refugees.[7] As a result, David Lloyd George asked his trusted Cabinet Secretary, Maurice Hankey, to join a six-day fact finding mission to Warsaw in July. In his report, Hankey suggested that "the French are a bad combination with the Poles" and that the Polish Army is not so much beaten as demoralised. The ill-advised advance to Kie[v] and the inevitable retreat have reacted disastrously on this young and inexperienced army."[8]

The fighting continued until the Red Army reached the gates of Warsaw on 14th August. However, the Poles won a decisive battle on the following day. Both sides needed to pause and the Russians withdrew towards Brest-Litovsk, whilst peace negotiations resumed between the governments.[9]

★★★

The British group were oblivious to what was happening on the Polish front, or to the efforts in London to secure their release. Eric Hayes's father approached a non-Royal Duchess, who took up his case and wrote to Alfred Knox. He replied:

Dear Duchess,

Your letter of 20th August has reached me here today. I am very sorry that I can add little to Mr Hayes knowledge of his son.

There are still, I calculate, nine officers and six other ranks of the British military and Railway Mission captured in Siberia. Prisoners with the Bolsheviks, originally nineteen were captured, but one Captain (Francis McCullogh), who is now writing in the *Nineteenth Century*, was released as a correspondent, and Colonel Johnstone and two others got off very recently. Only two of the fifteen belonged to my Mission – Captains Horrocks and Hayes. They were all captured West of Krasnoyarsk, but were taken to Irkutsk where they were seen by an officer about March, and were said to be then well treated. This officer (Captain Carthew) was sent up from Vladivostok to take them clothes and money. I hoped that they were to be repatriated through Vladivostok, but they have now all been transferred to Moscow. I am particularly sorry for Hayes and Horrocks, as they were both prisoners, I believe, for several months with the Germans previous to the Armistice.

I have done all I could since my return to worry high or subordinate officers at the Foreign Office and War Office. I have even written to the Times! I have been repeatedly assured that "everything possible is being done".

I have written to Mr Dawson (President of the Council of Action) who, according to the Press, is about to visit the Polish Bolshevik negotiations, to ask him to use his influence with the Bolshevik Plenipotentiaries.

Colonel Johnstone attributed the release (possibly wrongly) to a telegram he sent from Omsk to British Labour Delegation then in Moscow. I hope you will use your great influence to get something done by the Government.

Mr Hayes should apply to MIR General Staff, War Office, and ask to be kept informed of the latest information.

Yours sincerely,
Alfred Knox

★★★

Dealing with the tedium caused by the group's refusal to work became a delicate issue for Vining, but he came up with an inspired idea to rebuild the prison theatre. At the same time, Sergeant Rooney wrote a play that was translated into Russian and they performed this drama on the refurbished stage. After the audience's deafening applause, the commandant, who had been a tailor before the revolution, rushed round to the dressing room and congratulated the British group.

Unfortunately, this led to one of the few disciplinary incidents when the youthful Bernard Eyford was reported by a jealous rival for talking to one of the amenable actresses away from the theatre. Speaking to women prisoners was strictly forbidden and so the romantic officer and actress were both put into solitary confinement for a week.

This rule became very frustrating when two forlorn nurses arrived in the jail as hostages, one of whom had lived in England for eleven years and spoke perfect English. Several of the British officers knew their brothers, who had served in Kolchak's army. They wished to assist the destitute women, who walked about in rags with slippers plaited from dried grass, known as *lapiti*, but there was little that they could do to help them without risking a spell in solitary.

Other British arrivals were placed under Vining's wing, including six naïve Bolsheviks who had travelled from Britain and been unceremoniously arrested by the Moscow police. There was a welcome cheer for Captain Dwyer Neville of the Royal Air Force[10] when he suddenly appeared from nowhere. The Australian pilot had been captured with Lieutenant Colonel Eric Johnston eight months earlier, but contracted typhus at Tomsk. He had to stay behind in hospital when Johnston was sent to Moscow and released at the same time as Francis McCullagh.

The prison guards continued to give the British soldiers a hard time for not working and often reduced their food rations. At night, they carried out unannounced searches and removed many of their possessions without justification. On one such occasion, Vining had to give up the official British Railway Mission stamp, which he had used frequently to deceive illiterate officials.

At the end of August, a workmen's committee visited and demanded yet again to know why the British did not work. Vining responded by

reminding them of Russia's agreement to the Hague Convention governing the treatment of prisoners of war,[11] but this made little difference to
their situation. Two days later, on 2nd September, they were instructed
to gather all their possessions and assemble in the yard. At first, they
believed this was the start of their homeward journey but, depressingly,
it was merely a transfer to another of the many monasteries in Moscow
that had been converted into penal institutions.

It was a 20-minute march to the imposing Andronovsky Prison with
its high white walls, from where Emerson "could see the golden domes
of many of Moscow's thousand churches." They marched through the
imposing gateway with "beautiful wrought iron gates, crowned by a tall
bell tower"[12] and reported to the commandant's office immediately on
the left.

They were all placed in a single room on the second floor where
Eric Johnston and about 30 British prisoners were kept in April, before
they were exchanged as part of the O'Grady-Litvinov agreement. On
the wall, their predecessors had "painted a naval signal done in flags"[13]
marking their departure.

The conditions in their new prison were harsher than the Ivanovsky
and the guards were sharper. Night time searches resumed on a regular
basis; razors and cameras, which they had managed to keep in their
previous gaols, were now confiscated. Fortunately, Vining had hidden
his films inside a football, wedged tightly between the bladder and the
outer skin and these were never found.

They had an alternative football which they used in the courtyard while
they kept the "smuggler" safe. Soon after they arrived, they kicked the
football over the wall to check the outside perimeter. They decided that
escape from the prison would have been easy, but beyond the immediate
surroundings, "it would have become very difficult to make their way
without assistance."[14]

This former monastery boasted the oldest cemetery in Moscow.
Emerson walked amongst the evocative grave stones and noticed that
countless priceless statues and carvings had been vandalised. It was the
Russian custom to bury people wearing their jewels. Many of the monks'
graves had been robbed and the skeletons' contorted hands bore testament
to the disrespectful theft of their rings.

The constant nagging about work continued. Vining refused employment in the saw mill, but he did agree to build another theatre in a disused
stable block. Once it was finished, they put on another performance of
Joseph Rooney's play and this won them many friends among the other
prisoners and the guards.[15] There were more foreigners in Andronovsky
and they met the French son and brother of Madame Charpentier, who
continued to provide food and medical help twice a week.

The prisoners were not allowed sight-seeing visits into the city, despite
Vining's requests. They were allowed to join the fortnightly trip to the
baths, but these were considered to be a death trap. In the warmth of the
building, the lice transferred from the inside of clothing to the outside and
from there to other people. The British refused to go and instead used
the washing tubs in the laundry rooms after the workers had finished.

Occasionally they were taken for interrogation by the Extraordinary
Commission. Emerson suffered the same torture as Francis McCullagh
during several uncomfortable sessions with the Tcheka, but this was not
a unique experience. When he compared notes with the others in the
group, they were not certain whether the Soviets were trying to trick
them into admitting guilt for something, or turn them into double
agents, or just build an intelligence file on other members of the group.
The interrogators gave him and the other soldiers a "pamphlet telling
them to shoot their officers and join the Bolsheviks",[16] but these were
disposed of in the prison.

They heard that British delegations of shop stewards and Labour
party members were in Moscow for the second world congress of the
Communist International and that the sculptress, Mrs Clara Sheridan,
was visiting at the invitation of Lev Kamenev. They hoped these
representatives would help to attain their release, but none of them
visited the British captives. They would have been dismayed to know
that whilst they were being grilled by the Tcheka on 27th September,
the 35-year-old Mrs Sheridan was sculpting a clay bust of its murderous
Chief Felix Dzerzhinsky.

When they read her sympathetic views about the organiser of the Red
Terror, who had the blood of thousands on his hands, they were shocked
and appalled. Her obsequious description that "one can see martyrdom
crystallized in his eyes",[17] compounded by her feelings of "real sadness

that I may never see him again" were in total contrast to the evidence they had witnessed of the misery forced on millions of ordinary Russians by the Red Terror. They would also have been irritated that the Foreign and Colonial Office continued to negotiate a trade deal with the Soviet Government throughout September without securing their release.[18]

★★★

In October, the snow started falling in Moscow and the weather turned bitterly cold. The King of Khiva arrived with the tattered remains of his entourage, who wore long flowing robes and black sheepskin busbies. They were half dead from cold and exhaustion. Since they had fought with the British Army in the Caucasus, Vining gave them food and helped them to settle into the prison. As a result the Sultan constantly sought to draw him into his circle, but Vining was reluctant to extend the friendship beyond diplomatic favours.

Another British soldier was put under their care in October. Nineteen-year-old Private Lionel Grant of the Gloucestershire Regiment had become an isolated prisoner after his capture at Baku[19] and transfer to Moscow. He was hugely relieved to join the group and benefit from Vining's inspiring leadership.

All the British suffered from gastric problems, but Brian Horrocks was the only soldier to be laid low by a serious illness, when he contracted jaundice. He was sent to hospital for care, but by then there were enough Russian speakers in the group to converse with the guards, so his loss was not felt too badly.

After Madame Charpentier left Moscow, an American lady agreed to bring bread and supplies to them. Mrs Marguerite Harrison had arrived in Russia ostensibly as the representative of the *Baltimore Sun*, but this was a cover for her work as an American spy. She had been arrested on the same night as Francis McCullagh, with whom she had illegally attended a secret meeting in the Kremlin.[20] The Tcheka had coerced her to be a double agent and it was alleged that in June, she caused the arrest of a British journalist, Mrs Stan Harding.[21]

The technique used to turn British citizens into Soviet agents was revealed by a black prisoner who escaped on the same ship as Francis McCullagh. Benjamin Jeffers was a wine trader, accused by the

Bolsheviks of being a spy, who spent five months in Butirki, Sokolniki and Andronovsky prisons. In their attempts to persuade him to work for them, they explained: "If you catch a gentleman the first time we will give you 1,000 roubles and the next time we will give you 15,000 roubles...." To ensure he understood the consequences of failure, they added bluntly: "If you do not catch anybody, we will shoot you."[22]

Much to the embarrassment of the War Secretary, Winston Churchill, the British prisoners of war continued to be the subject of constant challenges in the House of Commons when the summer recess ended in October. Almost every day there was a question about their plight and the trade agreement. David Lloyd George was absent from the House on several occasions, but was pinned down by an advocate for British military intervention, Mr Noel Billing on 25th October.[23] The MP for Hertford asked: "Is it not a fact that the Right Honourable Gentleman himself stated in this House three months ago that no negotiations of any description would take place with Russia until these [British prisoners] were released, and that that was cheered to the echo in this House, and has he broken his word, or have circumstances altered?"

The prime minister retorted: "I do not think the Honourable Gentleman should assume that I have broken my word." However, the House knew that he had welcomed another Soviet delegation in August and several politicians had been involved in drafting the secret trade agreement sent by the Foreign Office to Moscow in September. They had also seen Krassin's response to the prime minister of 6th October[24] in which he confirmed that Vining's group was detained as bargaining chips in connection with Babushkin.[25]

The next day, Sir Frederick Hall, renowned for his zealous questioning of ministers and for devising clever supplementary question, asked the under-secretary of state for foreign afairs what were the number of British prisoners still in Russia and for details about their repatriation.[26]

The response from Mr Harmsworth was heavily qualified. Apart from Vining's group in Moscow, he was not sure about the numbers at Baku. He concluded that it was "impossible to say exactly how many may still remain in Russia," but the intention was to make an exchange along the lines described in their "message to Moscow of 9th October." The ingenious Hall then asked: "What security have we that British prisoners in Russia shall be repatriated into this country if we are not going to retain some of the Russian prisoners in this country"?

Mr Harmsworth replied that the proposed exchange would be simultaneous at the Finnish frontier. This opened the debate out and Sir William Davison pressed the government, by asking: "whether 16 or 18 British citizens are still kept as prisoners in Moscow by the Bolshevist Government; and will he inform the House what steps are being taken to secure their immediate release?"

★★★

In the Andronovsky Prison, the British group continued to hold their impromptu concerts in the evenings. After one of these occasions, they received a visit from a portly official from the Soviet Foreign Office. He introduced himself as Naoetava and said that he was the minister for entente affairs and that he had recently returned from England.[27] After asking about the health of Brian Horrocks, this courteous diplomat slipped in the news that they would leave for Petrograd on 20th October. There was stunned silence for five seconds as the news sunk in and then five minutes of loud cheering.

On the prescribed day, they waited for an escort but none arrived. Horrocks was greatly relieved to join them from hospital, which he described as worse than the prison. Just as they thought they had been deceived again, a squad of guards arrived at 8p.m. to escort them to Lubjanka.

In some ways, their departure was a sorrowful occasion as they had to leave behind many White Russian friends who they knew would only escape "without baggage", the sinister euphemism used to describe those who were executed without trial. Vining gave away many of their cooking supplies to these unfortunates and then ordered a cart to take their remaining possessions to the Tcheka's headquarters for the final paperwork. The commandant returned the personal items they had taken when they entered the prison, but he kept the precious stones they had bought in the Urals.

Vining and some of the others had bought amethyst, turquoise, beryl and alexandrite stones during their long halt at Novo-Nikolaevsk in December. They had hidden these in the seams of their tunics.

Unfortunately, Vining had allowed an old actress to repair his sleeves, forgetting about the stones and the treacherous thespian handed them over to the commandant in exchange for extra food.[28]

As they assembled in the courtyard, they felt bitterly sorry for the pale, sorrowful faces gazing after them. The poor wretches had no glimmer of hope as the worst of the winter approached. They gave them a final heartfelt wave before marching out of the gates and making their way down the icy cobbles with their three-legged companion on their final visit to the V-Tcheka, singing "Tipperary" at the top of their voices.

In Lubjanka, they were joined by four of the "grave offenders" who had been excluded (scandalously according to Lord Curzon) from the O'Grady-Litvinov agreement.[29] The quartet were members of the ill-fated Committee for the Relief of the British Colony in Petrograd.[30] Their secretary was George Gibson, a British businessman who worked for the United Shipping Company and as an agent for MI6. He had been arrested following the successful British raid on the Soviet fleet by Coastal Motor Boats on 18th August 1919.[31] The others included Charles James Maxwell, who had been manager at Hubbard's cotton mill, together with his niece and cousin Miss MacPherson. Emerson and the others made tea for their new companions and began a sing-song. The guards came in to tell them to stop, but they didn't.

Then the chief of staff of the Tcheka, Popov, arrived. He was a huge man over 6 feet 2 inches tall. He demanded payment for the cart they had ordered and quick as a flash, Vining replied that he could take it out of the money they owed them from July and asked for the remainder of their roubles to be returned. The chief of staff smiled and left. Afterwards, the guards told the British that it was the only time they had ever seen Popov smile.

The Ivanovsky monastery where the British prisoners were imprisoned from July to September 1920. (Courtesy of Perry Wieloch, 2017)

CHAPTER 16

HMS *Delhi*

Your Lloyd George is like a man playing roulette and scattering chips on every number.

LEON TROTSKY TO ROBERT BRUCE LOCKHART,
24TH FEBRUARY 1918[1]

Vining's group took so long to say farewell to their fellow prisoners that they missed the scheduled passenger train from Moscow and had to wait on the freezing platform for several hours. Eventually they were told to board a freight train and found themselves yet again climbing into a cattle wagon with a stove that had to be constantly stoked and eponymous wooden bunks that they had to share with an army of lice.

Finally they chugged out of Moscow at 2a.m. on 21st October. They had been given no food by the Soviet authorities and had handed over many of their comforts to their friends at the Andronovsky Prison. After a hungry journey that lasted 36 hours, their train arrived at Petrograd, where they were dumped on the platform and told to wait for the army to collect them.

They crowded into the nationalised buffet at the railway station. The waitress sold a cup of tea for one rouble, but demanded 300 as a deposit for the cups. They discovered that the black market still exchanged Imperial and Kerensky roubles. However, neither of these compared with the American dollar, which could be traded for 10,000 Soviet roubles.

Miss Maxwell and the other civilians who previously lived in St Petersburg were all picked up before the prisoners of war. Emerson had to wait such a long time that he thought they would end up sleeping at the station, but eventually they were taken to a former hospital which was "now a concentration camp for prisoners being repatriated."[2] The careworn custodian, Mrs Violet Froom, escorted them to a couple of large dormitories and to their joy there were proper mattresses on the beds.[3]

The next day, Vining met a local commissar named Patritsky, who explained that the prisoner exchange would take place in a week's time. He hoped that the British party would leave Petrograd with a more favourable impression than the one they had drawn from their internment in Moscow and he encouraged them to visit the theatre and the winter palace in the intervening time.

During this final week, they saw the Russian ballet at its best and were given tickets for the Royal Box at the Mariinsky theatre. They heard a magnificent performance from the renowned bass, Feodor Chaliapin, who ended the show singing the International, whilst bended on one knee, holding a red flag.

They visited the Hermitage[4] and Vining could not resist playing a few notes on the magnificent gold piano, which still had a "very sweet tone". Emerson wrote about his escorted tour in a letter to Dallas:

Russia, for me, finds as its focal point, the eye of the picture, an empty bathroom.

Through a twisting corridor, filled with gewgaws and trinkets of the Red regime and called the Bolshevist museum, I came to the Winter Palace at Petrograd.

The whole affair was so unexpected and so suggestive of the Arabian Nights, that it almost took my breath away. My guide, it appeared, had been employed in the Palace for about thirty years and it is unnecessary to state where his sympathies lay. He had attended the coronation in Moscow of Nikolai II as well as that of Alexander III before him.[5]

I shall not attempt to describe in detail the rooms. One could imagine the splendour of a state function there. Most of the paintings were in place, but many were overspread with crimson banners. These helped to convert the hall into a great Bolshevist auditorium. The portrait of Alexander III was concealed by a hideous picture of the beast who assassinated [sic] him. This came as a shock to me, even with my knowledge of the Reds, that they should thus honour a murderer.

We next visited the throne room of Peter the Great, which with its rich tapestries and art treasures had been looted by souvenir hunters from as far up the walls as one could reach. The historical pictures were mostly intact, but many of the fine paintings, especially those in which the aristocracy appeared, had been destroyed. Revolver shots and sabre cuts had mutilated many of them. The priceless rugs had been taken from the elaborately laid floor.

The private chapel was beautiful, but most of the fittings had been removed, leaving a scene of desolation.

Finally we reached the private apartments of the Royal Family. Seldom have I seen such beauty. The decoration and furnishings were almost hypnotic in their charm. There was nothing garish or gaudy and not a note of discord.

In the drawing room one could imagine the visitors who had been received by former Czars of all the Russians, the problems of state that must have been discussed with the Emperor's advisors as they sat before the marble fireplace. How tragic that such discussion should be so fruitless!

The Billiard Room was still complete, and in the library the books still rested behind the glass doors. One might expect the host to step back into the room at any moment.

The bathroom was beautiful, the Grecian type of white marble. The walls decorated with marine views. Everything was there but the water.

The bedroom had been used by Alexander III. It was also here that the loquacious Kerensky tried to play Napoleon after contracting a morganatic marriage.

Most of the leather covering had been torn from the chairs, as well as many of the curtains from the windows. Even the mattresses had suffered at the hands of devastating souvenir seekers. Now I know how the Venus de Milo lost her arms!

By the time we reached the sitting room of the Empress, I had already fallen beneath the spell of the tragedy of Russia. It was essentially a woman's room. The furniture, the mural decoration, the refined beauty, a few photographs of intimate family life still remained.

The portrait of the Czarina had been slashed by a Cossack sabre and a framed photograph of a beautiful Grand Duchess had been pierced by a bayonet. The window seat looked so inviting that one could easily imagine the Empress and her young daughters gazing out upon the palace courtyard or across the River Neva.

A subtle perfume still pervades the place. One could not help but think of the same family huddled together in a filthy Siberian shack, where they were slaughtered like a flock of sheep by their fellow countrymen. The Czar of all Russia perished in the same manner as thousands of poorer and humbler Russian families perished at the hands of the Bolshevists.

As I stepped out into the street my reverie was given a dramatic punctuation by an old peasant woman who stopped me and asked: "You are English – well where is Nikolai?"

But that bathroom! Beautiful it was as skill and art could make it, complete in every detail, but there was no water. That is the Russia of today.

Despite appreciating these cultural highlights, the British were not fooled by the privileges Patritsky afforded them. Speaking to the militia men guarding the palace, who were all royalist to their core, they were told that Russia was worse than it had been under the Czar. None of the smart shops were open in *Nevskiy Prospekt* and the boarded, or broken, windows made the city seem deserted. Ten thousand wooden houses were being destroyed to furnish fuel for the remainder of the city because the timber industry in the nearby forests had come to a complete stand still and the coal mines were closed.

During their week in Petrograd, all of them received offers of marriage from Russian women. The most persistent propositions were made by English women married to Russian men, who pleaded with Vining and the others to marry their daughters, so they could escape.

Marriage laws under the Soviet Government were very lax. If a man wished to marry a woman and she agreed, all they needed to do was to write their names in a book. Divorce was even easier, all they did was to strike either of the names off the book and it was done. However, it would be impossible for the British soldiers to choose one deserving case over another and after much soul searching, they declined all the offers.

A week after their arrival, Patritsky confirmed that they would leave the next day. They could not sit still that evening and sang their songs even more heartily than before. After thanking their tireless matron, they departed in two trams the next morning. These took them across the river Neva to the Finland railway station. An hour after leaving Petrograd, they arrived at the rail head at Bielo'ostrov, where Vining hired a couple of carts to carry their baggage to the frontier.

They walked for fifteen minutes and came in sight of the border marked by the Sestro River. A footbridge with wire fencing on both sides spanned the tributary. At each end of the bridge there were stern soldiers with rifles slung over their shoulders. The halfway point of the bridge was considered to be neutral territory. There, in an overcoat stood an official British Representative, who called the men forward by name.

Due to the risk of rabies, dogs were not allowed to be taken into Finland, so there was a "great stew" about Teddy. His owner decided to shoot him rather than give him up, but Vining resolved to make a desperate effort to smuggle him through. They emptied a kit bag into which the reluctant pup was carefully hidden, much to his annoyance. Whilst they carried him across the bridge, he started to complain, so Vining and some of the others closed ranks and sang "Tipperary" at the top of their voices to drown out his fretful yelps.

Walking past the Suomi soldiers in their grey uniform, they still had to pass through the customs house where all their bags were checked for Bolshevik propaganda. Whilst some of the party made a lot of noise and distracted the officials, the bag with Teddy inside was skilfully manoeuvred around the desk and placed with the checked baggage. With a huge sigh of relief, they left the station and released the thankful hound whose stumpy tail went around in circles as he gave everyone a good licking.

At Terrijoki, they were driven in sleighs to a quarantine camp overlooking the Gulf of Finland. This was formerly a collection of wooden summer houses owned by the rich and famous from Petrograd. Vining was told that his group would have to remain in this isolated setting for two weeks to confirm they were clear of disease. However, this was not the whole truth because the prisoner exchange protocol stated that the British were not allowed to proceed until the Russian prisoners had completed their crossing the other way.

This convoluted exchange was described in the House of Commons by the under-secretary of state for foreign affairs on 26th October.[6] The Russian political prisoner, Babushkin and seven other Bolshevik prisoners from England were transferred from SS *Ariadne* to HMS *Dauntless* at Danzig and were held on board the Royal Navy destroyer until the safe arrival of the British prisoners from Petrograd and Baku was confirmed. To complicate matters further, the SS *Brandenburg* was conveying 1,286 Poles and 108 Letts from Vladivostok to Danzig, where the Poles disembarked and the Letts proceeded to Riga on board the SS *Saratev*.[7]

After the British soldiers in Petrograd crossed into Finland, attention switched to the Caspian. On 5th November, the Royal Navy prisoners were released by the Azerbaijan Government and left Baku, followed by the British consul and civilian prisoners two days later. Once the Admiralty received information of their safe arrival at Tiflis, HMS *Dauntless* took Babushkin to Hangö on the Finnish coast on 13th November and the Bolshevik prisoners were then transferred to the custody of the British representative at Helsinki the next day.[8]

★★★

It was bitterly cold in Emerson's camp. He was allowed to take a small boat out to sea and look across the diaphanous water to the town of Kronstadt. His Finnish guide explained that this was a known escape route from Russia and that they were expecting many more to attempt the crossing when the water froze in deepest winter.

Apart from the occasional boat trip, there was little to do in their accommodation. The tedium was more frustrating than their detention in Russia. They were allowed to send telegrams to their families at home and all but two of the group received replies. Emerson sent a telegram to Dallas, who was staying with her cousins in Blackpool when she received his glorious message. As soon as she received the telegram, she planned her journey by train to meet him in London.

Private Lionel Grant wrote a letter to his regiment on 12th November complaining about the delay because "negotiations are suspended". He described how in Baku he had initially escaped when the Royal Navy mechanics were detained at the end of April. He explained that when he was eventually captured in July, he was placed in solitary confinement and then sent to Moscow where he was tried as a spy and despatched to a concentration camp. "Life in the prison was a horror... No one was allowed to lie down from 8am to 9pm, nor to leave the cell unless on working party".[9]

Finally news came through that Babushkin had crossed into Russia and they were released from their quarantine to spend a night in Vyborg,[10] where they rented a room each. The stillness of sleeping alone was a complete shock to Emerson. He also found the beds were too soft and comfortable, so he stayed awake for most of the night.

★★★

On 17th November, they left the frontier region and travelled to Helsinki, where they were met by Major John Scale, the regional head of MI6,[11] who had debriefed them at Terrijoki. Here they said goodbye to their Hungarian cooks and to the civilian prisoners. Vining and the other officers were taken to the British Embassy for lunch with the British officials, whilst Emerson and the soldiers were given a *smorgasbord* in a local hotel.

That same day, David Lloyd George met his Cabinet at 10 Downing Street. The agenda of the meeting[12] was dominated by the issues holding up the resumption of normal relations with Russia. The first item was the Displaced British Subjects; a relatively small number of British residents in the Soviet Union who were unwilling, or unable due to age, infirmity, or poverty to leave the beleaguered country.[13] The second was the outstanding disputes between Poland and Russia, including: General Wrangel's diminishing army in the Ukraine; the final settlement about the Polish frontier; and the question of the Baltic States.

Apart from the prime minister, the key protagonists were the President of the Board of Trade, Sir Robert Horne, Winston Churchill, Lord Curzon and the Lord Chancellor, Baron Birkenhead. To begin with, the two Secretaries of State confirmed that matters were in hand to send 300 British troops to the Baltic. These forces were to be placed at the disposal of the League of Nations for their plebiscite in Vilna district in connection with the Polish Lithuanian dispute.

The main discussion, which lasted for an hour and a half, turned to the resumption of trade relations with Russia. Sir Robert Horne made an impassioned plea based on the critical economic situation, with business confidence very low and unemployment very high in Britain. He suggested that no progress had been made since the San Remo conference in April where Britain, France, Italy and the United States had agreed a resolution in favour of restoring trade. Many people knew the other Allies were already ahead of Britain in this field with the USA leading the way.

Sir Robert reminded the Cabinet that British export goods were still prohibited despite extensive negotiations with the Soviet Foreign Minister, Chicherin, dating back to June. He stated: "I feel strongly the only way we shall fight Bolshevism is by trade. It thrives best in uncivilized conditions. The longer Trotsky keeps the terror up, the longer he keeps up Bolshevism."

Lord Curzon replied: "I do not dispute the proposition of the President of the Board of Trade. My criticism is not devoted to the economic point of view of the agreement, but to the conditions … which we have laid down repeatedly as fundamental…."

The prime minister interposed that Chicherin's stalling simply meant that he wanted to be sure of getting Babushkin. Lord Curzon said that Babushkin had crossed the frontier, but there were "still over 100 British not yet returned. We have that on the authority of Major Wining [sic], a Siberia prisoner who has reached Helsinki. He says there are a considerable number of prisoners in Moscow. And the authority of Mrs Froome [sic] who has been in Petrograd looking after our nationals there who states that there were 75 prisoners in Petrograd."

The prime minister, who was clearly supporting the president of the Board of Trade, reminded the foreign secretary: "When I mentioned the possibility of our going to war to support Poland, a shudder passed through the House and those who were clamouring against Bolshevism immediately shewed the white feather... I have heard predictions about the fall of Soviet Government for the last two years, Denikin, Judenitch, Wrangel have all collapsed but I cannot see any immediate prospect of the collapse of the Soviet Government."

The "very warm"[14] discussion extended into a second day when Winston Churchill made one final, "frantic appeal" against the agreement. The Lord Chancellor had tried to seduce the Cabinet by saying that "a big diamond syndicate is buying £10 million worth of diamonds from Russia, which are at this moment in sacks at Riga. Their object is to prevent the continued depreciation of diamonds due to Bolshevik selling, but they will insist that the money shall be spent in England, provided the agreement goes through".[15] However, Churchill claimed these "diamonds were all stolen, many from the dead bodies of the Russian aristocracy."[16]

Curzon, Churchill and Alfred Milner, Secretary of State for the Colonies, voted against the agreement, but the majority of the Cabinet sided with the prime minister. Churchill asked for it to be "recorded in the Cabinet Minutes that no Cabinet Minister was fettered as regards making anti-Bolshevist speeches – and went down that night to the Oxford Union, where he delivered a violently anti-Bolshevist speech." According to Sir Maurice Hankey, he "was quite pale and did not speak again during the meeting" and declared that he was "unequal to discussing other items on the agenda affecting the Army".[17]

★★★

That same day the Royal Navy picked up all the British hostages in a pair of battle ships. The civilians boarded HMS *Wolsey*, but Vining's group, dressed in all manner of strange garments, were invited on to the Royal Navy's "most modern and powerful cruiser," HMS *Delhi*,[18] the flagship of Vice Admiral Sir James Fergusson. As he led everyone across the gang plank, Vining saluted both the quarter deck and the Admiral, who was waiting with all the ship's officers to greet them with great enthusiasm.

When the cruiser weighed anchor, the Admiral gave Vining a tour of the ship. He was very proud that she was the first of her class to be built with a flared trawler bow, rather than a straight bow. Whilst at sea the immaculate crew demonstrated the impressive armaments on board; firing the voluminous 6-inch guns at dummy targets and an enormous depth charge that broke some of the crockery in the Ward Room.

The prisoners were treated with great sensitivity by the Royal Navy during their passage to Denmark. Vining received a "marconigram" inviting his group to lunch at the British Embassy in Copenhagen. When they docked, the Royal Marines band played "Auld Lang Syne" as they said farewell and took the train to the centre of the capital city. There, they were met by Danish diplomats, who accommodated the whole party in the Hotel Angleterre and invited them to dine at Wievells restaurant after their lunch at the British Embassy. The irony of them staying in the same hotel where Jim O'Grady and Maxim Litvinov negotiated the Anglo-Russian prisoner agreement did not pass them by.

After a short recuperation, they took an overnight steam ship and docked at Harwich at 6a.m. on 22nd November 1920, just over a year after they had been ordered to "remain until the last" in Omsk. On this final leg of his journey, Emerson worked out methodically how far he had travelled since arriving in London from America two years earlier. Philadelphia to London – 3,500 miles; London to Dublin and Glasgow by train – 1,000 miles; Glasgow to Vladivostok by ship – 13,000 miles; Vladivostok to Omsk by train – 2,700 miles; Omsk to Krasnoyarsk by train, sledge and foot – 880 miles; Krasnoyarsk to Helsinki via Moscow by train, truck and foot – 3,260 miles; Helsinki to London via Copenhagen by Royal Navy cruiser – 1,860 miles. The total was over 26,000 miles, equivalent to the circumference of the world around the Equator.

At Harwich, they had to say farewell to Teddy, who went into quarantine. Rooney ran up to a British policeman to shake his hand. An

Army officer tried to steer Vining towards Colchester, but he knew this would add more delay, so he slipped the net and took his party straight to London on the steam train.

Arriving at Liverpool Street Station at about 12.30p.m., they were met by a gaggle of reporters and photographers. They were still wearing khaki, but had very little kit and all appeared lean and extremely pallid. Horrocks and a few others were met by their parents. As Emerson stepped out, he saw Dallas and a broad grin spread across his face from ear to ear. His heart beat faster, but he controlled his emotions in front of the others, so the meeting was stiff and after an embarrassing hug, he pulled away from her.

They were cautious about what they revealed to the journalists because they knew a Victoria Cross winner had been court martialed for communicating with the media without permission after returning from North Russia.[19] They did contradict the narrative of recent "official" visitors to Russia, who had been there as welcome guests of the Bolshevik Government and explained that these apologists were allowed to see only "what they are intended to see and nothing more." They added in chorus "People in England have no idea of the dreadful state of things that exists in Russia."[20]

Vining and Hayes went straight to the War Office where they surprised the officials "who were expecting us by a later train."[21] The others reported to London District headquarters and most were demobilised that afternoon and the remainder were put on long leave. They received three months for service in Russia and were awarded two extra months for being classed as prisoners of war.

Bob Lillington took a train to Edinburgh where he reunited with Ludmilla, but most of the prisoners, including Emerson, recuperated in London. It was very hard for Emerson to adjust to his freedom. Fortunately, Dallas's shared experiences of Vladivostok and her understanding of shell-shock as a nurse meant that their relationship prospered. During these first few days, they visited galleries and museums and each night, they attended the theatre, or the opera.

They found that they shared so much in taste, style and love of culture that it took no time for Emerson to ask for her hand in marriage and Dallas did not hesitate in her affirmative reply. They both felt strongly about a wedding in London, so on 8th December, they married at St Giles' registry with a few friends in attendance.

Within a month, the group had scattered all over the world[22] to Argentina, Australia, Canada, India, Ireland, and the USA. Before they separated, they held a farewell dinner in the Cafe Royal, when they were joined by Hector Boon and other members of the British Railway Mission. Tears of joy were shed that somehow they had all survived their incredible ordeal that put Napoleon's retreat from Moscow in the shade. Every one of them acknowledged the part Leonard Vining played as their inspirational leader for more than twelve months. It was extraordinary that this was not recognised by the government with an appropriate award in the subsequent military honours list. All he received was a short note of thanks from a civil servant.[23]

The British prisoners captured in Krasnoyarsk on board HMS *Delhi* after their release in November 1920. (Courtesy of Angus MacMillan)

After returning to England, the prisoners had dinner in the Cafe Royal and signed the back of Emerson's photograph. The signature of the future Corps Commander, Brian Horrocks, is on the bottom left of the photograph. (Courtesy of Angus MacMillan)

Sergeant Bob Lillington of the Royal Hampshire Regiment with his wife Ludmilla at the wedding of their son after World War II. (Courtesy of George Lillington)

Inter-Allied Railway Agreement

The Inter-Allied Railway Agreement was signed on 9th January 1919, but did not become operational until March. It gave purpose to the US and other Forces, by setting out how the railways were to be improved:

> The general supervision of the railways in the zone in which the Allied forces are now operating shall be exercised by a special Inter-Allied Committee which shall consist of representatives from each Allied power, having military forces in Siberia, including Russia, and the chairman of which shall be a Russian.

> The following boards shall be created, to be placed under the control of the Inter-Allied Committee:

> > A Technical Board consisting of railway experts of the *Nations* having military forces in Siberia, for the purpose of administering the technical and economic management of all railways in the said zone.

> > An Allied Military Transportation Board for the purpose of co-ordinating military transportation under instructions of the proper military authorities.

> > The protection of the railways shall be placed under the Allied military forces. At the head of each railway shall remain a Russian manager or director with the powers conferred by the existing Russian law.

> The Technical Board shall elect a president, to whom shall be entrusted the technical operation of railways. In matters of such technical operation the president may issue instructions to the Russian officials mentioned in the preceding clause. He may appoint assistants and inspectors in the service of the board, chosen from among the nationals of powers having military forces in Siberia, to be attached to the central office of the board, and define their duties. He may assign, if necessary, corps of railway experts to more important stations. In his assigning

railway experts to any of the stations, interests of the respective Allied powers in charge of such stations shall be taken into due consideration. He shall distribute work among the clerical staff of the board, whom he may appoint at his discretion.

The clerical staff of the Inter-Allied Committee shall be appointed by the Chairman of the Committee, who shall have the right of distributing work among such employees as well as of dismissing them.

The present arrangement shall cease to be operative upon the withdrawal of foreign military forces from Siberia, and all the foreign railway experts appointed under the arrangement shall then be recalled forthwith.

The American representative on the Committee was Charles Smith. He came to an arrangement with his Japanese counterpart, Tsuneo Matsudaira, and the other Allies that John Stevens would lead the technical board. Stevens, a renowned American engineer, originally became involved at the invitation of the Provisional Government led by Alexander Kerensky in 1917. He was made official adviser to the Minister of Communications at Petrograd and established the American Russian Railway Service Corps for the purpose of helping to improve the efficiency of the Russian railways.

The members of his team, who came principally from the Northern Pacific and the Great Northern Railways, remained in Japan until March 1918, when they deployed to the Headquarters of the Chinese Eastern Railway at Harbin. The American experts dominated the senior appointments on the Boards, with Colonel George Emerson in charge of the Russian Railway Service Corps, working ostensibly for General Dimitri Horvat, the Russian General Manager of the Railway and member of the Inter-Allied Railway Committee.

DECREE No. 27 of the Military Revolutionary Committee of Irkutsk, dated the 7th February 1920[1]

There have been found by oversearching in many places in the town stores of arms, bombs and machine-gun ribbons, &c., and the mysterious removal in the town of these things (war ammunition), and the scattering of portraits of Koltchak [sic] in the town have been revealed.

From another side, General Voitsekhovski, answering to the proposal to surrender, in one of the points of his "Answer" mentions the handing over of Koltchak [sic] and his staff.

All these data admit that there is in the town a secret organization aiming at the deliverance of one of the grievous criminals against the labour classes – Koltchak [sic] and his party. This insurrection is destined to failure, but nevertheless it may be followed by a number of innocent victims and by an explosion of vengeance of the revolted masses, which would not allow the repetition of such an attempt.

By duty of preventing these useless sacrifices and of defending the town from the atrocities of civil war, and likewise basing themselves on the data of enquiry and on the decrees of the Council of the Commissaires of the Russian Soviet Federal Socialistic Republic having declared Koltchak [sic] and his Government outlaws, the Military Revolutionary Committee of Irkutsk herewith decrees: –

(1) The former Supreme Governor, Admiral Koltchak, [sic]

and

(2) The former President of the Council of Ministers, Pepeliaeff, [sic]

TO BE SHOT

Better is the execution of two criminals a long time worthy of death than hundreds of innocent victims.

(Signed) A. SHIRIAMOFF, *President of the Military Revolutionary Committee.*

A. SNOSKAREFF, *Member of the Military Revolutionary Committee.*

M. LEVENSON, *Member of the Military Revolutionary Committee*

OBORIN, *Manager of Affairs*

Fulfilled at 5a.m. on 7th February, 1920, in the presence of the Extraordinary Committee of Inquiry, Commandant of the town of Irkutsk, and the Commandant of the Prison of the Government of Irkutsk, in testimony of which we append our signatures below.

(Signed) TCHUDNOVSKI, *President of the Extraordinary Committee of Inquiry*

BURSAK, *Commandant of the Town of Irkutsk.*

Draft Agreement between His Majesty's Government and the Soviet Government of Russia for the Exchange of Prisoners

The British Government and the Russian Soviet Government, being desirous of effecting an exchange of combatant and civilian prisoners and others and of facilitating the return of their nationals respectively, have agreed as follows:–

Article 1 – Repatriation of Russian Combatants.

The British Government will repatriate all Russian combatant prisoners in the British Empire or in any territory over which the British Government at present exercises direct authority.

Article 2 – Repatriation of Russian Civilians.

The British Government will repatriate all Russian civilians in the British Empire or in any territory over which the British Government exercises direct authority, whether they are at liberty, interned, or imprisoned, who are willing to return to Russia.

Article 3 – Repatriation of certain specified Russians.

The provisions of Articles 1 and 2 will apply to Russians captured in the Caucasus or the Caspian and in Persia whose names, so far as they can be identified, appear on a list of such persons submitted by the Soviet government to the British Government.

Article 4 – Repatriation of Russians from Archangel.

The British Government undertakes, subject to provisions of Article 8, to secure the delivery to the Soviet Government of the Russian combatant prisoners and civilian officials who are in the custody of the Archangel Government and who have been captured at any time since the landing of the British forces in north Russia. This undertaking will apply to all those whose release is desired by the Soviet Government and who themselves desire to leave the territory under the control of the Archangel Government. This undertaking will include also the persons whose names appear on the list already submitted by the Soviet Government, which is set out in Annex A to this agreement, in so far as they can be identified.

Article 5 – Transport Facilities.

The British Government undertakes to provide transport facilities for all persons who will be repatriated in accordance with the provisions of Articles 1, 2, and 3 of this agreement. The British Government further undertakes to render every possible assistance, so far as sea transport is concerned, if it should become necessary to do so, for the repatriations of Russian nationals who are at present either prisoners in or who are unable to leave Denmark, Holland, Belgium, and Switzerland. This undertaking is subject to the conclusion by the Soviet Government of agreements with Governments of the above-mentioned States. For the repatriation of the persons concerned.

The British Government further undertakes to make representations to the Government of the Baltic States for the granting of the necessary facilities for the safe conveyance of all persons who are to be repatriated in accordance with the provisions of the foregoing Articles.

Article 6 – Proposed International Commission in Berlin.

In the event of the establishment of an International Commission in Berlin for the repatriation of Russian prisoners of war in Germany, the British Government undertakes to support, so far as it lies within its power to do so, the claims of the Soviet Government to be represented on such a Commission and to have equal rights with other members of the Commission. These rights are understood to include communication with the Soviet government by their representative and the making of arrangements with the Commission for the speedy repatriation of those Russian prisoners of war at present in Germany who desire to return to Soviet Russia.

Article 7 – Repatriation of British Prisoners.

The Soviet Government will repatriate all British combatants and civilian prisoners and all other British nationals at present in Soviet Russia who wish to return to any portion of the British Empire.

Article 8 – Repatriation of Russian combatants of the Archangel forces.

In return for the undertaking given by the British Government in Article 4 above to secure the delivery to the Soviet Government of those nationals captured in North Russia, whose names appear in Annex B, the Soviet Government on its part will return to the Archangel Government all officers, doctors, and military clerks of the 5th North Rifle Regiment and the 2nd Battalion of the Artillery Division captured on the Onega who wish to return to North Russia. This undertaking includes those persons whose names appear on the list at Annex B to this Agreement. Arrangements for this exchange of prisoners will be subsequently arrived at by means of direct communications between the military authorities on the spot.

Article 9 – Operation of this Agreement.

Notwithstanding any delay which may take place before the putting into force of the arrangements contemplated in Articles 4, 5, 6, and 8, the British and Soviet Governments respectively undertake to carry out the provisions of Articles 1, 2, 3, and 7 immediately after the signing of the Agreement.

Annex A provides a list of 26 names of Red prisoners including: Ivan Krivenko and Alexey Alexandrowitch Michailov. Annex B lists the names of ten officers of 5th North Rifle Regiment and 2nd Battalion of Artillery Division, including Colonel Mikheieff and the Regimental Priest Sibirtseff.

The Cabinet

Negotiations with M. Krassin

Memorandum by the Secretary of State for War

In accordance with conclusion 3 (paragraph ii *b*) of a Conference of Ministers held on 28th May, I circulate herewith a statement of the particular points on which the War Office desires a settlement to be reached with the Soviet Government.

W. S. C.

The War Office

11*th June,* 1920.

The Army Council consider that the following demands should be made of the Soviet Government.

Some of these demands are in the nature of enquiries for information, the onus for proving the reliability of which must rest with the Soviet Government itself; others are of such a nature that the Allied Powers should demand to supervise their execution themselves.

The Army Council are of opinion that the latter demands, *i.e.,* those the carrying out of which the Allied Powers can actually supervise, are of such an important nature that failure to comply should be made the reason for breaking off all negotiations with M. Krassin, either of a trading or any other nature. These demands are put first in the subjoined list under Heading A, and are followed by the demands which only the Soviet Government can answer, under Heading B.

A – *Demands, the carrying out of which the Allied Powers must supervise themselves.*

(i) The disarming of the Soviet Labour Armies, and a guarantee that they should only be used for *bona fide* labour purposes; and a further guarantee that they should cease to be controlled by, or to have any connection with, the Soviet Commissariat for War.

(ii) Withdrawal of Bolshevik troops form the Tashkent–Merv–Askabad area, and the disbandment of the army reported to be forming near Orenburg.

(iii) The dispersal of Bolshevik concentrations which are reported on the Karelian Isthmus, and on various points opposite the Polish front.

(iv) Withdrawal of troops from the Caucasus

(v) The reduction of the Soviet army to a peace footing to be fixed by the Allies.

Note – The best way of satisfying ourselves that the above demands have been carried out appears to be the dispatch of a competent Inter-Allied Commission to Soviet Russia, who would be allowed to visit all the territories concerned, and ensure that the Allied Demands had been faithfully executed.

B – *Demands (or enquiries) which the Soviet Government should be required to answer.*

(i) If the Soviet Government professes ignorance of the intentions of their local authorities (*i.e.*, the Revolutionary Committee who executed Admiral Koltehak at Irkutsk in February, 1920, the Naval Commander at Enzeli who demanded the handing over of the Volunteer Fleet, &c.), what guarantees can they give that, in future, their subordinate commanders will not again exceed their instructions?

(ii) Will the Soviet guarantee to stop anti-British propaganda in Afghanistan?

(iii) How far does the Soviet Government control the actions of the new "Far Eastern Republic" which it is reported has been set up at Verkhne-Udinsk? Is this Republic absolutely independent of the Soviet Government, and does the Soviet Government agree to recognize this independence, and not interfere with any military agreements between the said Republic and any other foreign power or powers?

(iv) If Captain Frecheville and Lieutenant Couche have not been tortured and murdered as reported, where are they?

(v) All British prisoners of war captured in Siberia and elsewhere are to be returned forthwith alive and well; what steps is the Soviet Government taking to carry this out?

(vi) Will the Soviet Government admit their liability for compensation for illness caused to British subjects by ill-treatment at the hands of the Bolsheviks?

Note – The immediate acceptance of B (v.) should be the *sine quâ non* of further negotiations.

Philadelphian Home
from Reds' Captivity

Emerson A MacMillan, Electrical Engineer, Was Prisoner in Siberia, Moscow and Petrograd. Brings Back a Canadian Bride. By Raymond G Carroll, *Special Telegram to Public Ledger*

New York, Jan 29 – After six months of open arrest in the Siberian cities of Krasnoyarsk, Omsk and Irkutsk, three months of close confinement in Moscow and two weeks of open arrest in Petrograd, Emerson A MacMillan, an electrical engineer from Philadelphia, arrived today on the steamship Cedric.

Mr MacMillan, hardy, young and possessed of a discerning mind, saw Soviet Russia with different eyes than HG Wells, Mrs Clara Sheridan and others who have written somewhat optimistically from observations based upon a setting staged by Lenin, Trotsky and company, the dictators of northern Europe and Asia.

"Before falling into the hands of the Reds towards the close of 1919," said Mr MacMillan, "I was nine months in Siberia attached to the Inter Allied Economic Mission. In May 1918, I had enlisted from Philadelphia in the Royal British Engineers. From March 1919 on until our capture by the Reds I was in Russia both as an engineer and in an executive capacity for the mission".

Lived a Year Among Russians

Thus in Mr Macmillan we have a man who lived for more than a year in actual contact with the Russian people. He speaks their language, and what he knows of conditions he learned first-hand. His was no sight-seeing tour. He took part in Admiral Kolchak's ill-fated retreat, and after his capture along with others of the mission he was thrown among both the peasants and townsfolk who are forced to put up with the present regime of tyrants and the human fragments of the old order still languishing in Russian prisons. In Moscow Mr MacMillan was imprisoned in the Ivanovsky monastery, which has been converted into a detention jail for political prisoners.

"True they started well enough by sending us to the baths," he said, "but a bath attendant robbed one of our party of 30,000 roubles. Officially we had previously been relieved of half of our money. While the rules of the prison were exceedingly strict we were allowed to walk and talk with the other prisoners in the courtyard during the daytime. It was an extraordinary collection of individuals. There were princes and barons, generals and governors, members of the Imperial Duma and lord mayors, professors and adventurers from almost every country on the globe. There were a number of former industrial magnates and some of the most prominent persons in Russia. Most of them spoke at least two languages, and many of them four and five. Because of their prominence the Bolsheviks had hesitated to kill them.

Detained Without Trials

"The majority of the prisoners I talked with had been in jail ever since the advent of the Lenin-Trotsky government. Few of them had had trials. They were simply indefinitely detained. One man introduced himself as Count Kotzebue, and wanted to know what had become of the czar. Many Russians still believe that Nicholas is sat in England. I was also interested in the case of an old peasant woman who was among the nobility serving a two year sentence for having usurped the Soviet authority of trying to sell three cabbages. The shoemaker who repaired the prisoners' boots at one time had been one of the wealthiest shoe manufacturers in Russia.

"There was a small library operated in connection with the prison. On making an inquiry in Russian for a certain book I was pleased to be answered in English. The librarian proved to be Prince Gorchakov. A Romanian general proved to be an excellent companion, also Count Seichenine, who had been a prisoner more than five years. He was held as a reprisal prisoner to be shot if certain Reds in Hungary were shot. The count was finally taken out and he did not return. When we read in a newspaper that certain Bolshevists in Hungary had been executed the mystery surrounding the non-return of the count was solved.

Food Poor and Scarce

"Food was exceedingly poor and scarce. Some days there was nothing for us. When we got it the issue was three-quarters of a pound of sour black bread a day, a thin fish soup, a bowl of weak grain porridge and a spoonful of sugar."

Mr MacMillan told of later being sent to another prison-monastery, where there was a more plebeian crowd and "from which we could see the golden domes of many of Moscow's 1000 churches." For exercise the prisoners were allowed to walk through a cemetery. He told of meeting an American aviator, who had been captured when serving as a soldier of fortune with the Polish army.

"One afternoon late in October", Mr MacMillan said "came orders transferring some of us to Petrograd. We were marched through the streets under guard, placed in freight cars and for two days consumed in the trip there was no food issued."

Attended Opera Under Guard

Mr MacMillan says that he attended the Soviet opera in Petrograd under guard. He was quartered in a concentration centre of the city set aside for evacuating foreigners. Small parties of prisoners were allowed to visit all of the museums, galleries, cathedrals, palaces and various places of interest. He availed himself of that opportunity. He told of miles of shops all shuttered up and declared it to be a most ghastly sight. The happiest day of his life, he says, was the day that word came for departure to Finland, where in the city of Helsingfors he was taken aboard a British battleship. He arrived in England early last month.

Not exactly the "happiest day in his life" for shortly after his arrival in London he was married to Miss Dallas K Ireland, a Canadian girl, who also had been attached to the Inter Allied Mission. The romance began a decade ago in St Catherine, Ontario where the couple met for the first time. Mr MacMillan accidently learned Miss Ireland was in the British capital, although he had not seen her in Russia. She had returned from the Far East through the Suez Canal, thus escaping the trip across Russia, which her husband says is not desirable at this time for any one. And he speaks from the book of experience.

Endnotes

Chapter 1

1   Dallas Katherine Ireland was born on 1st February 1892 on the US-Canadian border at Sault Sainte Marie and died on 9th August 1984, in Geneva, Switzerland. She was the daughter of William and Margaret Ann Ireland; her father was the headmaster of Niagara High School and then became a schools inspector. Dallas graduated in 1914 from University of Toronto University College, Class of IT4 and started nursing training in 1915. She qualified as American Red Cross Nurse Number 34286 on 24th December 1918.

2   The Inns of Court Officers Training Corps was established in 1909 as part of the Territorial Force to build the character of officer cadets. By the time Emerson reported for duty, the Corps had commissioned over 10,000 officers. Further details can be found in *The Inns of Court Officers Training Corps During The Great War*, by Lieutenant Colonel Francis Errington.

3   The Halifax Explosion occurred on 6th December 1917 when SS *Imo* struck SS *Mont Blanc* in the Narrows. The French cargo ship was laden with high explosives and their detonation killed approximately 2,000 people in the Richmond district, with a further 9,000 casualties. The blast was the largest man-made explosion before the development of nuclear weapons.

4   Berkhamsted in Hertfordshire lies on the River Bulbourne, a 7-mile chalk river that runs south-east towards Hemel Hempstead.

5   The Chiltern Hills cover parts of Bedfordshire, Buckinghamshire, Hertfordshire and Oxfordshire. They stretch 46 miles from south-west to north-east and are 11 miles across at their widest. The boundary in the north-west is marked by a chalk escarpment that coincides with the southern extent of the ice sheet that covered much of Britain 10,000 years ago.

6   The Women's Army Auxiliary Corps was formally instituted on 7th July 1917 and was renamed Queen Mary's Army Auxiliary Corps on 9th April 1918.

7   The *Daily Express* was owned by Lord Beaverbrook, who built it into the most successful mass-newspaper in the world. He strongly opposed the Allied intervention in Russia.

Chapter 2

1   Leonard Vining served in the Indian Army with the 25th Oudh and Rohilkhand Railway Battalion. In 1916, he was appointed as a Staff Transport Officer in the Royal Engineers.

2   For his Siberia assignment, Emerson was appointed Company Quartermaster Sergeant; his regimental number was WR210817.

3   The R-34 completed the first east to west crossing two weeks after John Alcock and Arthur Whitten Brown achieved the first non-stop transatlantic flight in their Vickers Vimy from Newfoundland to Galway. The R-34 was piloted by George Herbert Scott, who flew with a Royal Air Force crew and paying passengers from Scotland in four and a half days. The return journey on 10th July took 75 hours to complete.

4   During World War I, the requisitioning of fodder and cotton below market prices and the forcible recruitment of about 500,000 peasants into the Labour and Camel Transport Corps caused much discontent. Economic hardships after the war gave Egyptian nationalists an opportunity to press the United Kingdom for independence. They were boosted by US President Woodrow Wilson's appeals for self-determination for all nations. On 13th November 1918, thereafter celebrated in Egypt as Yawm al Jihad (Day of Struggle), the nationalists formed a delegation named Al Wafd al Misri, headed by Saad Zaghlul to negotiate independence, but the British refused to allow the Wafd to proceed to London. On 8th March, Zaghlul and three other members of the Wafd were arrested and deported to Malta, an action that sparked the popular uprising. This involved a demonstration with more than 10,000 teachers, students, workers, lawyers, and government employees marching from Al Azhar to Abdin Palace where they were joined by thousands more, who ignored British roadblocks and bans. Soon, similar demonstrations broke out in Alexandria, and other towns and General Allenby was summoned as the Special High Commissioner.

5   Allenby arrived in Egypt on 25th March in HMS *Carlisle*. This was a light cruiser laid down at Govan in April 1916 under an Emergency War Programme. The ship was launched on 9th July 1918 and after ferrying Allenby to Egypt, it went on to Vladivostok, where it evacuated the Royal Marine contingent that fought with the White Army. During World War II, it was converted to an anti-aircraft cruiser and earned battle honours in Norway 1940, Greece and Crete 1941, Libya, Sirte and Malta 1941–42, Sicily and the Aegean 1943.

6   Emerson's view of Mocha on the Yemen coast was not shared by other travellers. The state of the port city, which was the major market place for coffee, was

described before World War I by the German photographer, Hermann Burchardt as: "one of the most godforsaken little places in Asia. It looks like a city entirely destroyed by earthquakes."

7   At 82 miles in length and 31 miles wide, Socotra is described as "the most alien looking place on earth." The island lies 150 miles east of the Horn of Africa and 240 miles south of the Arabian Peninsula. The isolated island is home to a high number of endemic species which led to its recognition by the United Nations Educational, Scientific and Cultural Organization as a world natural heritage site in July 2008.

8   SMS *Wolf* carried six 1.5cm guns, three 5.2cm guns, four torpedo tubes and over 450 mines. She boasted a fake funnel, masts and sides for deception purposes. She made the longest voyage of a German warship in World War I between November 1916 and February 1918. For his success in capturing prisoners and prizes, her captain was awarded the *Pour le Mérite*.

9   The *Empress of Russia* had a distinguished record as an armed merchant cruiser and troopship during World War I. Her guns were brought to bear in a classic case of gunboat diplomacy to rescue diplomats in Yemen. In April 1917 she brought 2,000 members of the Chinese Labour Corps across the Pacific, some of whom were returning to China. After transporting American troops in the final year of the war, she left Liverpool on 12th January 1919 with about 30 volunteers for the Siberian campaign, including Rex Carthew of the Bedfordshire Regiment and Phelps Hodges of the Royal Artillery, who later earned fame for his escape across the Gobi Desert.

10 Emerson and Vining used the anglicised versions of place names. Tsingtao (Qingdao) is the main port in Kiao-Chou Bay (Jiaozhou Bay), on the coast of Shandong Province, halfway between Shanghai and Beijing. The siege of Tsingtao between 17th October and 7th November 1914 was the first action between Japan and Germany in World War I. The Japanese forces were supported by Royal Navy ships and 1,500 soldiers from the British Army, including 2nd Battalion South Wales Borderers. British casualties included 12 killed and 53 wounded.

11 Pouchow, now named Pukou, is one of 11 districts of Nanjing City astride the Yangtze River. Tientsin is now Tianjin.

12 Manchuria was an important region due to its rich natural resources. In 1858 and 1860, a weakening Qing Empire was forced to cede Manchuria north of the Amur and east of the Ussuri River to the Czar. As a result, Manchuria was divided into a Russian half known as Outer Manchuria, and a remaining Chinese half known as Inner Manchuria. Inner Manchuria also came under strong Russian influence with the building of the Chinese Eastern Railway through Harbin to Vladivostok. However, most of the southern branch was transferred to Japan in 1905 and became the South Manchurian Railway.

13 At the battle of Mukden (now named Shenyang) in 1905, a Russian Army of 340,000 was defeated decisively by the Imperial Japanese Army with only 270,000

troops. It was the largest battle in the world before World War I and its result shifted Russian foreign policy towards the Balkans.

Chapter 3

1 Robert Bruce Lockhart, *Memoirs of a British Agent*, p. 263. From February to April 1918, Bruce Lockhart argued against Allied military intervention in Russia because "My instinct told me that, weak as the Bolsheviks were, the demoralised forces of the anti-Bolsheviks in Russia were still weaker."

2 The Anglo-Japanese deployment was based on a treaty signed on 30th January 1902, which brought Japan into World War I on the side of the Allies. It was also useful to Japan during the Russo-Japanese war of 1904–05 for preventing France from assisting Russia.

3 The Czech Legion was formed with permission from the Provisional "Kerensky" Government in 1917 by Professor Thomas Masaryk, President of the Czechoslovak National Council from the Bohemians, Moravians and Slovaks scattered through the prisoner of war camps in Russia. They fought against the Germans on the Eastern Front and an agreement after the Treaty of Brest-Litovsk allowed for them to travel across Siberia to the port of Vladivostok from where, in theory, the Allies were to provide transport to France. On 29th June 1918, the Czechs took control of the Trans-Siberian Railway from Vladivostok to Penza, 300 miles from Moscow and the next day, France formally recognised the Czechoslovak Republic.

4 Japan issued a proclamation from Tokyo on 3rd August to the Russian people justifying its deployment of troops. The Japanese commander-in-chief was General Otani.

5 From *The Official Names of the Battles fought by the Military forces of the British Empire during the Great War 1914–1919*. This lists Ussuri Operations from 8th to 28th August 1918 and Ufa Operations from October 1918 to June 1919, but only one battle, Dukhovskaya.

6 WO 32/5676 1919 retrieved from The National Archives on 14 October 2017.

7 This is recorded in the chronology of the *Report on the Work of the British Military mission to Siberia*, 5th September 1918–27th December 1919, by Major General Knox to the Director of Military Operations in the War Office, dated 10th December 1919 (National Archives).

8 The 27th Infantry Regiment deployed from the Philippines.

9 The All-Russian Government, formed on 5th September 1918, was the result of a merger of three governments formed in June and July at Samara, Omsk and Vladivostok. A Directorate of Five was appointed to lead the government. This comprised one representative from the Social Revolutionary party, one cadet, two non-partisans and one populist. It claimed support from all sections of the population except the Bolsheviks and Monarchists.

10 The French mission spread the rumour that General Knox laid the ground work for the coup during his visit to Omsk. However, according to Jonathan Smele on p. 94 of *Civil War in Siberia: The Anti-Bolshevik Government of Admiral Kolchak 1918–1920*, the French "provide no firm evidence for their accusations." In his memoir *America's Siberian Adventure*, Major General William Graves cited a statement by Winston Churchill in the House of Commons as evidence that the British put Kolchak in power: "The British Government had called it into being, for our own aid, at a time when necessity demanded it."

11 Neilson was born in Glasgow and went to school at Uppingham. He was commissioned from Sandhurst in 1904 and joined his Regiment in India where he served for eight years before he deployed to Russia as an interpreter in the British Mission early in World War I. He was twice mentioned in dispatches and awarded the DSO in 1917. In the 1920 Siberian honours he was appointed CBE and also held the Russian orders of St Vladimir, St Stanislaus and St Anne. He left the Army soon after returning from Russia and died on 30th December 1962.

12 At the same time that the Czech Legion was created in 1918, Major Walerian Czuma began to form a Polish unit in Samara from prisoners of war and Polish settlers in Russia. It was named the Polish 5th Siberian Rifle Division.

13 The balance of forces comprised 24,130 bayonets, 43,505 sabres, 335 machine guns and 79 artillery pieces for the Red Army and facing them, General Gajda mustered 40,297 bayonets, 27,605 sabres, 687 machine guns and 112 artillery pieces.

14 The commander, James Wolfe Murray, was awarded the Distinguished Service Order on 18th April 1919 for bringing HMS *Suffolk's* 12-pounder guns rapidly into action and displaying an excellent example of coolness and bravery under fire during the battles in the Ussuri District, but the recoil cylinders froze in the winter, so they played little part in the Perm offensive.

15 A knout is a multiple whip which was used to punish criminals in Russia.

16 Vladimir Zenzinov, Pyotr Vasilyevich Vologodsky, General Boldyrev and Kadet Vladimir Vinogradov.

17 The Territorial Force was the volunteer reserve component of the British Army from 1908 to 1920, when it was renamed the Territorial Army. It is now known as the Army Reserve.

18 Bicycle troops were fashionable at the turn of the 19th century. They were seen as less expensive and more available than cavalry and given communication roles as messengers and scouts in the Boer War. Many countries formed cyclist units, including Imperial Russia where they were used with outrigger wheels, to mount patrols along the Siberian Railway during the war with Japan. At the start of World War I, British territorial cyclist companies were expanded into battalions, but as the mud of trench warfare diminished their utility, some of these, including 1st/9th Hampshire's, were re-designated as dismounted infantry.

19 The 1st/9th (Cyclist) Battalion, The Hampshire Regiment was created at Southampton in 1911 and mobilised on the day Britain declared War. Soldiers from Hampshire were renowned as tough, stubborn fighters with a natural eye for the

country and very good shots. The county produced a higher percentage of men than any other and earned 56 battle honours in France and Belgium and another 34 on other fronts. After a testing stint on coastal defence work, the battalion was converted to an A1 infantry role in 1915 and brought up to strength by its sister battalions, the 2nd/9th and 3rd/9th, before deploying to India in 1916.

20 Major General Elmsley was awarded the DSO for his command of the Royal Dragoon Guards on the Western Front and became an experienced brigade commander. Since his Siberian force was controlled by directives from London, he earned the distinction of being the first Canadian to command a British operational force. The Canadian contingent included: 255 officers; 3931 other ranks; 289 horses; and 118 Lewis machine guns. Twenty members of the brigade died in theatre including 19 from illness and accidents and one suicide.

21 This nickname derived from the Bengal tiger on the soldiers cap badges presented by King George IV to the 67th South Hampshire Regiment for 21 years of service in India between 1805 and 1826. The other half of the regiment was the 37th North Hampshire's, which was proud to be one of the six "Minden" regiments.

22 From an extract of a letter to his mother in West Meon, published in *The Hampshire Regimental Journal* of April 1919, pp. 86–87.

23 Hampshire Regiment Archives, *An Address to the Society of Freelances*, Brighton 13th January 1959 by A. A. Jupe.

24 The 1911 Census shows Leo Steveni at Rugby school as a 17-year-old visitor from Russia. The school record reveals that his father Oscar was a Timber Importer in St Petersburg. In 1915, he joined Major John Scale in the British Military Mission attached to the Russian War Office in Petrograd, exchanging intelligence. Returning to England after the revolution, he was supplied with a War Office Cipher and on 16th April 1918, ordered to travel via New York and San Francisco to Siberia. He was given secret orders by Colonel Arthur French to contact leading Russian elements opposing the Bolshevik regime and to report "their potentials as possible rallying points, in the event of an Allied intervention in the Far East". He spent nearly two years in railway carriage number 2013 conducting intelligence operations for the British Mission. For his work in Russia, he was awarded the OBE, MC, Order of St Stanislas (3rd and 3nd Class), Order of St Anne and *Ordre de L'Etoile Noir*. He later lived with his wife, Helen, at 55 Drayton Gardens, London SW10. On p. 282 of *Anglo-Soviet Relations 1917–1921, Volume II*, he is described by Richard Ullman as "a thorough going reactionary, who desired a complete restoration of the Czarist regime."

25 Peter Fleming, *The Fate of Admiral Kolchak*, p. 115.

26 Carthew was born in Carlisle on 8th March 1892 and was working in Canada as a real estate agent at the start of the war. He immediately volunteered to join the British Army and was commissioned in December 1914. He was awarded the Military Cross for conspicuous gallantry as a company commander with 6th Battalion, the Bedfordshire Regiment during the battle of Arras in April 1917. He deployed to Siberia with Phelps Hodges and 30 others on the *Empress of Russia* in

January 1919. Further details are available on The Bedfordshire Regiment in the Great War website: http://www.bedfordregiment.org.uk/.

27 Report on the Work of the British Military Mission to Siberia 1918–19, National Archives WO 32/5707.

28 Russian Island, lying across the Vladivostok bay, was the location of a barracks built for a Russian division during the war. British instructors, including a platoon of the Hampshire Regiment, assisted General Constantine Sakharov, with the first intake of 500 officers and NCOs graduating on 15th February 1919.

29 Some British trainers from Vladivostok did join an "expedition" against Bolsheviks on 15th April 1919. However, after a surprise night landing by four companies and a machine gun detachment, the enemy "offered little opposition and dispersed into the hills."

30 Jameson just managed to escape with his crews before the Bolsheviks captured Perm in June. He returned to Vladivostok on 8th August and departed from Russia on HMS *Carlisle*. For his inspiring leadership on the River Kama, Jameson was appointed a Companion of the Distinguished Service Order. The two commanders of the boats were both awarded the Distinguished Service Cross and eight petty officers and ratings were honoured with the Naval Military Service Medal, or the Distinguished Service Medal (*London Gazette*, 5th and 8th March 1920).

31 T. H. Jameson, *Expedition To Siberia 1919*, p. 35. For a full list of Russian medals awarded to British service personnel in Russia, see Ray Brough's *White Russian Awards to British and Commonwealth Servicemen During the Allied Intervention in Russia 1918–1920*. The consul's political duplicity was not the only example of the British Government treating the Siberian intervention in a different way to the North and South Russian campaigns.

Chapter 4

1 The Baldwin Locomotive Works was a successful builder of steam locomotives and other railway equipment in Philadelphia when Emerson lived there in 1918.

2 The 259th Battalion was in disgrace from their deployment on 22nd December 1918, in Victoria when two companies refused to board the SS *Teesta*. However, they were marched up the gang plank at the point of a bayonet, and once on board, ten riflemen were arrested and charged with mutiny. Nine were found guilty at their court martial with their sentences ranging from 28 days to three years penal servitude for Arthur Roy. For further details, see J. E. Skuce's *CSEF Canada's Soldiers in Siberia 1918–1919*.

3 Ian Moffat, Forgotten Battlefields: Canadians in Siberia 1918–1919, *Canadian Military Journal*, Autumn 2007, http://www.journal.forces.gc.ca/vo8/no3/moffat-eng.asp#n62

4 *The Times* of 27 May 1919 reports: "Monsieur Pichon the French Minister for Foreign Affairs revealed to the Chamber of Deputies the significant contingents

of foreign troops assisting Admiral Kolchak was 118,000 effective soldiers, on 26th March 1919. These were made up as follows: Czechoslovaks 55,000; Poles 12,000; Serbians 4,000; Romanians 4,000; Italians 2,000; British 1,600; French 760; Japanese 28,000 (later increased to 75,000); Americans 7,500; Canadians 4,000.

5 According to David Foglesong in *American's Secret War Against Bolshevism*, the American representative in Siberia, Consul General Ernest Lloyd Harris, supported Kolchak because he promised to uphold the financial commitments agreed to by previous non-Bolshevik governments. Whilst Graves was maintaining a policy of impartiality and non-interference, Harris was making every effort to persuade Washington to recognise the Kolchak government as the official government of Russia.

6 Eichelberger subsequently became a legendary Army commander in the Pacific during WWII. In Siberia, he was awarded the Distinguished Service Cross for his bravery in the field; negotiating the release of American soldiers held hostage and personally providing covering fire for patrols under attack.

7 General Graves wrote his book, *America's Siberian Adventure 1918–1920*, to set the record straight about the orders under which American troops served in Siberia. According to this memoir, Eichelberger informed him about the front line deceit on 22nd August 1919.

8 The Royal Garrison Artillery was formed from fortress-based regiments located on British coasts at the end of the 19th century. From small beginnings, it grew into a very large component of the British Forces, armed with heavy calibre guns and howitzers with immense destructive power, positioned some way behind the front line. Their officers' uniforms were the same as the Royal Field Artillery except that they wore trousers rather than breeches.

9 Peacock was awarded an MBE for repelling the attacks on the train and successfully bringing it to Omsk.

10 Further details of the Inter Allied Agreement are in Appendix 1.

11 President Wilson awarded 20 Distinguished Service Crosses to soldiers serving in Siberia for actions of extraordinary heroism between the end of May and 13th July 1919.

12 Sergeant Robbins, Private Tommie and Lieutenant Kendall, who eventually retired as a US Army Lieutenant General, were all awarded the Distinguished Service Cross for resisting this unwarranted attack and for capturing a force with vastly superior armament.

13 In his memoir, General Graves deals with several polemical issues including the relationship with the State Department and the American Red Cross. Despite his initial reservations, Graves considered his nurses "to be a great help, and I was very glad to have them as they were very self-reliant, and gave me no trouble by requests for better conditions, which I would have been glad to have given them, if I could."

14 The SS *Nippon Maru* was the first ship built for the Toyo Kisen Kabushiki Kaisha Oriental Steamship Company in Yokohama by Sir James Laing in Sunderland.

At 6178 tons, she started the service from Yokohama to San Francisco in 1899, but was adapted for military purposes in 1904 during the war between Japan and Russia.

15 See Anthony Cross, *Forgotten British Places in Petrograd/Leningrad*, pp. 135–147. After her return to England, Lady Muriel Paget drew attention to the desperate appeals for assistance being made by women such as Maria Bochkareva, who founded the Russian Women's Battalion of Death. She raised more funds and returned to help in Russia again, taking with her Dr Sarah O'Flynn, a former suffragette with an outstanding war record, who was one of the first women doctors to serve in the Royal Army Medical Corps and saved the lives of many soldiers wounded at Gallipoli.

16 Florence Farmborough, *Nurse at The Russian Front: A Diary 1914–18,* p. 390.

17 *Feldshers* in Russia are assistant physicians, who provide primary and surgical care in rural areas. *Sanitars* are medical orderlies.

18 The American Red Cross operated in Siberia for 20 months with more than 500 American doctors, nurses and volunteers serving their cause. On the credit side, they administered a far-reaching program of military and civilian relief and established, or aided, dozens of hospitals, clinics and dispensaries. They also offered nursing education classes to Russian women, established orphanages and created employment opportunities on their farms and in their offices.

19 For more on this issue, see Jennifer Polk, *Constructive Efforts: The American Red Cross and YMCA in Revolutionary and Civil War Russia, 1917–24.* Polk concludes that the American Red Cross "nullified much of its goal by so generously supplying medicine and clothing to the Kolchak troops without trying to get further and give the helping hand to those further along the line who, as human beings, suffered just as much from a sword or bullet wound, or the raging fever of typhus."

20 Diary entries for 29th September and 9th October, Frederick Lee Barnum Papers 1919–1920, Columbia University Rare Book and Manuscript Library.

21 Letter dated 21st August 1919, Box 1, Bessie Eddy Lyon Collection, Hoover Institution Archives, Palo Alto, California.

22 Captain O'Driscoll Report dated 23rd December 1919 within file WO 32/5707, retrieved from the National Archives, Kew.

Chapter 5

1 HMS *Kent* arrived on 3rd January 1919 and took over from the first Royal Navy ship on station in Vladivostok during the British Campaign, HMS *Suffolk*. Both ships were Monmouth Class armoured cruisers distinguished by three "tremendous" funnels.

2 Brigadier Archibald Jack was a 45-year-old New Zealander, educated at Otago Boys' High School, who served with the 9th Battalion New Zealand Regiment in the Second Boer War and then worked for the railways in South Africa, China and Argentina. In 1916, he sailed to England in the SS *Drina* with his wife Gertrude and their 3-year-old son, but the ship was torpedoed off Milford Haven. He was

given a temporary commission as a Lieutenant Colonel in the Royal Engineers and posted first to Romania and then to the Caucasus. In April 1918, he was appointed to command the British Railway Mission in Vladivostok and take the lead British role in the Inter-Allied Railway Agreement.

3 The Yenisei is in fact the fifth longest river in the world. At about 5,500km, it is slightly shorter but has 50% more flow than the Mississippi–Missouri. It rises in two major headstreams: the Lesser Yenisei rises in Mongolia and is joined on its way by the *Bolshoi* Yenisei. Its river system, which includes Lake Baikal, holds more water than any other in the world.

4 The Trans-Siberian Railway crosses 11 time zones.

5 Germany signed the Treaty of Versailles on 28th June. The official diary of the British Military Mission failed to mention this important event, merely recording that Private Lucas was suffering from venereal and the US hospital was unwilling to help. Emerson was also in Omsk when Austria signed the Treaty of Saint-Germain-en-Laye on 10th September.

6 The British Military Mission was made up of officers, who had volunteered for service in Russia earlier in the year. Many of them had considerable war experience. They were supposed to relieve the Middlesex and Hampshire Regiments in May and allow them to return to England. However, the Mission was reliant on volunteers from the infantry battalions to bolster numbers and to provide their security.

7 Fifty-five Canadians travelled to Omsk under the command of Lieutenant Colonel Thomas Morrisey, who had been awarded the DSO in the 13th Canadian Infantry Battalion on the Western Front in 1916.

8 According to Lieutenant Colonel Edward Steel, the Omsk rouble was down to 400 to the pound by 5th September.

9 Imperial War Museum Oral History 9145 Reel 5, Charles Ernest Shobbrock.

10 Victor Rudolph Ullman was born in Riga in 1886, joined the Canadian infantry in 1915 and arrived on the Western Front in July 1916. On 15th September, he received two gunshot wounds and was buried by the explosion of a shell, but recovered in hospital in England. The following year, he was gassed at Fresnoy in May and suffered three days of frothing and expectoration. After recovering, he returned to the Front Line and was shot in his left leg in August 1918, whilst leading an attack for which he was awarded the Military Cross. After the Armistice, he was seconded to the British Military Mission in Siberia where he worked in the Anglo-Russian Brigade until its dissolution. In October 1919, he contracted typhus in Chita, but recovered fully and returned to Canada where he lived until 1957.

11 Brian Horrocks, *A Full Life*, p. 46.

12 Francis McCullagh, *A Prisoner of the Reds*, p. 324.

13 The Royal Mint's major preoccupation until WWI was maintaining the circulation of gold as a global currency. Colonel Sir Robert Arthur Johnson KCVO KBE remained as Deputy Master until his death in 1938.

14 Report on the Work of the British Military Mission to Siberia 1918–19, National Archives WO 32/5707.

15 WO 95/5433 British Military Mission Diary entry for 13th July 1919.

16 For his work commanding the British Railway Mission, Jack was awarded the CMG in March 1919, the CBE in June 1919 and the CB in January 1920. He led a charmed life and after the War miraculously survived being shot through the head in Havana and being caught in the Sevenoaks railway disaster of 1927, before he died in February 1939.

17 The American YMCA had operated in Omsk throughout the civil war. According to Jennifer Polk, Russian military commanders such as Generals Gajda, Golitzine and Rozanov sought its assistance after they saw what it was doing for the Czech Legion. "Not all requests were filled, but over the winter and spring, the YMCA extended services and provided inexpensive or complimentary goods and supplies to members of the Russian armed forces. The association's reach extended from Perm and Ekaterinburg to Vladivostok."

18 From Ray Brough's Roll of Honour, the seven Hampshire soldiers who died in Siberia were: Private F. S. Leonard Vladivostok, 5th February 1919; Private C. Davies Vladivostok, 16th March 1919; Private R. Ellis Vladivostok, 17th March 1919; Sergeant C. A. Lawes, 28th April 1919; Private L. R. Burt Ekaterinburg, 29th May 1919; Private A. May Ekaterinburg, 19th June 1919; Private W. H. Taylor Omsk, 30th July 1919.

19 War Diary entry 2nd August of 355697 Cyclist Stanley Green of 12 Platoon C Company. Russia began World War I with the largest gold reserve in the world, amounting to 1,695,000,000 roubles. Considerable amounts were used to pay foreign debts and order war matériel. By the time of the Bolshevik revolution, this had reduced to 1,101,690,000, of which 120,799,000 was paid to the Central Powers. The majority of the Bolshevik gold was kept in Kazan, but during the civil war, the bullion passed via Ufa and Chelyabinsk in what Jonathan Smele describes as "possibly the largest heist in history" (Footnote 215 on p. 399 of *Civil War in Siberia*). Kolchak began transporting bullion to the state bank at Vladivostok in May 1919, where it was either sold for foreign currency or shipped to Japan, China and the USA as security for loans.

20 Lieutenant Colonel Edward Anthony Steel DSO RHA and RFA died on Friday 17th October of influenza, complicated by the severe chest wounds he had suffered at the Somme in 1916. He was the only British officer to die in Omsk during the British campaign in Siberia and was buried with full military honour in the Cossack cemetery. His coffin was borne by three Russian officers and three British captains in the Royal Field Artillery (Phelps Hodges MC, Cecil Cameron DSO CBE and George Faber OBE MC). His memoir was published posthumously by his grieving father, with the extract about "the land of tomorrow" on p. 154. The book includes stirring tributes from senior British and Russian officers for the work he completed with the White Russian artillery.

21 For further details see Douglas Baldwin's Interconnecting the Personal and Public: The Support Networks of the Public Health Nurse Mona Wilson, *Canadian Journal of Nursing Research*, Volume 27, Number 3.

22 In her diary entry of 27th September 1919, Mona Wilson wrote that Dallas was "so unhappy here and so in wrong with the Red Cross" (Public Archives, Prince Edward Island Acc 3652).

Chapter 6

1 Report on the Work of the British Military Mission to Siberia 1918–19.
2 General Knox wrote a series of respectful letters to Admiral Kolchak providing advice on the military campaign. These are included with his final report, which was handed over to the War Office by his personal staff officer, Major Cecil Cameron DSO CBE RFA and can be retrieved from the National Archives (WO 32/5707).
3 Of the many sources which describe the way Lenin and Trotsky built the Red Army and fought the civil war in 1919, the author has benefited most from the 1935 book by W. P. and Zelda Coates, *Armed Intervention in Russia 1918–1922* and from Basil Liddell Hart's *The Soviet Army*.
4 According to Smele, *Civil War in Siberia*, p. 317, the Central Committee meetings of 15th June and 7th July in Moscow supported the local military committee's proposal to pursue Kolchak, rather than switch to the south.
5 An account of a conversation between Winston Churchill and one of Kolchak's secret agents, General Golovin was distributed to a British Labour delegation visiting Russia and leaked to the *Daily Herald*, which accused the Secretary of War and Air of treason on 3rd July 1920.
6 Churchill appealed directly to Woodrow Wilson about changing his policy and supporting the Kolchak government. However, the American president remained adamant about non-interference as he made clear in his telegram to the Paris Peace Conference on 19th February 1919: "Greatly surprised by Churchill's Russian suggestion. I distinctly understood Lloyd George to say that there could be no thought of military action there and what I said at the hurried meeting Friday afternoon was meant only to convey the idea that I would not take any hasty separate action myself, but would not be in favor of any course (contrary to that which) may mean the earliest practicable withdrawal of military forces. It would be fatal to be led further into the Russian chaos. Woodrow Wilson."
7 General Graves's journey is described in his book *America's Siberian Adventure 1918–1920*.
8 Before the war, Petropavlovsk was a prosperous market town on the River Ishim; the centre for the trade of hides and frozen meat.
9 In the official papers relating to the foreign relations of the United States with Russia in 1919, there is a section of 115 documents on American attempts to avoid entanglement in the factional strife in eastern Siberia. Reading these, one can easily conclude that if it was not for General Graves, America would have been drawn into a full-scale war that might have matched her losses on the Western Front in 1918.

It is surprising that the State Department encouraged an increased commitment, whilst the War Department urged caution. It was not as if the State Department was not aware of the facts. On the 25th March, 1919, the American consul cabled to Washington a conversation with Kolchak, who admitted that: "The Military, the Political and particularly the international situation in the Far East are such that the Russian Government, although having administration in that region, is practically unable to exercise power and authority over this part of the country."

10 The Kolchak regime understood that the only way they could win the war was to draw in the US in the same way that Britain and France had pulled them into the war against Germany in 1917. This date is drawn from the "Narrative of Events in Siberia" in the War Office file retrieved from the National Archives.

11 Major General Greenly's interview was discussed in a meeting of the Cabinet on 27th January 1920.

12 This unkind description of Admiral Kolchak by General Knox in his final report to the War Office, referred to the Supreme Ruler's trait of listening to poor advice from incompetent Russian officers. It should be placed in the context that Knox was rude about most people and that overall, he believed that Kolchak was the only man who could lead the White Russian movement.

13 Taken from Ernest Léderrey's *The Red Army During The Civil War, 1917–1920*.

14 The Middlesex left behind one officer and 21 soldiers, who had volunteered to stay behind. Their Roll of Honour lists 14 soldiers commemorated in the Vladivostok cemetery: Annels, T. CSM PW/2618 MSM sickness, 31 July 1919; Boniface, B. Private G/39718, 15 August 1919; Bungay, J. Private 208204, 9 February 1919; Cruse, E. J. Private G/39145, 29 January 1919; Fellger, R. Private L/15784, 2 July 1919; Martin, A. J. Private G/39414, 22 January 1919; Tong, A. Private G/39726, 17 May 1919; Wells, H. Private G/39750, 8 February 1919; Wrigley, W. Private 102791, 31 August 1919; Crossley, G. W. Private G/99184, 17 December 1918; Fuller, J. Private TF/208200, 16 January 1919; Harding, C. Private G/49205, 20 November 1918; Webb, S. J. Sergeant G/39394, 13 September 1918; Wade, E. C. Private 16 September 1918.

15 A moujik is a Russian male peasant.

Chapter 7

1 Brian Horrocks's memoir *A Full Life*, includes his experience as a prisoner of war in Germany and also his participation in the Russian civil war. Details of Captain Hayes are taken from the *History of the Royal Norfolk Regiment 1919–1951*, by P. K. Kemp and from his personal papers donated by Jeremy Fairbank to the Special Collection of the University of Leeds (GB 206 MS 783).

2 A verst is an old unit of length used in Russia. At the time of Peter the Great, it was set at 500 sazhens, equivalent to 1.067km, or approximately, two thirds of a mile.

3 Smele, *Civil War in Siberia*, p. 210.

4   Appendix C to General Knox's report in the National Archives; his letter to General Golovin is dated 27th September 1919.

5   A full understanding of the origins of the *Tcheka* and its use of the Red Terror to govern Russia is provided by George Popoff in part three of his 1925 book, *The Tcheka: The Red Inquisition*.

6   The epic escape of Captain Phelps Hodges and Lieutenant Paul Moss can be found in the former's memoir, *Britmis: A Great Adventure of the War*.

7   Taken from Brigadier Blair's Report from Omsk dated 24th August 1919, retrieved from the National Archives.

8   A *Zemstvo* was an institution of local government set up in Russia during the 19th century. The All-Russian Zemstvo Union was established in August 1914 to provide a common voice for all the *Zemstva*. A municipal Duma was a town assembly with legislative responsibilities in the governing system of Imperial Russia.

9   General Gajda was beaten but allowed to leave for Shanghai. His civilian counterpart was not as fortunate; Mr Yakhushev's body was washed up on the shore several days after the failed coup.

10 The mutual respect between the British and American railway missions is clear from a letter from the head of the US Railway Advisors, Lieutenant Colonel B. O. Johnson to Brigadier Jack on 17th October 1919, in which he writes: "We Americans were rather a conceited lot, but our experience with you has taught us that our English speaking cousins have every bit as much so-called American 'pep' and resourcefulness as we thought we had, if not a little more." (Jack Papers retrieved from the Imperial War Museum).

11 The prime minister's announcement was a disaster for thousands of Allied troops still in Siberia, seeking safe passage because it removed the political support that was so vital for their security in a foreign land and gave succour to the Bolsheviks, who heard about it from their agents in London.

12 The SS *Monteagle* had taken the Canadian Expeditionary Force home in July.

13 From the diary of Captain Hamilton Maurice Howgrave-Graham OBE.

14 The gold was taken in payment for millions of pounds of war loans.

15 For more on the Canadian contribution to the Siberian campaign, see Ian Moffat's Forgotten Battlefields: Canadians in Siberia 1918-1919, *Canadian Military Journal*, Autumn 2007, http://www.journal.forces.gc.ca/vo8/no3/moffat-eng. asp#n62.

16 For more on the influence of labour agitators in the Canadian Expeditionary Force in Siberia, see Benjamin Isitt's *From Victoria to Vladivostok: Canada's Siberian Expedition 1917–1919*, UBC Press 2010.

17 For example, Germany and Austria were struggling against insurrections and in Hungary, Bela Kun established the Hungarian Soviet Republic on 21st March 1919. He was soon at war with the Kingdom of Romania and Czechoslovakia, both aided by France. The Hungarian Red Army achieved some success against the Czechoslovaks; however, it was defeated by the Romanians. Lenin's government

promised to invade Romania and link up with Kun, but military reversals suffered by the Red Army in Ukraine halted the invasion before it began. The Romanian counter attack organised by the Allied Commander in the Balkans, French Marshal Louis Franchet d'Espèrey, led to the overthrow of the Hungarian Soviet Republic and the establishment of a government of social democrats on 1st August 1919.

18 According to Benjamin Isitt, the situation in Russia provided "Canadian workers with an interpretive framework and an example of agency, to challenge the authority of employers and legitimacy of the state."

19 This Canadian Pacific Line ship, built by Alexander Stephen and Sons in 1900, shuttled troops across the Atlantic during the war. At 500-feet long, she had accommodation for 1,460 passengers.

20 The return of the battalion was reported widely in the press. A typical item was published on the front page of the *Southampton and District Pictorial* on Thursday 11th December 1919 entitled "1/9th HANTS HOME-COMING".

Chapter 8

1 *Armed Intervention in Russia*, p. 228. On 13th November in the House of Commons, the prime minister added that the government "cannot contemplate" and has made "no provision" for "additional expenditure on Russia."

2 Many of the despatches from the Omsk retreat were not published until the following year. Under the editorial leadership of C. P. Scott at this time, the *Manchester Guardian* had an undiminished reputation for independence and integrity. His source for this quote was Leo Steveni.

3 These were their nicknames in Siberia. Horrocks was commissioned into the Middlesex Regiment on 8th August 1914 and spent most of the war as a prisoner of the Germans, for which he was awarded the Military Cross in 1920. Hayes was born in Lincolnshire and educated at Carre's Grammar School, Sleaford, but he was commissioned into the Norfolk Regiment, known as the Holy Boys because the badge of Britannia on their cross belts was mistaken during the Peninsula War for the Virgin Mary.

4 McCullagh was commissioned into the Royal Irish Fusiliers at the same time as Gerald Templer who served with Dunsterforce in Southern Russia and subsequently found fame as the commander-in-chief during the Malayan Insurgency. The Royal Irish Fusiliers had many nicknames, but perhaps the most famous was the Faughs, from their battle cry "Faugh-a-Ballagh", or Clear the Way, from when they charged the French at the battle of Barossa on 5th March 1811 and Sergeant Masterton wrested a regimental eagle from a French ensign with the famous words "Bejasus boys, I have the cuckoo!"

5 Taken from the report of the campaign by the Senior British Military Commander, Major General Alfred Knox; retrieved from the National Archives. McCullagh's report on propaganda, Appendix O, is not included in this file. The covering note

explains: "Owing to delays in transit, this appendix has not been received and will be forwarded later." McCullagh was awarded an MBE for his work in Omsk and this was published in the Siberian honours list of 14th January 1920, but he was not informed until later that year.

6 The Army Service Corps earned its "Royal" prefix in 1918. Their troops were the only rear echelon support personnel to be considered combat soldiers. However, this did not prevent them from being given less adulatory nicknames in World War I, such as "The Jam Stealers".

7 Records of these Canadians are available in the National Archive, including the *London Gazette* Supplement of 6th September 1919 (p. 11324): Railway Traffic Officers Class II and Temporary 2nd Lieutenants General List on 17th May 1919: Herbert Edward Prickett (member of 1918 Canadian Expeditionary Force 229052 with medal card, WO 372/16/86998); Second Lieutenant Edward John Stephens of 33 Barbican, London 13 September 1895–25 January 1967 WO 372/19/36444 – Canadian Expeditionary Force 2152447); Second Lieutenant Bernard Freithieff Eyford, of Prince Albert, Saskatchewan, (WO 372/7/3957).

8 *London Gazette,* 1st February 1919: At Velu on 26th/27th September 1918 2nd Lieutenant James Dempster, ASC, 2nd Divisional Motor Transport Company. By his example and disregard of danger saved an ammunition train with conspicuous gallantry. During the shelling of an ammunition train, before and after the train had received a direct hit upon a truck of shell, which exploded. A dump on the other side of the track was hit and exploded also. He with a few men, man-handled trucks down the track to clear them from the burning train. He showed conspicuous gallantry, and was entirely responsible for saving the ammunition.

9 Vining, *Held by the Bolsheviks: The Diary of a British Officer in Russia 1919–1920,* p. 221.

10 In the 1911 Census, George Robert Lillington, known as Bob to his family, was living with his family in Portsmouth. His father, Stephen owned a plumbing business with his brother W. C. Lillington.

11 Tundra is a Russian word for land where the sub-soil is perma-frost and the growth of vegetation is hindered by low temperatures.

12 Now known as Novosibirsk.

13 Report on the Work of the British Military Mission to Siberia 1918–19, National Archives WO 32/5707. General Kappel's British liaison officer was John Neilson.

14 *The Times* correspondent Robert Wilton was accused of bias towards the White cause, but this did not stop the British military commander, General Knox, from withdrawing his accreditation later in the campaign.

15 During his research for this book, the author has discovered evidence in the Hampshire Regiment Archives that some of the Imperial Treasury was removed from Omsk by 9th battalion in September; see Cyclist Stanley Green's diary excerpt in Chapter 5.

16 The *Manchester Guardian* published Leo Steveni's account of the retreat in three episodes on 20th, 21st, 22nd July 1920.

17 In Russia, Christmas is celebrated on 7th January and is viewed primarily as a religious event. On Christmas Eve, families attend long church services and then return home for a traditional "Holy Supper", comprising twelve dishes; one for each of the Apostles.

Chapter 9

1 Miles Lampson was the British consul in Siberia after Sir Charles Eliot. Subsequently, he became the Right Honourable, The Lord Killearn.
2 Lenin often visited the internationally renowned Natural History Museum at Minusinsk, when he lived in exile in the nearby village of Shushenskoye.
3 Vining had no idea that Captain Phelps Hodges had already embarked on the southern route and was halfway across the Gobi Desert on his way to Peking.
4 The author is grateful to Mike Sampson and the Tiverton Civic Society for help with the story about William Yates. Further details can be found in the *Western Times*, 12th February 1926 (Honour for a Tiverton Pastor) and the *Exeter and Plymouth Gazette*, 5th April 1926 (Funeral of Respected Tiverton Minister). The 1911 Census shows that William Yates lived at 3 Portland Place Quay, Exeter.
5 One week after Vining and his compatriots were captured, the list of Siberian Honours was published in the *London Gazette* of 13th January 1920. The only member of the abandoned British group to receive anything on this list was Captain Francis McCullagh, who was awarded an MBE, but he did not find out about this until he left Russia. In the British Railway Mission, Brigadier Jack was awarded the CB and Lieutenant Colonel Eric Johnston was made CBE. The demoted Major Neilson, forever associated with the *coup d'état* which brought Kolchak to power, was also awarded the CBE. Two weeks later the *Gazette* published the award of a Military Cross to Captain Horrocks in recognition of gallant conduct and determination displayed in attempting to escape from German captivity and for bearing illegal punishments. The irony of this award being announced soon after his capture in Siberia did not strike Horrocks for some time.
6 For more on the Danish Red Cross mission and other Danish representatives in Soviet Russia, see Bent Jensen, "Missiia Datskogo Krasnogo Kresta v Rossii, 1918–1919 gody," *Otechestvennaia istoriia* 1997, no. 1 (Jan–Feb), pp. 27–41.
7 The other members of Colonel Eric Johnston's party reported missing to London on 22nd December were: Majors N. I. Mills and H. G. O. Smith of the Royal Engineers and Captain Dwyer Neville of the Royal Air Force.
8 Lieutenant Colonel Francis Harvey DSO, East Yorkshire Regiment wrote the British Military Mission Report on Training dated 2nd December 1919. After his reconnaissance mission, Harvey returned to Vladivostok where he commanded the training on Russian Island until he caught influenza. He was treated in the American hospital from 11th to 18th June, just before Dallas arrived.

9 The British Military Mission Report from Omsk records the arrivals and departures on a daily basis. On 17th May 1919, the following Captains arrived from Vladivostok: Charles Connor Moore, Essex Regiment; George William Philip Newkey Burden, East Lancashire Regiment; George Valdemar Faber MC, Royal Artillery; Eric Charles Hayes, Norfolk Regiment; Brian Gwynne Horrocks, Middlesex Regiment; Dennis Pilkington Kilpin, Machine Gun Corps; William Leonard Leslie, King's Shropshire Light Infantry; Harold Keith Salveson, 42nd Deolis (Indian Army); Norman Alfred Stilling, Duke of Wellington's (West Riding Regiment).

10 In his book, *The Fate of Admiral Kolchak*, Peter Fleming, elder brother of the author who invented James Bond, describes Captain Norman Stilling as an officer of the British Military Mission who, stranded in Irkutsk, contrived by bluff and adroitness to invest himself with the sort of diplomatic immunity, which a consul would enjoy. Whether he was working directly for British military intelligence or not, Stilling's secret report was eventually presented to the Cabinet on 17th June 1920 by Winston Churchill, who wrote: "I circulate herewith an interesting account, by an officer of General Knox's mission, of the events, which led up to the execution of Admiral Kolchak at Irkutsk."

11 There are several different values attributed by contemporary authors to the Imperial Treasury that accompanied Kolchak and was handed over by the Czechs in Irkutsk. The amount fluctuated according to currency and exchange rates.

12 Two days later, whilst Kolchak was calling for help from Nizhne Udinsk on 29th December, General Graves received a secret telegram from Washington that informed him: "very confidentially that it is expected that within a few days you will receive orders for the withdrawal of your entire command. Keep matter very secret until orders are received by you."

13 According to W. P. and Zelda Coates on p. 237 of *Armed Intervention in Russia 1918–1922*, this was published on 22nd July 1920.

14 In his report presented to the British Cabinet by Winston Churchill, Stilling stated that many of the officers who Kolchak refused to abandon, deserted him at various stages of the journey and arrived at Harbin on Allied echelons.

15 The Prime Minister David Lloyd George, met a Russian delegation in Paris on 19th January 1920 with Paul Deschanel, the incoming president of France, as well as representatives of the other main Allied powers. That evening, he chaired a Cabinet meeting in his room at Claridge's Hotel in Paris. Those present included the Lord Chancellor and the Minister of Labour, as well as Lord Curzon (Foreign Affairs), Churchill (War and Air), Long (First Lord of the Admiralty) and the heads of the Royal Navy and Army. After commenting that the policy of the new French regime would be "of a somewhat chauvinistic character," Lloyd George discussed the situation in Russia at length. Churchill again called for more troops to be deployed to the south, but Field Marshal Sir Henry Wilson said that the "troops did not exist. Egypt and India were each calling for five more battalions

and troops were also required at home." The minutes of this meeting record no mention of the British prisoners, or Kolchak's capture.

16 The struggle for power in Irkutsk between the Bolsheviks and the Social Revolutionaries, supported by the Czech Legion, provided the political backdrop to the capture of Admiral Kolchak. For more on this aspect of the story, see Scott B. Smith's *Captives of the Revolution: The Social Revolutionaries and the Bolshevik Dictatorship 1918–1923* and Jonathan Smele's *Civil War in Siberia.*

17 General Janin was blamed by the other Allies for the failure to protect the Supreme Leader. However, all the Allies must share blame in equal measure. The High Commissioners (including Lampson of the United Kingdom, Kato of Japan and Maugras of France), who instructed Janin to guarantee the Admiral's safety, did not provide him with any of their own national forces to back this up and then left Irkutsk precipitately, allowing the Bolsheviks a free hand to deal with Kolchak. Janin also blamed the Japanese detachment at Glaskov for shirking the task of rescue.

18 Stilling Report presented to British Cabinet.

19 Peter Fleming suggests that the Bolshevik Revolutionary Committee was in a similar situation to that facing the Czar's custodians in Ekaterinburg in 1918.

20 The "sharpest" interlocutor, according to Jonathan Smele, was the Bolshevik lawyer, K. A. Popov, who grudgingly conceded that Kolchak remained "entirely dignified" throughout his final testimony.

21 See Appendix 2 for the Decree of the Military Revolutionary Committee of Irkutsk, dated 7th February 1920 that ordered the execution of "the former Supreme Governor" and "the former President of the Council of Ministers." The execution was witnessed by president of the local *Tcheka* and the town commandant.

22 According to Smele, *Civil War in Siberia,* the last Czech contingent departed from Irkutsk on 1st March.

23 This included relief and supplies for hospitals and orphanages as recorded in the minutes of an executive committee meeting on 17th February 1920 (found in American Red Cross archive papers, Box 915, 987.04).

24 By then, Lieutenant Colonel Charles Wickham DSO had taken over as chief of the British Military Mission. He had been General Knox's "untiring" head of administration since October 1918. His correspondence to the War Office, retained in the National Archives, reveals that he sent comforts by train in February to the "missing" British soldiers, but these failed to reach Vining.

Chapter 10

1 Telegram to General Ironside (Archangel) 76959; WO 33/966 number 1528.

2 Nansen was the first man to cross Greenland's inland ice. After WWI, he was placed in charge of the exchanges of 400,000 prisoners of war between Russia, Germany,

and the former Austria-Hungary. He was awarded the Peace Prize for his work on behalf of prisoners of war and starving people. In 1922, he became the first global high commissioner for refugees and the League of Nations subsequently provided what became known as "Nansen passports" to stateless refugees to enable them to cross national borders.

3   Jim O'Grady was active in the union of cabinet makers; he was the only Roman Catholic MP in the Labour Party.

4   The government under Georgy Lvov sent a note to the Allied governments promising to continue the war, but this resulted in mass demonstrations of workers and soldiers on 20th April and the resignation of the Foreign Minister Pavel Milyukov.

5   Scavenius was foreign minister three times during a challenging period in Denmark's history and prime minister during the German occupation in World War II.

6   The Danish consul was the last international diplomat in Krasnoyarsk. He acted as intermediary on delicate negotiations between Vining and the Bolshevik commissars and his staff passed news of the outside world to the British prisoners of war.

7   For example, Curzon instructed O'Grady to offer Litvinov other concessions such as food supplies instead of agreeing to secure the release of prisoners in Germany. See Curzon's telegram to O'Grady of 19th December 1919, British Documents Volume III, Number 608.

8   Hardinge had been viceroy of India during WWI and returned to his previous post as permanent under-secretary at the Foreign Office before he became ambassador to France in 1920. He held the unusual distinction of being the only non-royal recipient of six British knighthoods.

9   "The Negotiations at Copenhagen between Mr O'Grady and M Litvino[v] for the Exchange of British and Russian Prisoners of War and Civilians" retrieved from the National Archives file number CAB 24/97/61. The draft agreement attached to Hardinge's memorandum can be found at Appendix 3.

10 The Archangel Government refers to the Provisional Government of the Northern Region, which was subsumed within Admiral Kolchak's Provisional All-Russian Government. The leader of this so-called Archangel Government from January 1919 was Lieutenant General Yevgeny Miller. After the Allies withdrew from the region and the Omsk Government fell in November 1919, Miller remained for three months before he escaped to Norway with the remnants of his forces.

11 Sir Halford Mackinder was MP for Glasgow Camlachie. He was a former president of the Oxford Union and director of the London School of Economics.

12 Cabinet minutes reveal that Downing Street spent far more time on the Bolshevik problem than they did on Ireland, Afghanistan, Turkey, the League of Nations, or the economic situation in Europe.

13 Mackinder's report is dated 21st January 1920 and filed as 18/E/170 21. The four exiled members of the All Russian Council were Sozonov, Maklakov, Savinkov and Prince Lvov. He met the fifth member, Chaikovsky, in London.

14 "The Report on Bolshevik Influence on Muslims" by the Intelligence Department of the High Commission of Constantinople covered a memorandum by Mr Low, retrieved as file 18/OJ/2 in the National Archives.

15 This quote from a leader in Lord Beaverbrook's *Daily Express* typified the extensive media criticism of those who advocated a military campaign against the Bolsheviks.

16 The full report from the informant, who was "said to have been in personal touch with some of the most prominent Bolsheviks", can be found in the secret Home Office "Monthly Review of Revolutionary Movements in Foreign Countries Report Number 16" at the National Archives.

17 Ullman, *Anglo Soviet Relations 1917–1921 Volume II*, p. 343, taken from Report CX/P/353.920 6th January 1920 in file 174866/91/38; FO 371/3961.

18 This story is included in a letter to David Lloyd George by the Chairman of the Committee to Collect Information on Russia, Lord Alfred Emmott on 24th December 1920; see Parliamentary Archives LG/15/7/3.

19 The details of the prisoner exchange agreement remained secret, although the news of its existence spread throughout Russia, including Krasnoyarsk, where Vining's group was informed about it by the commissars.

20 Richard Ullman suggests on p. 343 of *Anglo Soviet Relations 1917–1921 Volume II* that the "grave offences" clause "gave the Foreign Office much concern, for it feared that the Soviet regime would interpret it as meaning not only offences in criminal law, but also those which in the West would be called political." This concern was well-founded, as will be seen in Chapter 15.

21 The final agreement was published as "Agreement Between His Majesty's Government and the Soviet Government of Russia for the Exchange of Prisoners, 1920". See Appendix 3.

22 National Archives T1/12514/12904; Foreign Office W/38 dated 18th March 1920 letter to the Secretary to the Treasury.

23 National Archives T1/12514/12904; Treasury response to the Foreign Office, file 12904 dated 16th April 1920.

Chapter 11

1 Harry Ferguson, *Operation Kronstadt*, p. 7.

2 The 1905 revolution affected the whole of Russia. Francis McCullagh was a non-military observer in Manchuria during the Russo-Japanese war, which coincided with the revolution. The following year, he published a book about his experiences, *With the Cossacks: Being the Story of an Irishman Who Rode with the Cossacks throughout the Russo-Japanese War.*

3 Libya was invaded by Italy on 3rd October 1911. The colonising troops conducted a brutal counter-insurgency campaign which lasted for more than 20 years.

4 According to Vining's diary, the Czech Commandant of Ekaterinburg took the place of McCullagh in Krasnoyarsk.

5 Since McCullagh had abandoned Vining's collective and was trying to escape alone, there was potential for a confrontation with the British group over access to the commissars. The risks they took to cover his tracks would have added to a sense of antagonism and might have led to a sense of passive hostility towards the Irish spy.

6 The remnants of the White Army under command of General Kappel became known as the "Kappel'evsky".

7 In fact, Yurovsky survived this illness and lived until 1938. Francis McCullagh was the only independent western journalist to interview the Czar's assassin. The unique account can be read in chapters 13 and 14 of his book, *A Prisoner of the Reds*.

8 For more on the Extraordinary Commission and the methods used by the Soviet secret police, see George Popoff's *The Tcheka*, published in 1925.

9 McCullagh, *A Prisoner of the Reds*, p. 86.

10 Minutes of Evidence Taken before the Committee to Collect Information on Russia, Volume I, p. 36.

11 McCullagh, *A Prisoner of the Reds*, p. 317.

12 Ibid, p. xii.

13 The torture McCullagh experienced was mild compared with the reported practices in other cities. In the winter, one of the secret police methods of torture was to pour water on naked prisoners and turn them into living statues. In some regions, prisoners were skinned alive, scalped, "crowned" with barbed wire, impaled or crucified.

14 McCullagh was interrogated by two very senior officials in the Soviet secret police. Ivan Xenofontov was one of the earliest members of the Bolshevik party, joining in 1903. He was a founding father of the *Tcheka* following the assassination of Moisei Uritsky and became First Deputy Chairman, only subordinate to Felix Dzerzhinsky. He died from stomach cancer in 1926. Solomon Mogilevsky subsequently became head of the Soviet Foreign Intelligence Service from 1921 to 1922. He died in an unsolved air crash near Tiflis in 1925.

15 On p. 401 of *Anglo-Soviet Relations 1917–1921 Volume 3, The Anglo-Soviet Accord*, Ullman reports that 124 British prisoners of war and 727 civilians arrived in England and several thousand Russians were repatriated, within a few months of the O'Grady-Litvinov Agreement being signed.

16 There are three references to Captain McCullagh's evidence in the "Interim Report of the Committee to Collect Information on Russia". These are on p. 4 in the section on arrests and on p. 6 in the section on how the Secret Police examinations were conducted. His full interview can be read in the "Minutes of Evidence Taken before the Committee" Volume I, pp. 36–42.

17 McCullagh sent a telegram to London from Moscow shortly before he was arrested in which he explains the plight of Vining and the other prisoners he left behind in Krasnoyarsk. This can be found in WO 106/1277 reference, 26th March 1920.

Chapter 12

1 Jeffers was a black wine trader imprisoned by the Bolsheviks for five and a half months in Moscow. This quote is from his evidence to Lord Emmottt's Committee to Collect Information on Russia.

2 *Sifnoi teiff*, the Russian term for epidemic typhus, was spread by lice, rather than fleas (murine typhus), or mites (scrub typhus). Signs and symptoms started with a sudden onset of fever that might reach 39 degrees Celsius, or 102 degrees Fahrenheit. Other symptoms included headaches, coughs and severe muscle pain. Five to nine days after the symptoms start, a rash begins on the body and spreads everywhere apart from the face and palms. Other signs include sensitivity to light, delirium and coma.

3 There are no exact records of the number of Russian deaths caused by the typhus epidemic during in World War I and the subsequent civil war in Siberia, but it is estimated that more than three million died from the disease.

4 T and B cigarettes were the brand name of Tuckett and Billings Tobacco Company in Canada. George Tuckett cornered a large part of the tobacco market during the Civil War and in 1866 he teamed up with John Billings to start a tobacco plant in Hamilton, Ontario. Their initials were turned into the eponymous nickname "Tab".

5 Through the efforts of public health pioneers such as Hélène Sparrow and Rudolf Weigl, much more was known about the role of lice in the spread of the typhus. These ectoparasites are different to head lice and do not interbreed with them because they lay eggs in clothes, not at the base of hairs. The eggs hatch, after about ten days' incubation, into nymphs that grow into adults.

6 The Bolshevik Government agreed to the safe withdrawal of the Czech Legion to Vladivostok in exchange for their strict observance of neutrality in the conflict with the White Army and a pledge to return the Imperial Treasury that they had appropriated from Admiral Kolchak.

7 MacMillan's letter dated 2nd March 1920 from Krasnoyarsk was written by hand on Canadian YMCA paper. The British prisoners also received comforts from the National Service Committee, which sent Christmas packages to the "Brave Soldiers From Their Canadian Friends."

8 On p. 8345 of *The London Gazette* dated 10th August 1920, it was announced that four of the British officers abandoned in Krasnoyarsk had their ranks and appointments removed on 13th March 1920, whilst they were still serving King and Country in Russia: Captain L. E. Vining Indian Defence Force, Deputy Assistant Director of Railway Traffic, Class BB; relinquish the temporary rank of Major; Temp 2nd Lieutenant H. E. Prickett General List, Railway Traffic Officer Class FF; relinquish the temporary rank of Captain; Temp 2nd Lieutenant E. J. Stephens General List; Class GG and relinquish the rank of Lieutenant; Temp 2nd Lieutenant F. E. Eyford General List; Class II and relinquish the temporary rank of Lieutenant.

9 In fact, Trotsky was not the first to say this to the apathetic doctors in Ekaterinburg. Francis McCullagh had acted as interpreter for Colonel John Clarke, head of the British medical services who had been sent forward by General Knox a year earlier. Dr Clarke had attempted to explain to the Russian doctors that heat was just as good as "unprocurable insecticides." See p. 95 of *A Prisoner of the Reds.*

10 The habit of destitute Russians sleeping together on floors of publicly heated buildings, such as a railway stations, meant that the epidemic had a far greater effect in Siberia than anywhere else.

11 Since the infected lice lived in clothing, the prevalence of typhus was also affected by weather, poverty and lack of hygiene. Lice, and therefore typhus, were more prevalent during winter and early spring. In these seasons, people wore more layers of clothing, providing the lice with extra places to hide.

12 *Prisoner of the Reds*, p. 321.

Chapter 13

1 The foreign secretary's note about prisoners was one of many on the subject of Russia that were submitted to the prime minister and his Cabinet in May 1920. Separately, Winston Churchill still held out hope of defeating the Bolsheviks and on 11th May sent a secret report of conditions in Soviet Russia by Brigadier A. J. Turner CMG DSO of the British Baltic Mission. Turner's caveat was apposite: "One hesitates to commit to paper any opinion regarding the state of affairs in Russia … only two sources of information exist: firstly, Soviet representatives, or visitors of distinctly Bolshevik views; and secondly, Russians and prisoners of other nationalities of very strong conservative or reactionary tendencies." It is believed the number 150 is a typing error, rather than misleading Danish information.

2 The distance indicates that this is now the station at Krasnopolyansk, close to Kansk.

3 Ilanskaya is now named Ilansky, located on the Ilanka River, 173 miles east of Krasnoyarsk.

4 For more on the Soviet secret police, see Donald Rayfield's *Stalin and His Hangmen: The Tyrant and Those Who Killed for Him.*

5 The Engadine valley in Switzerland was the destination of choice for many British invalids recovering from tuberculosis.

6 The location where the line was cut was most probably the River Kitoy, south of Telma. This was the scene of fierce fighting between the Bolsheviks and General Voitsekhovski's force. He had taken over the remnants of Kappel's army after the general died of severe frostbite on 26th January. His force had dwindled to about 10,000 loyalists, but four days later, Voitsekhovski won a crucial five-hour battle at Zima with the help of the Czech garrison and then captured the town of Polovina 80 miles west of Irkutsk on 5th February. After threatening to rescue Admiral Kolchak in Irkutsk, he had to disengage his troops after the Czech Legion came to terms

with the Bolsheviks and informed Voitsekhovski that they would repulse any attack. The weary White soldiers passed around Irkutsk and struggled across the frozen Lake Baikal before making their way to Chita, where they were joined by the tattered remains of General Sukin's force that had journeyed along the northern route.

7   The main signature on the execution decree was A. Shiriamoff, president of the Military Revolutionary Committee.

8   The 5th Red Army arrived in Irkutsk on 8th March and marched ceremonially through Irkutsk's triumphal arch, exactly one week after the last Czech contingent left the city.

9   After the overthrow of General Rozanov on 31st January, the American forces had a relatively quiet time in Vladivostok until the departure of their last echelon on 1st April aboard the SS *Great Northern*. The ship left for the capital of the Philippines, Manila, with the American commander, General Graves, serenaded by a Japanese band playing, with some irony, "Hard Times Come Again No More".

10 This is attributed to the American historian Canfield F. Smith.

11 Vining sent his message to China believing that the British Mission in Vladivostok had closed down. In fact, WO 1061277 "Withdrawal of Military Mission from Siberia" shows that Brigadier Blair and the remainder of the Mission did not leave for Shanghai until 11th May 1920. The final chief of the British Military Mission, Charles Wickham, sent the missing appendices for the War Office report G (Training in Irkutsk), H (Training at Tomsk), K (Logistic Support to the White Army) and N (Medical Relief Work). Concerning the report on propaganda, he simply stated: "On account of the capture of Capt. F. McCullagh, by the Bolsheviks, appendix O is not available." He subsequently returned to the United Kingdom and became the first inspector general of the Royal Ulster Constabulary.

12 In Vining's published diary, this officer is referred to as Captain C. A letter from General Knox in the University of Leeds Special Collection confirms this is Captain Rex Carthew. He arrived in Omsk on 23 April 1919 and returned to Canada, via Vladivostok, on board the SS *Empress of Russia* on 10 July, 1920.

13 Graves, *America's Siberian Adventure 1918–1920*, p. 184.

14 The author is still trying to establish for certain at what point Bob and Ludmilla parted during the evacuation from Omsk and the details of Mrs Lillington's journey. He is grateful to their grandson, George Lillington, for establishing Ludmilla's most probable route which is described in this chapter. All that is certain is that they were reunited Scotland and lived in Edinburgh for five years before settling in Portsmouth, where they brought up two sons. Bob continued to serve in the Hampshire Regiment, earning his Territorial Efficiency Model before WWII.

15 These observations are from Horrocks's memoir, *A Full Life* and Vining's diary, *Held By The Bolsheviks*.

16 Phelps Hodges, *Britmis: A Great Adventure of the War*, p. 77.

17 This quote is from Harvey's report of the British Training Mission, held in the National Archives.

18 Graves's *America's Siberian Adventure 1918–1920*, p. 186.

19 See Chapter 10; the full report is in the Directorate of Intelligence (Home Office): A Monthly Review of Revolutionary Movements in Foreign Countries Report Number 16, February 1920.

20 The Admiralty's secret Weekly Intelligence Summaries issued by Naval Intelligence Directorate reported the dispositions of His Majesty's ships in operational theatres round the world. They also provided informed comment on littoral and land campaigns as well as political crises of national interest. The documents are all marked clearly "To be destroyed When Replaced by a Subsequent Number." However, the Cabinet failed to destroy them and so they are available for anyone to access through the National Archives.

21 This is from Report Number 72 for the week ended 1st May, which informed the Cabinet there were about 60,000 troops due for repatriation from Vladivostok and that the "French Commission, who are in general charge of the repatriation, expect to get the last of the Czechs away by the beginning of August 1920." In fact the last of the Czech Legion did not depart until later in the year.

22 The Russian Soviet Federative Socialist Republic lasted as a sovereign state until 30th December 1922, when it became one of 16 republics within the newly created Union of Soviet Socialist Republics.

23 The American military commander, Major General William Graves believed that in the eastern part of Siberia, the White leaders, including Semeonov, Kalmikov and Rozanov, were far worse than the Bolsheviks. However, in his memoir, *A Full Life*, Horrocks suggests that the atrocities were "six of one and half a dozen of the other."

24 Playing cards was made a crime because it might make one ambitious to acquire the property of his neighbour and therefore become a "speculant". The ultimate speculant crime was buying, or selling goods, for which the penalty was death by shooting.

25 The British team thus became the first international team to play in Soviet Russia, two and a half years before the Finnish Workers' Sports Federation football team that has been credited with that recognition.

26 Vining, *Held by the Bolsheviks*, p. 195.

27 Stephen Roskill, *Hankey: Man of secrets Volume II 1919–1931*, p. 170.

28 Ibid.

29 CAB 24/106/51 CP 1350, Negotiations with M. Krassin, dated 27th May 1920.

30 Roskill, *Hankey*, p. 171.

31 Attributed by the Cabinet Secretary to Winston Churchill.

Chapter 14

1   Hansard, House of Commons Debate, 14th June 1920; Volume 130, cc869–870.

2   Lieutenant Commander Joseph Kenworthy worked in the Plans Division of the Admiralty during World War I. He won the seat of Central Hull as a Liberal candidate in a by-election in 1919 and resigned from the Royal Navy to enter Parliament.

3   As the MP for Newcastle-under-Lyme, Josiah Wedgwood became a leading backbencher before World War I. He had a distinguished military career in the Royal Navy and Army, earning a DSO during the landing at Cape Helles in the Dardanelles Campaign. At the start of 1918, he was sent to Siberia to encourage Russian participation in the War and gather intelligence about the influence of the Central Powers. In the 1918 election, he won his seat unopposed and subsequently joined the Independent Labour Party.

4   Charles Palmer was a journalist who won a shock victory in a Shropshire by-election in February 1920, standing as an Independent in a three-way contest with the Coalition Liberal and Labour candidates. He died in October 1920, four months after challenging the prime minister about the British prisoners of war in Siberia.

5   According to a secret translation from a conference held on 31st May 1920 (National Archives 24/10/107/21 CP 1421), General Wrangel's troops were holding out in the Crimea with the help of British soldiers. This force, which comprised the remnants of Denikin's army, was looked upon by Russian workmen "as a gang of mutineers, who are relying on foreign aid and are carrying out a fruitless struggle, which only increases bloodshed against the Russian people and their lawful government."

6   A copy of this memorandum is in Appendix 4. It reveals that Churchill was tracking the plight of Vining's cohort whilst they were in Irkutsk. The document was originally filed as CP 1451 and is now available at the National Archives under CAB 24/107/50.

7   *Sine quâ non* is the essential element, or condition.

8   Hansard, House of Commons Debate, 13th July 1920, Volume 131, c2133.

9   See secret telegram to Lord Kilmarnock 11th July 1920 received at 9.20p.m. (FO 371/3961 207842, dated 12 July 1920). This reports the contents of a telegram from Litvinov to Chicherin seeking funds (50,000 francs) for the *Daily Herald* which: "acts as if it were our organ … it has gone considerably more to the Left and decidedly advocates direct action."

10 On 10th July, *The Nation* ran the headline: "The Price of Mr Churchill".

11 For more on the calls for impeachment, see Donald Boadle's *Winston Churchill and the German Question in British Foreign Policy 1918–1922*, p. 116.

12 *Taiga* is a Russian word for the extended coniferous snow forest on the edge of the Arctic. In eastern Siberia, this is principally made up of larch trees.

13 This memorandum was sent on 30th June, according to the president of the Board of Trade, Sir Robert Horne, during a meeting held by the Cabinet at 10 Downing Street on 17th November.

14 Forty-eight-year-old Georgy Chicherin was a wealthy noble who supported the 1905 revolution and fled abroad to avoid arrest. In 1917, he was detained in Brixton prison for his anti-war writings before Trotsky secured his release in exchange for the safe passage of British subjects in Moscow. After negotiating the Brest-Litovsk treaty, he held the post as the People's Commissar for Foreign Affairs for 12 years, before handing over to Maxim Litvinov. He spoke all the major European languages and was a workaholic who, despite his portly frame, was extremely frugal.

15 The note listed four conditions to be fulfilled before trade could begin: A mutual undertaking to refrain from interference in the internal affairs of the other, including, in particular, Soviet attempts to encourage the peoples of Asia in action hostile to the interests of the British Empire; The immediate exchange of all remaining prisoners; Recognition in principle by the Soviet Government that it was liable for compensation to private citizens who have supplied goods or services to Russia for which they have not been paid; The mutual granting of trade facilities with the provision that each government could exclude agents of the other *non grata* to itself.

16 On p. 403 of *Anglo-Soviet Relations 1917–1921 Volume 3, The Anglo-Soviet Accord*, Ullman writes: "Of all the British subjects in Soviet hands, those at Baku received the most notice by the British public." And at note 5, he explains: "It is an index of the extraordinary popular concern over the Baku prisoners that questions about them were asked on twenty-seven of the fifty nine days on which the House of Commons sat between 13 May 1920, when the plight of the prisoners first became generally known and 21 August when the House rose for the long summer recess."

17 Not to be confused with his namesake, George Nathaniel, who was the foreign secretary and styled as Curzon of Kedleston.

18 *Daily Mail,* 26th and 27th July 1920.

19 Hansard, House of Commons Debate, 1st July 1920, Volume 131 c624.

20 The British Mission in South Russia was reduced in size after General Denikin handed over to General Wrangel in April 1920. Brigadier Jocelyn Percy commanded 150 officers and 450 other ranks, but he was not supported with a political representative. For a better understanding of the British campaign in South Russia, see Clifford Kinvig's *Churchill's Crusade: The British Invasion of Russia 1918–1920.*

21 A *pood* is 36 pounds, equivalent to 2.72kg. These facts are confirmed in a report submitted by Alexei Rykov to the Congress of National Economic Councils, Moscow 22nd to 25th January 1920. Extracts from Rykov's speech, "*Ekonomicheskaya Zhizn*" (Economic Life) were passed to David Lloyd George as an enclosure by Lord Emmott later in the year (Parliamentary Archive LG/15/7/3).

22 *Babushka* is a diminutive old lady, or grandmother.

23 *Gorat* is a town.

Chapter 15

1 Popoff, *The Tcheka: The Red Inquisition*, p.18

2 Ibid; p. 120. The headquarters of the M-Tcheka was known as "The Death Ship" due to its architecture.

3 The soup was named after the fish eyes that floated on the surface. This sense of hunger is confirmed on p. 221 of Vining's *Held By The Bolsheviks,* where he writes "we are so hungry that we devour eagerly all that is supplied us and feel very much like Oliver Twist did, only that it is useless asking for more."

4 In the "Interim Report of the Committee to Collect Information on Russia", Lord Emmott wrote: "With regard to parasites Mr Cooke said that "verminous" was not a strong enough word to describe the conditions of the prison of the Extraordinary Commission … the lice were there by the million." The other signatories in this report were the Conservative MP for Bassetlaw, Sir Ellis Hume-Williams; the Liberal MP for Middleton and Prestwich, Sir Ryland Adkins; and the Labour MP for Rhondda East, David Watts Morgan.

5 The *Nackenschuss* technique is described on p. 230 of Vining's diary and on p. 11 of Lord Emmott's "Interim Report of the Committee to Collect Information on Russia". The committee quotes from Mr Joshua Grundy, a foreman mechanic, who: "told us that when the time came for shootings, it was his duty to awaken the prisoners and take them to the cell door… Eight days before I was let out I took 16 men to be shot in one night, from 12.30 to 3 o'clock in the morning."

6 The Soviet trade delegation at the beginning of August was headed by Lenin's deputy Lev Kamenev. The conflicting British policies were summarised succinctly in Viscount Curzon's question in the House of Commons on 9th August, when he asked the prime minister: "How the Soviet delegation to this country is composed; whether any further news has come through with regard to our officers and men retained as prisoners at Baku; whether the Government have any information as to whether Bolshevik money is being spent in revolutionary interests in Great Britain and, if so, what steps are being taken to deal with it and with those who are responsible; and whether it is proposed to continue negotiations irrespective of the Polish question while such a state of affairs exists?" Hansard, House of Commons Debate, 9th August 1920.

7 CP 1540 dated 26th June 1920, "British Attitude Towards the Poles and Wrangel", Memorandum by the Secretary of State for War, National Archives CAB 24/108/42.

8 CP 1724 dated 3rd August, "Personal Report by Sir Maurice Hankey on His Visit To Warsaw July 1920", National Archives CAB 24/110/24.

9 A peace conference was opened at Riga on 21st September with preliminary terms signed on 12th October 1920. The new Poland included a Russian minority of four million people, for which she was to pay a heavy price in World War II.

10 Second Lieutenant Dwyer Augustus Neville was commissioned into the Royal Flying Corps on 7th February 1917 and transferred to the newly created Royal Air Force on 1st April 1918. He served in 41 Squadron equipped with the SE5a for fighter and escort duties. The SE5a was capable of superior performance to its

rival Sopwith Camel; however, problems with its Hispano-Suiza engine meant that there was a chronic shortage. Just before the fifth battle of Ypres, he was forced down in aircraft number C9133 on an offensive patrol over the Comines Canal on 22nd September 1918, as the Allies approached the Hindenburg Line. He was taken prisoner by the German Army, but was repatriated on 13th December 1918. He then volunteered to serve in Russia and ended up in Omsk in November 1919. Born in Australia on 18th April 1892, he died on 6th October 1979 and is buried at Buderim Cemetery Queensland Australia. National Archives WO 339/88651, http://www.airhistory.org.uk/rfc/people_indexN.html.

11 The Hague Convention of 1899 began as a result of a proposal by the Russian Czar, Nicholas II; it created the first formal agreement about the rules of war. The first convention comprised three treaties and three declarations, which came into force on 4th September 1900. The second of the treaties contained the laws to be used in wars on land between the signatories and specified the treatment of prisoners of war. These were updated at the 1907 Convention, which provided the basis for the conduct of belligerents during World War I.

12 This description is taken from Marguerite Harrison's *Marooned in Moscow*, p. 110.

13 Vining, p. 241.

14 Ibid, p. 243.

15 Taken from L. Bowler's *An Englishwoman's Experiences in Bolshevik Prisons*.

16 Vining, p. 240.

17 Mrs Clara Sheridan was the widow of Captain William Frederick Temple Sheridan, the great grandson of the famous playwright, Richard Brinsley Sheridan. Her husband served with the Rifle Brigade and was killed leading an assault at the battle of Loos in September 1915; five days after the birth of their son. She became a renowned sculptress through her busts of Herbert Asquith and Winston Churchill and was escorted to Russia by Maxim Litvinov on 11th September 1920. Apart from Dzerzhinsky, she also completed busts of Lenin, Trotsky and other Bolshevik leaders. The diary of her daring mission was serialised and published in *The Times* starting on Monday 22nd November 1920.

18 In its Cabinet Papers of September 1920, the National Archives, holds a note sent by the Foreign Office to Kamenev on 11th September (CAB 24/111/50) and a secret Draft Trade Agreement with Russian Soviet Government, revised by the president of the Board of Trade after consideration by the Russian Trade Committee with an alternative Article 8 proposed by Sir Hubert Llewellyn, 30th September 1920. CAB National Archives, 24/114/87 CP 2086, previously CP 1778

19 Private Grant had been wounded in France in 1916 and torpedoed in the Mediterranean in 1917 before serving in India, Mesopotamia, Salonika and Baku with 7th Battalion, Gloucestershire Regiment. British involvement in Baku had originally centred on the fight against the Ottoman Empire. During the first battle, from 26th August to 14th September 1918, General Dunsterville led the defence of the port with British losses totalling 200 men and officers killed, missing or wounded. The North Persian Force and Bicherakov Cossacks re-entered Baku on 17th November with the 7th Battalion, Gloucestershire Regiment based in

Baku until it returned to England via Constantinople in August 1919. There is a memorial to the British service men buried at Baku 1918–19, with the names of four officers and 44 men. These range from a Royal Navy Shipwright 4th Class and Royal Marines Light Infantry Private to a Major in the Staffordshire Regiment. There is also one Punjabi from the Indian Army.

20 On p. 279 of *A Prisoner of the Reds*, Francis McCullagh confirms the arrest of Mrs Marguerite Harrison on Good Friday 1920. In chapter 11 of her book, *Marooned in Moscow*, she writes about her association with McCullagh and the Reverend Frank North, who helped British citizens from the Anglican Church in Moscow. She also writes about her visit to British prisoners in Andronovsky in April when the regime was less severe than later in the year. On p. 219, she claims to have sent weekly food packages to Mrs Harding and bread to the British prisoners in Andronovsky prison.

21 According to a British Parliamentary Report (Russia No 1 1922 HMSO Cmd 1602), Mrs Stan Harding proceeded to Russia as the representative of the *New York World* in June 1920. Prior to her journey, she met Maxim Litvinov in Copenhagen and obtained a letter of introduction and safe conduct from the People's Commissar for Foreign Affairs to work in Russia. On arrival in Moscow, she was accommodated in a house allotted to people from abroad, but was invited by a reporter named Mogilevsky, who had travelled in the same group as her, to move to a more central apartment. However, he deceived her and took her to the headquarters of the V-Tcheka at Lubjanka 2 where she was arrested, stripped, searched and then placed in a solitary cell with a "verminous" plank bed. She was then interrogated for several hours and accused of being the head of the British Secret Service in Russia. For nine weeks, she underwent continuous ill-treatment at Lubjanka, where she was held in solitary confinement. Her inquisitors tried to coerce her to work for them and informed her that Mrs Margueritte Harrison was responsible for her arrest. In September, Mrs Harding was transferred to Butyrka Prison (Butirki in some British reports), where she met Miss Maxwell, who had been arrested on the grounds of conspiracy against the Soviet Government. She finally escaped from Moscow on 26th November 1920 as part of the Trade negotiations. Marguerite Harrison's false reports did not save her and she was re-arrested in October, suffering first in Lubjanka and then in the Novinsky Prison for Women, eventually being released on 29th July 1921, in exchange for American famine relief.

22 "Minutes of Evidence Taken before the Committee to Collect Information on Russia Volume I", on Tuesday 15th June 1920, p.43.

23 Hansard, House of Commons Debate, 25th October 1920, Volume 133, cc1313–4.

24 National Archives CAB 24/112/38, originally CP 1938, "Resumption of Trading Relations with Russia" dated 6th October 1919. Krassin's response to the prime minister states that the Russian Government "is prepared to return without exception all British war and civil prisoners who are still in Soviet Russia (including convicts and also those who have been taken in Siberia and temporarily detained in connection with the arrest of Mr Babushkin and others by the British Government) on condition that the British Government will permit the immediate return to Soviet Russia of Mr Babushkin and his friends...."

25 In late 1918, the Soviet Government sent MEA Babushkin as their consul to Khorasan, the largest province in Persia. However, he and his wife and his whole staff were arrested by British troops on 25th October, before he could establish formal relations. See Pezhmann Dailami "The Bolshevik Revolution and the Genesis of Communism in Iran, 1917–1920" *Central Asian Survey*, 11:3, 51–82, 1992 *DOI: 10.1080/02634939208400780*.

26 Hansard, House of Commons Debate, 26th October 1920, Volume 133, cc1516–21.

27 Vining, *Held by the Bolsheviks*, p. 250.

28 Ibid; p. 251.

29 See Chapter 10, note 20.

30 The Committee for the Relief of the British Colony in Petrograd was established by wealthy British citizens to aid the less fortunate. It also provided funds for the British network of agents. The *Tcheka* arrested the chairman, Mr Gerngross, on 2nd June 1919 and the others after the raid on the Soviet fleet.

31 For a full account of the raid on the Soviet fleet, see Ferguson's *Operation Kronstadt*.

Chapter 16

1 Robert Bruce Lockhart, *Memoirs of a British Agent*, p. 231.

2 Vining, *Held by the Bolsheviks*, p. 262.

3 Mrs Violet Froom was Matron of the British Colony Hospital in a wing of the Pokrovsky Hospital on the Vassili Ostroff. This was established by Lady Georgina Buchanan, the British ambassador's wife in 1914 before Lady Muriel Paget's Anglo-Russian Hospital on the other side of the river in St Petersburg. After the two British hospitals closed and the medics evacuated to England, the courageous Violet Froom took over the role previously filled by the Committee for the Relief of the British Colony in Petrograd. According to Harry Cuffwright, she acted as "Ambassador, parson and everything combined" (see "Minutes of Evidence Taken before the Committee to Collect Information on Russia Volume III" and Meriel Buchanan's *Ambassador's Daughter*).

4 There are 1,045 rooms in the Hermitage, which was built in 1754 and took eight years to complete.

5 Alexander III, a doughty soldier, came to the throne after the liberal reformer Alexander II was killed in 1881 by a bomb thrown at his feet by a member of the terrorist group, *Narodnaya Volya*. In contrast to his father, he was known for conservative domestic policy, industrial development and the alliance with France that was invoked in 1914. He extended the powers of the secret police before he was succeeded by his indulgent and sentimental son, Nicholas II in 1894.

6 Hansard, House of Commons Debate, 26th October 1920, Volume 133, cc1516–21.

7 The details of the prisoner exchanges are recorded in a series of Secret Admiralty Weekly Intelligence Summaries that should have been destroyed, but were retained by the Cabinet Office, declassified and placed in the National Archives. Numbers 16 to 20, from 20th October to 20th November, provide the key information and

also report the grave concerns of the commander-in-chief of the Mediterranean about threats to British interests in Georgia from the Turkish Nationals and Bolshevik Armenian operations. They also record the fact that Royal Air Force aircraft bombed Bolshevik ships at Enzeli and Kasian on 18th November, with the enemy responding ineffectively with anti-aircraft guns.

8 That same day, Sevastopol was evacuated and 123,000 refugees arrived in Constantinople in 73 ships.

9 This letter is held by the Soldiers of Gloucestershire Museum under the file for Private Lionel Ricketts Grant No 5420/267024.

10 During a short civil war after Finland declared itself independent, Vyborg was held by Finnish Bolsheviks until it was captured by government forces on 29th April 1918. Twenty-one years later, more than 70,000 people were evacuated from the region when the Soviet Union invaded Finland. The Winter War was concluded by the Moscow Peace Treaty, which transferred Vyborg and the whole Karelian Isthmus to Soviet control, where it was incorporated into the USSR on 31st March 1940.

11 John Scale DSO OBE had been head of MI6 in Russia before the revolution and was involved, allegedly, in Rasputin's death in 1916. Bruce Lockhart briefly mentions meeting him with Major General Knox and John Neilson on his way back to Russia before his ill-fated assignment. For Major Scale's role in the raid on the Soviet fleet in August 1918, see Ferguson's *Operation Kronstadt*.

12 "Conclusions of a Meeting of the Cabinet held at 10 Downing Street SW1 on Wednesday November 17 1920 at 1130", written by Lieutenant Colonel Sir Maurice Hankey GCB, Secretary, retrieved from the National Archive Cabinet Papers, CAB/23/23.

13 Many of these citizens were associated, in the minds of the Soviet authorities, with the privileged classes of Imperial Russia. It did not help their cause if they had been born and brought up in Russia and spoke little or no English. The British Government contributed a small amount into a fund, whose purpose was to provide assistance to the Displaced British Subjects in cases of particularly urgent need (in some accounts these are Distressed British Subjects). However, their troubles grew steadily worse and eventually, Lady Muriel Paget and Dr Sarah O'Flynn travelled to Leningrad to bring assistance. Their relief organisation built a dacha at Detskoye Selo, which served as a retirement and convalescent home.

14 Roskill, Stephen, *Hankey: Man of secrets Volume II 1919–1931*.

15 Ibid.

16 Ibid.

17 Ibid.

18 HMS *Delhi* was the fourth *Danae*-class cruiser that was designed to counter the threat of new German ships in the middle of World War I. It was laid down on 29th October 1917 at Armstrong's High Walker Shipyard at Elswick and launched on 23rd August 1918. It served with a crew of 450 in the Baltic and according to Admiralty records was at Danzig on 23rd October, with *Dauntless, Dunedin, Viscount, Wolsey, Woolston* and *Wessex*. After it suffered extensive battle damage in World War II, it was scrapped in 1948.

19 For a full account of the court martial of Lieutenant Colonel Sherwood Kelly VC CMG DSO at Westminster Guildhall on 28th October 1919, see Appendix 3 of Clifford Kinvig's *Churchill's Crusade: The British Invasion of Russia 1918–1920*.

20 On p. 14 of *The Times* of 23rd November 1920, next to the second instalment of Mrs Sheridan's diary, a column is headed "From A Russian Gaol; Britons Who Served With Kolchak; Horrors of the Omsk Retreat". The report states: "There are certain provisions in King's Regulations and the Manual of Military Law which lay down what a soldier may not talk about so far as his military service is concerned. Of political opinions he is assumed to have none, so that whatever a man who went out with the British Railway Mission may have in his mind to say, there are inevitably parts of it that he cannot discuss, so long as he wears the King's uniform."

21 *Held by the Bolsheviks*, p. 271. Vining was also interviewed by the "invaluable" Mr Lionel Gall, who had become Secretary of the Foreign Office Committee to Collect Information on Russia after he finished implementing the O'Grady-Litvinov Prisoner Agreement.

22 Before returning to America, Emerson and the others in the group were encouraged to submit letters to the Foreign Office for reparations from the Soviet Government. Emerson wrote his letter on 11th December and posted it in the City of London. Three months later in Philadelphia, he eventually received an acknowledgement from the Russian Claims Department at the Board of Trade in Cornwall House, Stamford Street, London SE1. The Deputy Director wrote: "I have to enclose herewith a form to enable you to submit your claim for registration in this Office in case in the future His Majesty's Government may be able to do anything to protect your interests in the matter." Sadly, Emerson never received compensation for his stolen items in Moscow.

23 Vining remained in the Indian Army as a staff transport officer, but his career did not flourish as a result of his enterprise. However in WWII, he finally received some of the recognition that he deserved. In 1941, he deployed to Eritrea after the capture of Aamara and became responsible for all movement and transportation. He organised the clearance of Massawa, so it could operate as a port again and the railway and ropeway networks. After three months of hard work, his commander submitted a citation which was approved by the General Officer Commanding Troops in Sudan. On 16th April the following year, he was informed of the award of the MBE for gallant and distinguished service.

Appendix 2

1 This translation is the one included at Annex H to Winston Churchill's secret memorandum to the Cabinet dated 17th June 1920, titled "The Execution of Admiral Koltchak [sic]".

Bibliography

Papers and Reports

Agreement between Governments of UK and Russian Federation Volume 16, Number 2, published January 1920, amended 1920, retrieved from the Prince Galitzine Memorial Library, St Petersburg, May 2017

Agreement Between His Majesty's Government and the Soviet Government of Russia for the Exchange of Prisoners, HMSO 1920, Cmd 587 (Russian text is in Dokumenty vneshnei politiki, Vol II, pp. 364–67)

American Red Cross archive papers, Box 915, 987.04

Bessie Eddy Lyon Collection, Hoover Institution Archives, Palo Alto, CA

European War Secret Telegrams, Series II, Volume II, 1st February 1919 to 31st May 1919, Harrison & Sons, London 1920, FO 371/3961 File 174 866/91/38

Frederick Lee Barnum Papers 1919–1920, Columbia University Rare Book and Manuscript Library https://clio.columbia.edu/catalog/4079877

Interim Report of the Committee to Collect Information on Russia, 4th November 1920 Cmd 1041, University of Warwick https://wdc.contentdm.oclc.org/digital/collection/russian/id/5272

Lloyd George, Papers in the Parliamentary Archives, LG/15/7/1-7

Lord Emmott Collection held by Nuffield College Library Archives, University of Oxford; ff 419–430 11/8 ff (1–430); Volumes I – III of "Minutes of Evidence Taken before the Committee to Collect Information on Russia At 22 Carlisle Place, Westminster between 10th June and 17th August 1920"

Janin papers, Ministere de Guerre

Manuscripts of Florence Farmer to Clara D. Noyes, 6 Oct 1919, in Library and Archives Canada, Ottawa, ON, Florence Farmer fonds, C—1911–20 & 1968

Maklakov Papers and Melgunov Civil War collection, Stanford

Medical Archives of the Johns Hopkins Medical Institutes, Baltimore, MD William S. Thayer American Red Cross Mission to Russia, 1917–18

Miliukov Papers and Khagondakov Memoirs, Columbia

Milner Papers, New College, Oxford

Papers of Brigadier Jack and Warrant Officer T. E. Ivens in the Imperial War Museum 88/46/1

Public Archives, Prince Edward Island Acc 3652
Report on the Work of the War Prisoners' Aid of Young Man's Christian Association in
   Russia from May 1917 to September 30 1918 dated 15th November 1918, Anderson
   Papers, Box 5
Report (Political and Economic) of the Committee to Collect Information on Russia,
   HMSO, Cmd. 1240, 31 May 1921
Russia No 1 1922: Correspondence with the Russian Soviet Government respect-
   ing the Imprisonment of Mrs Stan Harding in Russia presented to Parliament by
   Command of His Majesty HMSO Command 1602, retrieved from Warwick Digital
   Collection
Rykov, M. Report to the Congress of National Economic Councils, Moscow, 22–25
   January 1920
Secret Admiralty Weekly Intelligence Summaries (WIS) Numbers 16–20, 23rd October to
   20th November 1920. Issued by Naval Intelligence Directorate, Naval Staff
The American Red Cross in Siberia; undated manuscript, Box 140, American Red Cross
   Collection, Accession XX482-9.19/21, Hoover Institution Archives, Palo Alto, CA
The Official Names of the Battles fought by the Military forces of the British Empire during
   the Great War 1914–1919, HMSO

The National Archives, Kew

CAB 24/97/61 CP 559, The Negotiations at Copenhagen between Mr O'Grady MP and
   M Litvino[v] for the Exchange of British and Russian Prisoners of War and Civilians,
   dated February 1920
CAB 24/106/51 CP 1350, Negotiations with M. Krassin, Note by Lord Curzon, dated
   27th May 1920
CAB 24/107/50 CP 1451, Negotiations with M. Krassin, Secret Memorandum by the
   Secretary of State for War, dated 11th June 1920
CAB 24/107/89 CP 1488, The Execution of Admiral Kolchak, Secret Memorandum by
   Winston Churchill, dated 17th June 1920
CAB 24/108/42 CP 1540, British Attitude Towards the Poles and Wrangel, Secret
   Memorandum by the Secretary of State for War, dated 26th June 1920
CAB 24/110/24 CP 1724, Secret Personal Report by Sir Maurice Hankey on His Visit
   to Warsaw July 1920, dated 3rd August 1920
CAB/23/23, Conclusions of a Meeting of the Cabinet held at 10 Downing Street SW1
   on Wednesday November 17 1920 at 1130
CAB 24/105/54 CP 1254, Present Conditions in Soviet Russia, Secret Memorandum by
   the Secretary of State for War
CAB 24/107/21 CP 1421, Secret Translation Provisional Answers to questions raised by
   the Head of the British Government at a Conference held on May 31st 1920
CAB 24/111/50, Foreign Office Note to Kamenev on 11th September 1920
CAB 24/114/87 CP 2086 CP 1778, Draft Trade Agreement with Russian Soviet
   Government, revised by the president of the Board of Trade after consideration by
   the Russian Trade Committee with an alternative Article 8 proposed by Sir Hubert
   Llewellyn, 30th September 1920
CAB 24/112/38 CP 1938, Resumption of Trading Relations with Russia, Krassin's 6th
   October response to Lord Curzon

Directorate of Intelligence (Home Office): A Monthly Review of Revolutionary Movements in Foreign Countries Report Number 16, February 1920

Foreign Office FO 538, Allied High Commission, Vladivostok, 1918–1921

Foreign Office FO 371, Political Departments, General Correspondence from 1906–1966

Foreign Office FO 608/203, Secret Agent Report, 1919

Foreign Office FO 925/370777, Skeleton map of Russia and northern Asia lithographed at the Intelligence Division, War Office November 1897 with corrections January 1918 together with Foreign Office Brief of British Policy in Siberia dated 20th December 1918

Notes of a Cabinet Conference, held in the Prime Minister's Room, Claridge's Hotel, Paris on Monday, January 19 1920 at 5.30 pm

Sir Halford Mackinder report, dated 21st January 1920; filed as 18/E/170 21

The report on Bolshevik Influence on Muslims by the Intelligence Department of the High Commission of Constantinople covering a memorandum by Mr Low retrieved as file 18/OJ/2

Treasury T1/12514/12904, Lord Curzon correspondence about a gift for Mr O'Grady, 1920

Weekly Appreciation of Matters of Naval Interest, Number 72 for the week ended 1st May 1920, dated 5th May 1920

WO 32/5676, Ward Report of 20 November 1918

WO 32/5707, Report on the Work of the British Military Mission to Siberia 1918–19

WO 32/5707, Peacock Report and Narrative of Events in Siberia

WO 33/966, European War Secret Telegrams

WO 106/1275, Director of Military Intelligence File covering secret cypher telegrams between the Head of the British Military Mission to Siberia, Major General Knox and the Head of the British Railway Mission, Brigadier Jack.

WO 154/341, Two redacted pages from the official war diary of the British Military mission to Siberia

WO 339/54065, Norman Stilling's file

University of Leeds Archives

Special Collections: GB 206 MS 783 Eric Hayes Papers (the gift of Jeremy Fairbank April 1986); LRA MS 1228 Maxwell, Charles James Papers (Daphne Henniker 1992)

Liddle Collection: LIDDLE/WW1/RUS/27 Jameson, Thomas Henry Papers; LIDDLE/WW1/RUS/39/08 Farthing, Lieutenant Colonel CH Papers; LIDDLE/WW1/GS/0815 Hulton Papers (JP Hulton son); LIDDLE/WW1/GS/1429Sir Reginald Savory Papers

Books and Articles

Atkinson, C. T. *The Royal Hampshire Regiment 1914–1916* (University Press, 1952)

Baldwin, Douglas O. "The American Red Cross in Vladivostok: The Adventures of Nurse Mona Wilson" in *Sibirica* 1 (1994–95), pp. 85–107; also in *Canadian Journal of Nursing Research*, Volume 27, Number 3

Bisher, Jamie. *White Terror: Cossack Warlords of the Trans-Siberian* (Routledge, 2005)

Boadle, Donald. *Winston Churchill and the German Question in British Foreign Policy 1918–1922* (The Hague Martinus Nijhoff, 1973)

Bobrick, Benson. *East of the Sun: The Conquest and Settlement of Siberia* (Heinemann, 1992)

Bradley, J. F. N. *Civil War in Russia 1817–1920* (BT Batsford, 1975)

Brändström, Elsa. *Among Prisoners of War in Russia and Siberia* (Hutchinson, 1929)

Brough, Ray. *White Russian Awards to British and Commonwealth Servicemen During The Allied Intervention In Russia 1918–1920* (Tom Donovan, 1991)

Buchanan, Meriel. *Ambassador's Daughter (Foreword by Sir Robert Bruce Lockhart)* (Cassell, 1958)

Bukeley, Rudolph. "Work of the American Red Cross: The Great White Train" in *The Trained Nurse and Hospital Review* 3, September, 1919

Chichkin, S. N. *Civil War on the Far East* (USSR Defence Ministry Publishing House, Moscow, 1957)

Coates, W. P. and Zelda. *Armed Intervention in Russia 1918–1922* (Victor Gollanz, 1935)

Connaughton, Richard M. *The Republic of the Ushakovka: Admiral Kolchak and the Allied Intervention in Siberia 1918–20* (Routledge, 1990)

Denikine, General A., translated by Catherine Zvegintzov; *The White Army* (Jonathan Cape, 1950)

Dunsterville, Major General L. C. *The Adventures of Dunsterforce* (Arnold – Kingfisher Library, 1932)

Errington, Francis. *The Inns of Court Officers Training Corps During The Great War* (Printing Craft Ltd, 1922)

Farthing, Clement. "Lieutenant Colonel Clement H. Farthing BEM in Siberia, 1918–19: A Memoir" in *Sbornik* Number 8, 1986, pp. 93–99

Farmborough, Florence. *Nurse at the Russian Front: A Diary 1914–18* (Constable & Co, 1974)

Ferguson, Harry. *Operation Kronstadt* (Hutchinson, 2008)

Fleming, Peter. *The Fate of Admiral Kolchak* (Rupert Hart Davis, 1963)

Foglesong, David. *America's Secret War Against Bolshevism: Intervention in the Russian Civil War 1917–1920* (University of North Carolina Press, 2nd Edition, 2001)

Gehardie, William. *Memoirs of a Polyglot* (MacDonald 1973)

Gilbert, Martin. *Winston S. Churchill: 1916–22* (Heinemann, London, 1975)

Grand Duke Alexander of Russia. *Once A Grand Duke* (Cassell, 1932)

Graves, General William S. *America's Siberian Adventure (1918–1920)* (Peter Smith Publishers, New York, 1941 reprint)

Harrison, Marguerite E. *Marooned in Moscow* (Thornton Butterworth, 1921)

Hodges, Phelps. *BRITMIS A Great Adventure of the War* (Jonathan Cape, 1931)

Horrocks, Lieutenant General Sir Brian. *A Full Life* (Collins, 1960)

Hudson, M. *Intervention in Russia 1918–1920* (Leo Cooper, 2004)

Irwin, Julia F. "The Great White Train: Typhus, Sanitation and US International Development During the Russian Civil War" in *Endeavour* Volume 36.3, Elsevier Ltd, 2012

Isitt, Benjamin. *From Victoria to Vladivostok: Canada's Siberian Expedition, 1917–19* (UBC Press, 2010)

Jameson, T. H. J. *Expedition to Siberia 1919* (Royal Marines Historical Society Special Publication Number 10, Portsmouth, 1987)

Janin, General Maurice. *Ma Mission en Sibérie 1918–1920* (Paris Payot, 1933)

Jensen, Bent. "Missiia Datskogo Krasnogo Kresta v Rossii, 1918–1919 gody" in *Otechestvennaia istoriia 1997*, no. 1 (Jan–Feb), pp. 27–41

246 • CHURCHILL'S ABANDONED PRISONERS

246 • CHURCHILL'S ABANDONED PRISONERS

Judson, William V. *Russia in War and Revolution: General William V. Judson's Accounts from Petrograd, 1917–1918,* edited by Neil V. Salzman (The Kent State University Press, 1998)

Jupe, A. A. "Round The World With The PBI", Royal Hampshire Regiment Archives, undated

Kemp, P. K. *History of the Royal Norfolk Regiment 1919–1951 Volume III* (Regimental Association, 1953)

Kennan, George F. *Soviet American Relations 1917–1920 Volume 1 Russia Leaves the War* (Faber & Faber, 1956)

Kettle, Michael. *The Allies and the Russian Collapse: March 1917–March 1918* (Andre Deutsch, 1981)

Kinvig, Clifford. *Churchill's Crusade: The British Invasion of Russia, 1918–1920* (Hambledon Continuum, 2006)

Knox, Maj-Gen Sir Alfred. *With The Russian Army, 1914–1917* (London, 1921)

Lansbury, George. *What I Saw In Russia* (Leonard Parsons, 1920)

Léderrey, Ernest. *The Red Army During The Civil War, 1917–1920* (Weidenfeld and Nicolson, 1956)

Lewis, David. *The Good Fight: Political Memoirs 1909–1958* (Macmillan, 1981)

Liddell Hart, B. H. *The Soviet Army* (Weidenfeld and Nicolson, 1956)

Lloyd George, David. *War Memoirs Volume II* (Odhams Press, 1936)

Lockhart, Robert B. *Memoirs of A British Agent* (Putnam 1932)

Maclean, Fitzroy. *All The Russians* (Viking, 1992)

Mavor, James. *The Russian Revolution* (MacMillan, 1929)

McCullagh, Francis. *A Prisoner of the Reds: The Story of a British Officer Captured in Siberia* (John Murray, London, 1921 & EP Dutton, New York, 1922)

McLaine, W. "An Engineer in Soviet Russia" in *Amalgamated Engineering Union Monthly Report and Journal,* October, 1920

Moffat, Ian. "Forgotten Battlefields: Canadians in Siberia 1918–1919" in *Canadian Military Journal,* Autumn, 2007 http://www.journal.forces.gc.ca/vo8/no3/moffat-eng.asp#n62

Monaghan, Andrew. *Power in Modern Russia: Strategy and Mobilisation* (Manchester University Press, 2017)

Nicholson, G. H. and Powell, H. L. *History of the Hampshire Territorial Force Association and War Records of units 1914–1919* (Hampshire Advertiser Company, Southampton, 1921)

Norton, Henry Kittredge. *Far Eastern Republic of Siberia* (J Day & Co, 1927)

Novikov, P. A. *Civil War in Eastern Siberia* (Centrepoligraph Publishing House, Moscow, 2005)

O'Connor, Frederick. *On the Frontier and Beyond* (John Murray, 1931)

Pezhmann Dailami. "The Bolshevik Revolution and the Genesis of Communism in Iran, 1917–1920" *Central Asian Survey* 11:3, 1992, pp. 51–82 DOI: 10.1080/02634939208400780

Polk, Jennifer Ann. *Constructive Efforts: The American Red Cross and YMCA in Revolutionary and Civil War Russia, 1917–24* (University of Toronto, 2012)

Popoff, George. *The Tcheka: The Red Inquisition,* (AM Philpot Ltd, London, 1925)

Rayfiled Donald. *Stalin and His Hangmen: The Tyrant and Those Who Killed for Him* (Random House, 2004)

Richard, Carl J. *When The United Stated Invaded Russia: Woodrow Wilson's Siberian Disaster* (Roman & Littlefield, 2013)

Roskill, Stephen. *Hankey: Man of secrets Volume II 1919–1931* (Naval Institute Press, 1972)

Ross, Edward Alsworth. *The Russian Soviet Republic* (Century, 1923)

Skuce, J. E. *CSEF Canada's Soldiers in Siberia 1918–1919* (Access to History Publications, Ottawa, 1990)

Smele, Jonathan D. *The Russian Revolution and Civil War 1917–1921: An Annotated Bibliography* (Continuum, 2003)

Smele, Jonathan D. *Civil War in Siberia: The Anti-Bolshevik Government of Admiral Kolchak 1918–1920* (Cambridge University Press, 1996)

Smith, Canfield F. *Vladivostok Under Red and White Rule: Revolution and Counter-Revolution in the Russian Far East 1920–1922* (University of Washington Press, 1975)

Smith, Scott B. *Captives of the Revolution: The Social Revolutionaries and the Bolshevik Dictatorship 1918–1923* (University of Pittsburgh Press, 2011)

Steel, Colonel J. P. FRGS Late Royal Engineers; *A Memoir of Lieutenant Colonel Edward Anthony Steel DSO RHA and RFA 1880–1919* (Simpkin, Marshall, Hamilton, Kent & Co, London, 1921)

Steveni, Leo. "From Empire to Welfare State", unpublished memoir in Liddell Hart Military Archives

Swettenham, John. *Allied Intervention in Russia 1918–1919* (Allen & Unwin, 1967)

Tread, Lt Col. F. J. F. *From Whitehall to the Caspian* (Oldhams Press, 1920)

Uldricks, Teddy. *Diplomacy and Ideology: The Origins of Soviet Foreign Relations, 1918–1930* (Sage, 1979)

Ullman, Richard H. *Anglo-Soviet Relations 1917–1921, Volume II, Britain and the Russian Civil War November 1918–February 1920* (Princeton University Press, 1968)

Ullman, Richard H. *Anglo-Soviet Relations 1917–1921, Volume III, The Anglo-Soviet Accord* (Princeton University Press, 1972)

Ustinov, Peter. *My Russia* (MacMillan, 1983)

Vining, L. E. *Held By The Bolsheviks: The Diary of a British Officer in Russia 1919–1920* (Saint Catherine's Press, 1924)

Ward, LtCol. John CB CMG MP. *With the Diehards in Siberia* (Cassell & Co, 1920)

Wright, Damien. *Churchill's Secret War With Lenin: British and Commonwealth Military Intervention in the Russian Civil War 1918–1920* (Helion, 2017)

Wykes, Alan. *The Royal Hampshire Regiment* (Hamish Hamilton, 1968)

Newspaper, Journal and Magazine Articles and Websites

Blackwood's Edinburgh Magazine, December 1921; An Englishwoman's Experiences in Bolshevik Prisons by L. Bowler

Exeter and Plymouth Gazette, 5th April 1926

http://www.airhistory.org.uk/rfc/people_indexN.html

http://21stbattalion.ca/tributetz/ullman_vr.html

Illustrated London News, 20th September 1919, Volume CLV, Number 4196

Manchester Guardian, 20th, 21st, 22nd July 1920 and various

National Census Online: http://www.ukcensusonline.com/

Peterborough Examiner, 7 December 1920, p. 9

Philadelphia Public Ledger, 30 January 1921

Portsmouth Evening News, 11 Oct 1955

Southampton and District Pictorial, 11th December 1919

The Bedfordshire Regiment in the Great War website: http://www.bedfordregiment.org.
uk/
The Edinburgh Gazette, 23rd August 1921, Japanese awards and honours
The Hampshire Regimental Journal, April 1919
The Nation, 10 July 1920, pp. 458–9
The Times various
The Windsor Daily Star, 7 July 1945, p. 12
Western Times, 12th February 1926

The London Gazette

The London Gazette, 1st February 1919, Military Cross
The London Gazette, 6th September 1919 and Supplement Number 11324
The London Gazette, 13th January 1920, Number 31732, HMSO
Supplement to *The London Gazette*, 30th January 1920, p. 1229
The London Gazette, 10th August 1920, p. 8345
Supplement to *The London Gazette*, 17th February 1921
The London Gazette, 14th February 1941, Indian Army Emergency Commissions
Supplement to *The London Gazette*, 16th April 1942, p. 1693
Supplement to *The London Gazette*, 12th October 1943, p. 4553

Hansard website

Hansard, House of Commons Debate, 14th June 1920, Volume 130, cc869–70, retrieved at:
https://api.parliament.uk/historic-hansard/commons/1920/jun/14/russian-prisoners
Hansard, House of Commons Debate, 1st July 1920, Volume 131, c624, retrieved at:
https://api.parliament.uk/historic-hansard/commons/1920/jul/01/soviet-trade-delegation
Hansard, House of Commons Debate, 13th July 1920, Volume 131, c2133, retrieved
at: https://api.parliament.uk/historic-hansard/commons/1920/jul/13/kit-and-messing-allowances
Hansard, House of Commons Debate, 9th August 1920, Volume 133, c20, retrieved at:
https://api.parliament.uk/historic-hansard/commons/1920/aug/09/soviet-delegation
Hansard, House of Commons Debate, 25th October 1920, Volume 133, cc1313–4,
retrieved at: https://api.parliament.uk/historic-hansard/commons/1920/oct/25/bkitish-prisoners
Hansard, House of Commons Debate, 26th October 1920, Volume 133 cc1516–21
retrieved at: http://hansard.millbanksystems.com/commons/1920/oct/26/trade-agreement-soviet-government

Index